KT-474-724

The Tea Tree Oil Encyclopedia

Featuring

Various Remedies

and Other Essential Oils

WISDOM IS WEALTH

First Published 1996
Printed and bound in the UK.

© Mrs K. Mackenzie 1995

KAREN MACKENZIE ASSERTS THE RIGHT TO BE IDENTIFIED AS THE AUTHOR OF THIS
WORK IN ACCORDANCE WITH THE COPYRIGHT, DESIGNS AND PATENTS ACT 1988

Printed and   BPC Wheatons Ltd
Bound by: Exeter, EX2 8RP

Published by: Karedon Publishing Company
Karedon House P O Box 2
LE67 6ZU   UK

Cover Printed by kind permission of Ken Byrnes, AusTTeam

ISBN 1 900806 00 2
A copy of this book is available from the British Library

*The Tea Tree Oil Encyclopedia is sold with the condition that it
will not, by way of trade or otherwise, be re-sold, copied, hired
out or otherwise circulated without the publishers prior consent
and without a similar condition including this condition being
imposed on All, world-wide: this applies to the present form and
in any form including binding, title or cover other than that in
which it is currently published. No extracts can be copied in any
form without the publishers consent, detailed in writing. These
statements are legally binding in the U. K., Europe, Australia,
U. S. A. and the rest of the world.*

THIS BOOK IS DEDICATED TO
Donald and Victoria

ACKNOWLEDGEMENTS

I would like to acknowledge my family, my friends and everyone in the Tea Tree Oil Industry who have given me such great support and assistance.

A very special thank you goes to Charles Wells, Nils Lundgren, Ken Byrnes, Michael McBride, Adrian Blake, Nina Turpin.

&

Christine Carson
Pam, Angie and Stephanie
And of course to you the readers.

NOTE TO READERS

You should commence using this book only after reading page 8

Essential oils are measured as follows:

Approx. 20 drops = 1 ml
Approx. 200 drops = 10 ml bottle
5ml = 1 teaspoon
10ml = 1 dessertspoon
20ml = 1 tablespoon

INTRODUCTION

When I first heard about Tea Tree oil, I could not believe it. It was too good to be true. Why had we not heard about it before?. The truth is we had, but then we chose to ignore it!!.

I have traced Tea Tree oil back to its roots in Aboriginal Australia, its popularity during the Second World War, right up to the present day World-wide acclaim. I have read the research papers, used it for first aid purposes, mixed it with other essential oils, made toiletries with it, treated my pets and even polished the furniture with it.

I am constantly amazed by its versatility and in effect ingenuity. I would never have believed that one essential oil could lend itself so successfully to so many different applications. No-one but nature could have created such a valuable broad-spectrum substance, and that is the beauty of Tea Tree oil - it is totally natural.

I wrote this book in an effort to bring Tea Tree oil to your attention; so you, like I, could read about its history, study the research work, utilise its many properties and make up your own mind about natures potent gift.

After all, Tea Tree oil was created for each and every one of us.

PREFACE

Every week we see new headlines in the daily papers "Headlice Shampoo - Cancer Scare"........ "The Age of the Superbug"........"Household Chemicals and Pollution Linked to Memory Loss"........ "Acne treatment - damages skin cells"....... and so it goes on.

We are finding that our body's are starting to rebel, against the synthetically based - chemical cocktails, that we come into contact with during the course of a day. Hairsprays, cosmetics, deodorants, polishes, detergents, perfumes, aftershave, first aid treatments, medicines, air fresheners to name but a few. On top of all this our systems are being weakened by the one vital element that should be giving us sustenance, our food. Yes! our factory farmed and most processed foods, are also adding more pollutants to our bloodstream. It is undeniable that our immune systems are beginning to suffer, where will it all end?.

Germs, bacteria and other parasites, are evolving to beat their chemical killers, superbugs, and goldenstaph, thrive. Mystery illnesses are on the increase. Do we then try to make stronger chemicals?, you bet we do!.

Are we forgetting one simple, fundamental fact?. Bacterium is a basic, one-celled form of life - our life!!. When we use harsh chemicals against it we can also unbalance and destroy our own body cells too.

I am not denying that synthetic medicine was, and is, a great gift. It is its indiscriminate use, in addition to all other synthetics and chemicals, that is causing a problem. Fifty years ago society started to turn its back on nature and the synthetic industry took centre stage. We seemed to forget that we were part of nature and to turn against it, we would be turning against ourselves. It is only now that we are beginning to pay the price.

Now, wouldn't it be marvellous if we could find a safe, non-toxic, non-irritant substance that replaced many of the strong chemicals in our cupboards?.

Well, we have! ....

Here is a product that is made by nature for nature. A completely natural, topical, anti-bacterial and anti-fungal substance. It has anti-inflammatory, immune system strengthening, pain killing and wound healing qualities. It also seems to exhibit anti-viral, expectorant and balsamic characteristics.

All this and it can be used as a powerful antiseptic, parasiticide, insecticide **AND** is also kind to our skin cells.

The pure Tea Tree oil of the *Melaleuca Alternifolia*, (with a Terpinen-4-ol content of 40>% and a 1,8 Cineole content of <5%) works with the body not against it, yet research shows it has rapid results against the new "20th Century Superbugs".

I still find it ironic that if man had made such a synthetic substance and had spent millions of pounds on the development programme, it would have been hailed as the wonder of the century. Everyone would have known about it, and everyone would be utilising its many properties. But because Tea Tree oil was created by nature, for centuries, it has been viewed with suspicion.

As soon as we, and the 'Professional World' once again wholeheartedly embrace natural methods, and use them alongside conventional Medicine, Industry and Agriculture, the sooner we will begin to stem the tide of the so called 'Mystery Illnesses'.

CAUTION: PLEASE READ CAREFULLY BEFORE USING THIS BOOK.

* This book should be used for first aid purposes only. It should not be used to diagnose conditions or to replace prescribed medication.

* Caution: People with a serious medical condition. Certain oils may affect epilepsy sufferers. People with high blood pressure should use neat oils, like Rosemary oil, sparingly: see an Aromatherapist if in doubt.

* If any essential oil has contact with the eyes, wash with copious amounts of cold water, if stinging persists seek medical advice. Do not rub eyes while handling essential oils.

* If an essential oil is swallowed in quantity, do not induce vomiting, a large quantity of milk may be helpful and activated charcoal. Seek medical advice.

* Keep Tea Tree oil/essential oils out the of reach of children.

* Tea Tree oil must not be taken internally without medical supervision.

* Everyone, including pets, who intend to use essential oils, must initially carry out a sensitivity test before use. Put one drop of selected oil ie. Tea Tree oil onto the wrist, cover with a plaster and leave untouched for 24hrs. If no adverse reaction, use as described. **A separate test must be done for each essential oil, and each 'formulation of oils'** (recipe from book) **used.**

* If prone to allergies use sparingly, initially.

* Pure essential oils and certain massage techniques should not be used by the elderly or in pregnancy, without a qualified practitioners supervision.

* **New-borns should have advice from a qualified Aromatherapist.**

* **Young babies should have less than 5% solution and from a qualified Aromatherapist.**

* **Babies (over 1 year) should not have more than 10% solution.**

* **Children should not use more than 20-25 % solution.**

* **People with sensitive skins or the elderly should not use more than 50% solution - without medical supervision.**

* If irritation occurs, dilute or discontinue use, depending on the discomfort.

* Homeopathy users should seek the advice of their practitioner, certain oils may affect a prescribed homeopathic remedy.

* Essential oils are flammable, do not put near a naked flame.

* Certain oils are solvents, they may damage plastics and polished wood.

* Initially, patch test everything, including soft furnishings or furnishings, before the whole object, or part, is cleaned with Tea Tree oil or a solution of.

* The author and publisher disclaim all responsibility for adverse reactions by not following guidelines, inappropriate usage or the use of inferior quality oils.

* **If in doubt, how to obtain a list of qualified Aromatherapists in your area, is featured at the back of this book, under useful addresses.**

CONTENTS   PAGES

CONTENTS   PAGES

Chapter One

The Roots

Although there is no documented evidence, it is widely understood that for centuries the Bundjalong Aborigines, who lived on the North Eastern side of the New South Wales region, around the Bungawalbyn creek, were well aware of the antiseptic qualities of their numerous 'Healing Trees'.

They treated various wounds and skin infections with an early form of poultice, made from the crushed leaves and warm mud from the banks of the creek. The poultice was excellent for drawing out infection and healing the skin. The Aborigines also used the 'healing' waters of the creek, bathing and washing in the natural antiseptic that the fallen leaves and twigs had created.

The many and various species of the *Melaleuca* and *Leptospermum* Genera became commonly known as 'Tea Trees', when in 1770 Captain Cook and his crew of 'The Endeavour' used the leaves, with their distinctive aroma to brew a spicy and refreshing 'tea'. It is most unfortunate that Captain Cook did not 'discover' the unique healing qualities of the 'Tea Trees', but according to his account of that time, drank the essence in varying concoctions, even alcoholic beverages such as beer.

*

Thus the name 'Tea Tree' became popular, especially with the first 'white' settlers who colonised the low lying areas around the Clarence and Richmond Rivers. From the 1790's onwards, they watched and learned from the Aborigines how to use the leaves and waters in various inhalations, poultices, and rubbing mediums.

Because these first settlers had little or no medical or botanical backgrounds, there was no real scientific evidence recording the healing qualities of the Tea Trees. The European community was very sceptical of the 'stories', the Aborigines were often thought of as primitives from an uncivilised world. In the eyes of the settlers "....they didn't want to work or better themselves, ...they were always disobedient and lazy". Thus the Aboriginal healing remedies, along with their way of life, were treated with contempt.

As new settlers arrived they struggled to clear the harsh native vegetation, to make way for settlements and dairy farms. They cursed every Tea Tree for its hardy and persistent hold on its own natural habitat. The Tea Trees tenaciously survived drought, fire, flood, even frost and resisted any attempt to destroy them. Fortunately for the rest of the world, the only way they could have been eradicated was by the physical removal of every part of the tree, including its extensive root system.

It is ironic, that while the settlers battled to destroy the Tea Trees, they were only too willing to use the crushed leaves for poultices, inhalations and to stem infection and disease.

It is to our loss that the Tea Tree, although used as an effective 'bush remedy' by subsequent generations of farmers, did not reach our attention until the early 1930's. It was not even mentioned in the BRITISH PHARMACEUTICAL CODEX until 1949, where it was listed as *'Oleum Melaleuca'*.

*

In Australia it was not until the early 1920's that A.R. Penfold, FCS. Chief Chemist at the Museum of Applied Technology, Arts and Sciences in Sydney extracted the oil of the *Melaleuca Alternifolia* and announced that yes indeed!, it did have antiseptic, anti-bacterial activity.

The accepted anti-bacterial agent at that time was carbolic (known as Phenol). Imagine the stir it must have caused when it was determined that "an old Aboriginal remedy" was up to 13 times stronger! and was non-toxic and non-irritating - unlike Carbolic!

When in 1925 the results were finally published there was great enthusiasm among medics of that time and "Penfolds discovery" was immediately put to the test.

In 1930 the Medical Journal Of Australia published an article by Dr E. M. Humphrey, it stated that what he ...."found most encouraging was the way that the oil from the crushed leaves of the *Melaleuca Alternifolia* dissolved pus and left wounds and surrounding areas clean"....

He also noticed ...."that the germicidal action became more effective in the presence of living tissue and organic matter, without any apparent damage to healthy cells"....

He concluded ...."that it was a rare occurrence because most effective germicides actually destroyed healthy living tissue along with the bacteria"....

He suggested ...."that it would be particularly good for dirty wounds from street accidents"....

He also found ...."most encouraging the results on nail infections. Infections that had resisted various treatments for months were cured in less than a week!"....

...."The pus solvent properties of Tea Tree oil made it an excellent application for the fungal disease "Paronychia" which if left untreated could result in the deformity and even eventual loss of the nail"....

He urged the dental industry to ...."take seriously the antiseptic properties for infections of the gum and mouth".....

He noted that ...."just 2 drops of Tea Tree oil in a tumbler of warm water made it a soothing and therapeutic gargle for sore throats in the early stages"....

He wrote that ..."it would probably be effective for most of the infections of the "naso-pharynx"....

That it ..."was an immediate deodorising medium on foul-smelling wounds and pus-filled abscesses"....

And .... "if it was added to hand soap it would make the soap up to 60 times more effective against Typhoid Bacilli than the so-called 'disinfectant soaps' of the day"....

He felt ...."that if an ointment could be made from the oil it would help to eradicate several parasitic skin diseases"....

The Scientific and Medical world were intrigued. More research was funded and articles began appearing in additional publications such as the Australian Journal of Pharmacy and the Australian Journal of Dentistry. World-wide appetites were whetted. Articles were presented and published in the Journal of the Medical Association (USA) and the British Medical Journal.

As the reputation of Tea Tree oil spread there was a great deal of anecdotal evidence about its effectiveness in a wide range of topical applications, both medical and veterinary.
From diabetic gangrene in man to diseases of poultry and fish, it was recognised as a safe, effective, non-toxic, non-irritant, anti-septic disinfectant.

*

If Penfold was the 'Founding Father', Humphrey was certainly the 'Metaphorical Mother'. His enthusiastic writings opened up a multitude of medical and practical uses for Tea Tree oil. Others have tried, tested and enthused about its healing properties, but thanks to Penfold and Humphrey the world would no longer be denied the miraculous healing powers of the Aboriginal TEA TREE, *Melaleuca Alternifolia.*

Chapter Two

A Growth Industry

By the start of the Second World War, Tea Tree oil from the *Melaleuca Alternifolia* had earned its reputation as the miracle healer.

It was scientifically recognised world-wide for its successful treatment of a whole range of conditions including ear, nose and throat infections, mouth infections: Gingivitis, Pyorrhoea; gynaecological problems, nail infections: Paronychia; dental nerve capping, haemorrhages, wounds, first aid and a wide range of fungal and bacterial infections: Candida, Tinea, etc. not to mention all the many and varied veterinary applications as well.

A bottle of Tea Tree oil was a standard government issue in Australian Army and Navy first aid kits, especially for those soldiers serving in tropical countries. It was initially used in munitions factories to stop the high air-borne bacteria count, then it was found that, by adding it to the machine cutting oils it substantially reduced infections, especially those from abrasions caused by metal filings.

During these years the production of Tea Tree oil was considered of such importance that bush cutters were exempt from doing National Service.

Surgeons, doctors, dentists, vets and even housewives were utilising its many and varied healing powers. Colgate-Palmolive, a huge Australian conglomerate manufactured a Tea Tree oil germicidal soap that was very popular for a number of years.

Demand became far greater than supply. Even though there were approximately twenty to thirty stills in the Bungawalbyn area of New South Wales, they were mostly family run businesses, the cutting and harvesting was all done by hand, mainly from trees growing wild in the swampy bush-lands. Successful harvesting depended wholly upon manpower against the harsh elements of the Australian climate and the many hazards of working alongside the poisonous wildlife.

Throughout the war years all available stocks of good quality Tea Tree oil were taken under government control. There was little or none left for the developing market place. Scientists concocted cheaper synthetic altern-atives, although not as effective as Tea Tree oil for their germicidal qualities, they were much more readily available. In the post war era the pure oil of the *Melaleuca Alternifolia* was almost impossible to buy.

Right up until the late 1940's the pure Tea Tree oil was still highly regarded and sought after. It had been the heyday of the Tea Tree oil industry.

*

During the earlier years, as the popularity of Tea Tree oil was growing, so too was medical technology. In 1929 the Scottish Biologist Alexander

CHAPTER 2 - A GROWTH INDUSTRY

Fleming first observed the effect of penicillin on bacteria and the antibiotic was "born". By 1941 the drug was developed and established. By the 1950's it was heralded as the new 'wonder drug'. It was the age of synthetic and semi-synthetic medicine. Infections and usually fatal diseases were virtually wiped out, Tuberculosis, Pneumonia, Venereal disease to name but a few. There was hope where there had been despair. The new drugs went from strength to strength, everyone wanted them and everyone got them. Antibiotic's were the theme of the day, man rejoiced the fact that he had finally triumphed over nature. Natural remedies were classed as quack cures - modern medicine was now being built on synthetics and chemicals, and for more than a decade they reigned supreme.

*

In the 1960's the "Hippie" revolution started, suddenly there was a growing awareness and concern about chemical pollution; the addictions to synthetic drugs, their hazardous side effects, the body's reduced immunity to the superbugs (as indeed, the superbugs themselves became immune to the antibiotic's) and the dubious environmental implications all this entailed. Once more people were beginning to look for alternative 'natural' remedies to find a cure, and not before time the 'Herbal Renaissance' had finally begun.

Like the tenacious hold those newly discovered, Aboriginal "Healing Trees" have had on their natural habitat, so too the TEA TREE OIL of the *Melaleuca Alternifolia* was waiting in the background, forgotten but not gone. New research work was funded and the popularity of the Tea Tree was once again growing.

*

Up until the late 1970's all the Tea Trees were harvested by hand from the swampy, snake and spider infested, bush-lands around the Bungawalbyn Creek. The leaves and terminal branches were hacked off and transported out of the swamp to the stills, many of the wide-tyred trucks would not even attempt to make a track through the dense undergrowth, so the cutters themselves had to, manually, carry their yield out of the swamps to the awaiting transport. On a good day, one skilled worker could cut and load up the truck with up to a tonne of leaves.

Arriving at their destination the leaves would then be emptied into one of the large distilling vats and then the oil was distilled using a simple, but effective, wood fired steam-distillation method.

The steam passed through the leaves, bursting the oil bearing sacs and vaporising the oil. The vapours were condensed and mixed with the distillation water in the collection tank. The pure oil was then siphoned off into drums. Each standard vat could quite easily be filled by one skilled cutter and yield around 7-10 litres of pure oil.

As demand was once again on the increase, so too, the Tea Tree Industry itself started to expand. From the late 1970's farms were being set up and for the first time Tea Trees were being cultivated and the oil produced on a commercial scale.

*

By the late 1980's plantations and mechanical cutting had been introduced. By 1991 production was substantially increased to meet the ever growing demand for a high quality Tea Tree oil. It is interesting to note that the majority of the modern plantations still use a similar steam-distillation method that was used over fifty years ago.

Even now a considerable amount of research work is required to determine optimum yields and how to produce the best quality oil possible. The growing methods, the age of the leaves when cut and the distillation procedures can all determine an inferior or high quality oil. New areas in Australia, and even in Zimbabwe and the USA, are being tested for their ability to sustain the Tea Trees, outside New South Wales.

Towards the end of 1994 AusTTeam was set up by a group of plantation owners, growers, and marketing men to increase peoples awareness and understanding of Tea Tree oil. Out of approximately 8,000 acres of plantations, around 80% are owned by AusTTeam shareholders. They set high standards, for their members to reach, ensuring the rest of the world can enjoy the authentic pure Tea Tree oil of the *Melaleuca Alternifolia* whose composition falls well within the Australian Standard.

With increasing concern for the environment, global warming and the burning of fossil fuels, it may be comforting to know, that by using Tea Tree oil, you are not adding to the destruction of the trees, but actively helping in the replanting of the land, that was laid bare by the first 'white settlers' over 200 years ago. A single Tea Tree can be harvested for decades, growing healthier and more vigorous with each cutting. It takes each Tea Tree just 18-20 months to fully recover its growth from being cut to a stump. Nothing is wasted, once the oil has been extracted, the leaves can be composted and used as an 'organic' soil conditioner, even the water that was used in the vaporising tanks can be utilised in agricultural and veterinary applications.

CHAPTER 2 - A GROWTH INDUSTRY

The Tea Tree Industry, which planted over 12 million self-generating trees in 1989, has continued to increase the annual number of individual plantings well into the 1990's.

By 1995 over 8000 acres of plantations have been established, with a conservative estimate that if the market continues to expand, as it has done within the last 10 years, it is likely to produce over $100 million dollars worth of product, within the first part of the 21st century.

The Tea Tree oil of the *Melaleuca Alternifolia* has once again gripped and now firmly holds the attention of the world.

Chapter Three

The Real Oil

In the family *Myrtaceae* there are literally thousands of species and sub-species, most if not all, have aromatic leaves with glandular sacs containing essential oil. The Myrtle, Bayberry, Bottlebrush, Pimento, Clove *Eugenia*, Eucalyptus, the Tea Trees *Leptospermum* and the Tea Trees *Melaleuca* all belong to this family.

The *Melaleuca* genus itself contains over 150 varieties of very hardy 'Tea Trees'. The most well known of these, *Melaleuca Cajuputi* and *Melaleuca Quinquenervia*, provide us with the essential oils Cajuput and Niaouli, all have germicidal qualities, but only one *Melaleuca* Tea Tree provides us with a powerful, broad-spectrum germicide, that is also kind to the skin. It is only found in one relatively small area of New South Wales, Australia; it is very interesting that the same trees grown outside this area do not yield oil that is so suitable for therapeutic use.

The *Melaleuca Alternifolia*; Mela (Dark or black) Leucon (White) suggesting a black and white appearance. It is also known as the 'Pinleaf Tea Tree' and the 'Narrow Leafed Paperbark Tree'. 'Paperbark', because the bark actually looks like strips of paper, peeling from the entire height of the trunk. This 'paper' like bark is soft and relatively strong, it was used by Aborigines for bedding material and as swaddling, for their babies. The settlers used it as a building material. It was also used for caulking boats, packing fruit and even as a kind of roofing felt for buildings. Today, the Australians who are famed for their barbecues, use the bark as an aromatic 'pouch' for barbecuing meat and fish.

The therapeutic uniqueness of the *Melaleuca Alternifolia*, grown in New South Wales, and its effectiveness as a germicide stems from its complex composition.

In 1968 twelve components of Tea Tree oil were isolated. In 1978 forty eight components were identified. Presently, due to more precise chromatographic analysis, it has been revealed that there are actually ninety seven (plus) components, all working synergistically to create those unique healing properties.

The oil contains Terpenes, Pinenes, Cymones, Terpineous Cineoles, Sesquiterpines and Sesquiterpinene alcohol's. In addition there are at least four constituents that are not usually found in plants. These are Viriflorene .95%, *b*-terpineol .25%, L-terpineol-trace and Allyhexanoate-trace. Some of these constituents were completely unknown at the time of identification and names had to be created for them.

The exact composition and effectiveness of the healing properties are due to the climate, the amount of rainfall, the condition of the soil and many more environmental factors. Samples taken at random from different trees have shown that the Cineole content can vary from a low 2% to over 60%, all from botanically identical trees. The distillation methods can also effect the composition of the oil. A skilled cutter can usually identify just by crushing the leaves if a particular tree is high in Cineole, but a more scientific evaluation is now usually carried out. Every reputable Tea Tree oil company in Australia ensures that their own oil is independently analysed and confirmed to be within the Australian Standard.

*

One of the main ingredients, 1,8 Cineole is the constituent that is found in quite high levels in Eucalyptus oil and many other oils of the *Melaleuca* genus. It contributes to the 'Eucalyptus' aroma and camphor like qualities. If too high the Tea Tree oil is noticeably of Eucalyptus type and it is very probable that the oil has either been adulterated, or is not up to the high quality it should be. Cineole is also responsible for the skin penetrating qualities, this allows Tea Tree oil to be so effective in the eradication of boils and septic lesions. A very high content of over 15% is not recommended as it is a known skin irritant and allergen.

The major therapeutic constituent is without doubt Terpinen-4-OL. It is responsible for the powerful, yet gentle, germicidal qualities. Tea Tree oil containing more than 30% is very desirable, but again the range of the percentage can vary considerably from under 5% to over 40%, unlike the Cineole content, the Terpinen-4-ol should be as high as possible.

The Australian Standard of 1967 stated that the Terpinen-4-OL content should be higher than 35% and the 1,8 Cineole content less than 10%. Unfortunately this lead to an over production of oil that failed to meet the required standard. In 1985 the Australian Standard was revised and re-issued stating that the oils should have a Terpinen-4-OL greater than 30% and the 1,8 Cineole content lower than 15%.

A number of distributor companies within the U.K. fall well within these parameters. The better quality oils today have a 1,8 Cineole content between 2% and 6% with a Terpinen-4-OL content between 37% and 42>%. The aroma of a good quality Tea Tree oil should be spicy and mildly antiseptic. If the aroma has more than the slightest hint of Eucalyptus it has either been adulterated with a less expensive oil/chemical or has not been distilled to the high standard required. If this is the case you have a low quality oil, with low therapeutic properties - it should not be used for therapeutic or first aid applications. Please also be aware that there are many oils that technically can be called Tea Tree, Ti-Tree or Titrol oil. There are over 150 species of *Melaleuca* Tea Trees, but as stated before, only one has the low 1,8 Cineole and the high Terpinen-4-OL content.

If you are to be assured of a good quality Tea Tree oil, you should always remember to only purchase the ones with 'Melaleuca Alternifolia' actually displayed on the label, if it also has a high 40>% Terpinen-4-OL and low <5% 1,8 Cineole content printed on it too, so much the better.

*

With the growing demand for high quality oil, there will be some interesting labels displayed, one already noticed by Nina Turpin from her book "The Healing Wonder From Down Under" reads:

"100% pure Tea Tree Oil with added Vitamin E"

If there is anything at all, added to the Tea Tree oil in the bottle, it cannot be 100% pure!.

On the other hand if there was just .5% pure Tea Tree oil and 99.5% Vitamin E oil, this misleading label could still be used. Of course this oil would bear no resemblance to pure Tea Tree oil whatsoever. It would also have little or none of the antibacterial, germicidal properties that the unad-ulterated oil possesses.

All this reminds me of a very apt slogan I once saw, during my "love Affair" with consumer competitions;

"Nothing added, nothing removed,
Natures best cannot be improved."

*

In 1988, the occurrence of viridflorene in Tea Tree oil was confirmed by a combination of Gas Chromatograms/MS and Kovat's Indices. A year later, in 1989 a Gas Chromatographic/MS was used to examine the chemical composition of lab-distilled oils. Only the leaves and the terminal twigs of the *Melaleuca Alternifolia* were used. The compounds identified in this study can be seen listed as follows:

a -pinene (2.5%)

y-muurolene (trace)

a-p-dimethyistyrene (trace)

globulol (0.2%)

ledol (trace)

viridflorol (0.1%)

rosifoliol (trace)

spathulenol (trace)

cis-p-menth-2-en-1-ol (0.1%)

terpinen-4-ol (40.2%)

a-bulnesene (trace)

camphene (trace)

a-thujene (0.9%)

b-pinene (0.3%)

a-amorphene (trace)

p-cymen-8-ol (trace)

linalool (trace)

sabinene (0.2%)

a-cubebene (trace)

a-phellandrene (0.3%)

a-ylangene (trace)

1,4 -cineole (trace)

cis-sabinene hydrate (trace)

limonene (1.0%)

b-phellandrene (0.9%)

1,8-cineole (5.1%)

a-gurjunene (0.2%)

y-terpinene (23.1%)

trans-piperitol (trace)

terpinolene (3.2%)

cubenol (0.1%)

methyl eugenol (trace)

b-caryophyllene (0.1%)

aromadendrene (1.4%)

b-gurjunene (0.1%)

b-elemene (0.1%)

s-cadinene (1.2%)

allo-aromadendrene (0.3%)

a-humulene (trace)

viridflorene (1.0%)

a-terpineol (2.3%)

a-muurolene (0.1%)

trans-p-menth-2-en-1-ol (0.2%)

palustrol (trace)

bicyclogermacrene (0.1%)

y-cymene (2.8%)

myrcene (0.5%)

trans-sabinene hydrate (trace)

cis-piperitol (trace)

cadina-1,4-diene (0.1%)

a-terpinene (10.4%)

calamenene (0.1%)

nerol (trace)

a-copaene (trace)

trans-*b*-ocimene (trace)

1,2,4- trihydroxy-p-menthane (trace)

Also found were 10> sesquiterpene hydrocarbons (0.2%), 4 Oxygenated sesquiterpenes (0.1%), and 20> Unknowns (0.1%). The lab-distilled oil was slightly different to the commercially distilled oil. The commercial oil had more constituents namely, hexanol, allylhexanoate, camphor and piperitone.

Chapter Four

The Power &
The Gory

The skin is the largest organ of the body. It lives and it breathes - it is responsible for some of the body's most complex functions, such as temperature control, touch, pressure, pain, secretion and excretion (through the sweat and sebaceous glands).

The skin is made up of (approximately) 645 sweat glands, 95 oil glands, 19 million cells, 65 hairs, 21 feet of blood vessels, 75 feet of nerve endings and 19-20,000 sensory cells per square inch.

It is now scientifically accepted that substances can effectively reach the bloodstream by absorption through the skin's layers. Just as it can eliminate toxins, the skin can also absorb them. Nicotine (the nicotine patch) steroids and hormones have been successfully introduced into the bloodstream by transdermal absorption.

Transdermal absorption has three main advantages over orally ingested medication:

> 1) It is easy to maintain a steady concentration in the blood stream - the patch stays on, there is no need to remember to 'take' medication.

> 2) Medication bypasses the liver and the intestines. It seems not to have the same toxicity level when absorbed directly into the bloodstream, mainly because it does not wholly enter the digestive system.

> 3) It allows for long term therapy, as it is gentler on the system.

The skin also acts as an effective barrier against injury, invasion by harmful micro-organisms, pollution and the elements.
Although a very effective barrier, certain conditions can help and actually speed up the rate of absorption of substances through the skins layers.

> 1) The smaller the molecular particles of a substance the more easily it will be absorbed i.e. Tea Tree oil is more readily absorbed than olive oil.

> 2) If a substance is in contact with the skin for any length of time ie. Tea Tree oil can be absorbed in minutes when rubbed on to the skin, absorption also depends on conditions like temperature.

3) The warmer the skin is the more it will absorb, the pores open and glandular activity is increased, a substance will then be quickly absorbed through the sweat and oil glands on the surface of the skin.

4) There are certain substances which can react with each other and with the skin to stop absorption.......There is still a great deal of research still to be done on this subject, it has been found that the synergy of some of these chemical binding agents have actually INCREASED absorption. ......Tea Tree oil is very readily absorbed also because of the natural synergy of its components.

Face creams are chemically engineered for maximum absorption! by the chemicals they contain!!

5) Various gases may gain entry through the skin by the respiratory process, (the skin is a living breathing organ).

6) If the skin is covered after exposure to a certain substance then absorption is increased. The cover works in two ways; it can trap heat and so warms the skin and by holding the substance against the surface, it extends the contact time. This can be dangerous if toxic substances are being handled.

Absorption can be impeded by conditions such as the skin's natural exfoliation, substance evaporation, and certain binding agents, included in preparations (see item 4 above). All substances that do become absorbed through the skin are likely to gain access into the bloodstream.
The bloodstream is basically the body's "River of Life". Blood is pumped around the body picking up oxygen, nutrients and substances that have been absorbed, it then takes them into every cell. Like any river it can become polluted and feed the body with either life or death.

But why should the average person be worried about transdermal absorption? ....

There are over 20 square feet of surface area on the average body, that is a large area of possible absorption. If you think of all the substances that come into contact with your skin during the course of a day it is quite a cause for concern.

Antiseptics	Dyes	Solvents	Household Sprays
Shampoo	Make-up	Soap	Air Fresheners
Conditioner	Face Cream	Hair Spray	Bath/Shower Gel
Fly Spray	Perfumes	Moisturisers	Washing up liquid
Polishes	Nail Varnish	Hand Creams	Cleaning Agents
Air pollutants	Deodorants	Detergents	Nail Varnish Remover

All these and more are probable substances that we come into contact with during the course of a day. Even pollutants/poisons in the water supply like fluorine, chlorine, lead, nitrates etc. can be absorbed when we wash, have a bath or do the washing up, not to mention drink it.

Now look on the labels of the above listed products. Do you really want those substances in your bloodstream?. Do you even know what they are?

Propylene Glycol is sometimes added to moisturisers which is commonly known as a type of "anti-freeze" (....and it is, in some brands, added to commercial whipped desserts!). Aluminium, in some form, is added to most anti-perspirant deodorants. Scientists are now beginning to think that there is a link to the symptoms of Alzheimer's Disease and the absorption of aluminium; but it is still being absorbed into the body of everyone who uses these anti-perspirants.

Many perfumes contain as much as 70% Ethanol, a substance that reacts with the fatty protective layer of the skin, temporarily altering its structure and allowing penetration. Perfume can contain as many "nature identical" chemicals as bubblebath, soaps and moisturisers. The more dubious essential oils can contain chemical constituents that try to mimic their natural counterparts, and they are not always displayed on the label.

The hands are particularly vulnerable because the skin is quite thin and there are many visible main veins, which provide quick, easy access to the bloodstream. A plus point for wearing undamaged rubber gloves when handling chemical cleaners, insecticides and pesticides.

All the different products that we use may be increasing the chemical substances that are entering our systems. One thing we do know is that synergy does occur, that substances can work with one another to create a greater or different effect than if they were working completely alone. This could mean that the unknown 'mixture' of chemicals that meet up within the body may have unforeseen consequences for a susceptable person.

There is research work going on at the moment into household pollutants. A growing number of scientists now believe that some of these chemicals can actually cause memory loss - surely this means that they are being readily absorbed into our brain cells - so what about all the chemicals that we put onto our skin everyday - moisturisers, lotions, hair products and soaps. Surely these too must eventually be absorbed into our brain cells?.

For all you sceptics - try a simple well known test: Cut a garlic clove in half, rub the soles of your feet with both halves, now put your shoes and socks back on - in a few hours ask your partner if your breath smells - convinced?.

Because no-one really knows for sure about the skin in this capacity, or the repercussion of the chemical cocktails we bombard our systems with during the course of a lifetime. We could be facing a very major issue, even disaster, for future generations. The chemical cosmetics industry is vast, they themselves fund many of the scientific departments. They will not thank anyone for publicly informing the consumer about the possible dangers.

Society on the whole, even now, seems to ignore the natural household and cosmetic products available. It is still basically the age of the chemical. We may be slowly turning to organic farming methods and alternative therapies, but we continue to buy, and use, a multitude of chemicals in and around our homes, as well as on our bodies.

Until we know the effects all this is having on our systems, I for one will be doing my best to minimise the chemicals that my family and I come into contact with.

*

Tea Tree oil is a natural, safe alternative. It can be used on its own or as an ingredient in various household products; such as furniture and floor polish, white ring remover for polished surfaces, silver and brass cleaner, as well as topical first aid and toiletry items such as; natural healing ointments, moisturisers, and shampoo's. Chapter 5 - Home and Away Applications - will help you to stem the tide of synthetic chemicals, from ordinary household products, entering and flowing through your bloodstream.

Tea Tree oil is usually absorbed within minutes, it contains natural, safe compounds that help its passage through the dermal layers. It can effectively eradicate trapped bacteria, that cause boils and abscesses etc. It also seems to be quite potent in the fight against fungal and viral infections too. When applied, even in a greatly reduced dilution (as low as .25% in some cases), it can actively provoke irreparable damage to the wall of the invading germ cell (without affecting a healthy skin cell), causing the germ to die, instead of going on to multiply and so cause infection and disease.

But what are bacteria, fungi and viruses?........

BACTERIUM

PLURAL - BACTERIA FROM THE GREEK: 'BAKTERION' (SMALL ROD OR STICK)

Bacteria is the common name for a vast group of one-celled microscopic organisms. A bacteria cell is the smallest, simplest structural unit of living tissue that is capable of functioning as an independent entity.

They can exist in the hottest, coldest places on earth and at more than 10kms below the ocean and in the almost airless reaches of the upper atmosphere.

Bacteria are found in the air, food, water, soil, organic matter, in our body and on our body. Some are harmful, but others we need for our very existence.

The oldest sign of life on earth is a fossilised bacterial cell discovered in a rock in Africa. It is estimated to be over 3 billion years old.

Thirty trillion bacteria would only weigh 28gms. They are measured in microns; 0.001 micrometers = 0.00004".

Bacteria falls into two main groups, gram positive and gram negative. Gram staining, a technique for identifying the bacteria was perfected by Hans Christian Gram in 1884. The bacteria was treated with a special dye and chemicals. The bacteria could then be categorised into the two groups - Gram positive bacteria, which was deep violet in colour and was later found to be susceptible to penicillin and gram negative bacteria, which would appear deep red and would be susceptible to other antibiotics, such as streptomycin. The basis for such staining is still a mystery. It is interesting to note that Tea Tree oil can be effective against both types of bacteria.

WHAT ARE BACTERIA RESPONSIBLE FOR?

SORE THROATS	WOUND INFECTIONS
BOILS	TUBERCULOSIS
ABSCESSES	PNEUMONIA
DIPHTHERIA	TYPHOID
WHOOPING COUGH	DIGESTIVE DISORDERS
BUBONIC PLAGUE	LEGIONNAIRES DISEASE
FOOD POISONING	SALMONELLA POISONING
STOMACH ULCERS	CHOLERA
ACNE	Etc.

VIRUS

PLURAL - VIRUSES   FROM THE LATIN: 'VIRUS' (POISON SLIME)

Discovered in 1952, viruses are submicroscopic entities even smaller than bacteria, ranging from 20nm to 300nm. (one nanometre is one thousand-millionth of a metre). The average virus needs a special electron microscope in order to see it.   Most viruses are pathogenic, they enter living cells, take them over and multiply rapidly.   They are unable to multiply without a living cell, because of this, a few scientists did not class them as living organisms, but a mechanical process by which the cells mimic the mechanics of a virus and the cells themselves multiply as the virus. (Viruses may be a variety of DNA or RNA molecules that have arisen within living cells, they then quickly mimic the cells pattern).

As the virus takes over the host cell it begins to die (or transmute into a copy of the virus).   The virus quickly replicates to other cells in the body.

Viruses also have been shown to cause certain cancers in animals whether they do in humans is not yet fully conclusive.

WHAT ARE VIRUSES RESPONSIBLE FOR?

WARTS	GERMAN MEASLES
SMALL POX	INFLUENZA
MEASLES	COMMON COLD
POLIO	HEPATITIS
RABIES	MUMPS
HERPES	SHINGLES
CHICKEN POX	AIDS
LASSA FEVER	T CELL LEUKAEMIA
COLD SORES	GLANDULAR FEVER
YELLOW FEVER	Etc.

FUNGUS

PLURAL - FUNGI   FROM THE GREEK: 'SP(H)ONGOS' (SPONGE)

Fungi are a diverse group of organisms, they show characteristics of both lower plant life and lower animal life, but are not closely related to either. There are more than 100,000 different species of Fungus known to man, and they come in many and varied forms such as; moulds, mildew, mushrooms, yeast etc.

FUNGUS (Cont.)

Parasitic Fungi feed on living plants, animals and decaying organic matter.

Fungi also gives us antibiotics, vegetarian protein such as quorn and a base for some vitamins and minerals. We need yeast for fermentation of alcohol, bread, cheese, soy sauce etc.

WHAT ARE FUNGI RESPONSIBLE FOR?

CANDIDA ALBICANS	CRYPTOCOCCAL MENINGITIS
VALLEY FEVER	ATHLETES FOOT
THRUSH	RING WORM
IMPETIGO	BALANITIS
NAIL FUNGUS	SHAVING RASH
TINEA	DANDRUFF
Etc.	

Fungi can also be tumour inducing and cause respiratory disease.

PATHOGEN FROM THE GREEK: PATHOS - (SUFFERING) + -GEN (THAT WHICH PRODUCES)
Pathogens are micro-organisms that cause infectious diseases in humans and animal life. Especially bacterium or fungus.

PARASITE FROM THE GREEK: PARASITOS - (FELLOW GUEST)
A creature that lives on or inside another living creature, ie. fleas, worms and protozoa etc.

PROTOZOA FROM THE GREEK: PROTO - (THE EARLIEST FORM) -ZOA - (ANIMAL)
A single celled microscopic organism of the phylum or sub-kingdom proto-zoa. Diseases caused: Malaria, Trichomonal Vaginitis etc.

MICRO-ORGANISMS FROM THE GREEK: MIKROS (SMALL)
An animal or plant of microscopic or submicroscopic size. Especially a bacterium or protozoan.

MICROBE MICRO + GREEK: BIOS (LIFE)
A micro-organism. A minute life-form, usually causing disease. (A germ).

GERM FROM LATIN: GERMEN - (OFFSHOOT), FOETUS
A micro-organism - often pathogenic. (A microbe).

SEPTIC FROM THE GREEK: SEPTIKOS (ROTTING)
Causing to putrefy; the activity of bacteria.

ANTIMICROBIAL ACTIVITY

As stated in Chapter Three: The Real Oil; Tea Tree oil can differ quite considerably in quality. The average good quality Tea Tree oil will show the following Minimum Inhibitory Concentrations (MIC), against most commonly encountered pathogenic Gram negative / Gram positive bacteria and fungi usually in the range of between O.25-1.0% v/v.
ie. the lowest concentration which will inhibit the growth of a specified micro-organism.

Several hundred in vitro tests have been conducted. In summary, it may be concluded that Tea Tree Oil of the *Melaleuca Alternifolia* (<5% Cineole and 40>% Terpinen-4-ol) is active against a wide range of micro-organisms including the following:

GRAM POSITIVE BACTERIA

Staphylococcus aureus	0.25-1.25	
Staphylococcus epidermidis	0.5-2.5	
Streptococcus pneumoniae	0.25	
Streptococcus faecalis		1.0-1.25
Streptococcus pyogenes		1.0
Streptococcus agalactiae		1.25
Streptococcus propionibacterium	0.5	
Listeria mono	0.75	
Micro coccus luteus	0.75	

GRAM NEGATIVE BACTERIA

Escherichia coli	0.25-0.5	
Klebsiella pneumoniae		1.0-2.0
Citrobacter spp	0.5-1.0	
Shigella sonnei	0.5	
Proteus mirabilis	0.5-1.0	
Legionelia spp	<0.75-1.0	
Pseudomans aeruginosa		2.0-5.0>
Pseudomans fluorescens		5.0>
Vibrio furnissii	0.625	

FUNGI

Trichophyton mentagrophyies	0.75>	
Trichophyton rubrum	0.5>	
Aspergillus niger		1.0
Aspergillus flavus	0.25-0.75	
Candida albicans	0.25-1.25	
Microsporum canis		1.0
Microsporum gypseum		1.0
Thermoactinomycetes vulgarus		1.25
Chaetomonium globosum	0.5	
Penicillium SP	0.75>	

BACTERIA & FUNGI - THE INFECTIONS THEY CAUSE.

Organism	Type	Infection
Actinobacillus actinomycetemcomitans:	B-	Associated with actinomycosis (a fungal infection caused by this genus). Isolated from people with bacterial endocarditis (infection of the lining membrane of the cardiac chambers), cystitis, urethritis, and from abscesses of the brain, thyroid, and soft tissue.
Actinomyces Israelii	B+	Has been recovered from the human mouth, tonsils, and saliva. Causes abcesses usually in tooth socket after extraction.
Actinomyces viscosus	B+	Causative agent of actinomycosis, associated with poor hygiene.
Aspergilus niger	F	Cutaneous and pulmonary aspergillosis, aspergillomas, and otomycosis. Acquired through inhalation.
Bacteroides fragilis	B-	Usually constitutes about 95% of normal fecal and normal flora of the respiratory and genital tracts. Is isolated from tissues affected by the following conditions: mucous membrane ulcerations, tonsillitis, ear infections, appendicitis, surgical wounds, vaginitis, septicemia, endocarditis, meningitis (inflammation of the membranes that envelope the brain and spinal cord.)
Bacillus subtilis	B+	Present in soil, decomposing matter, dust and air, and is a frequent laboratory contaminant.
Bacteroides gingisalis	B-	Constitute a large part of the normal fecal flora. Occasionally associated with disease, most often as opportunists.
Branhamella catarrhalis	B-	Part of the normal oral and nasopharyngeal flora. Associated with mucous membrane inflammations, neonatal conjunctivitis, acute bron-chopulmonary infections.
Candida albicans	F	Part of normal flora of throat, skin, vagina, feces. May invade any tissues or organ and produce disease. Most common cause of contagious disease candidiasis (thrush, vaginitis). Also skin and nail infections, athlete's foot, pulmonary or bronchial infection, pulmonary fungus balls, endocarditis (most commonly in drug addicts following cardiac surgery), cystitis, septicemia, abscesses in many organs. Predisposing conditions include: diabetes, malignancy pregnancy usage of antibiotics, steroids, or cyto-toxic drugs.
Closiridium perfringens	B+	Food poisoning and severe diarrhoea. Present in genital tract of 5% of normal females. Cause uterine infections after instrumental abortions. Part of normal fecal flora and isolated from milk and soil.
Enterococcus faecalis	B-	Part of normal flora of the intestines but may cause disease when removed from this habitat into the bloodstream. Susceptibility to drugs varies widely

Organism	Type	Infection
Escherichial coli (E. Coli)	B-	Part of normal intestinal flora and is often used as an indicator of fecal-contamination of water. Most frequent cause of urinary tract infection. May also cause appendicitis, pneumonia, sinusitis, septicemia, endotoxic shock, wound infections, abscesses. Diarrhoea in travellers (esp. to Mexico, Central & South America, Europe & Asia).
Fusobacterium mortiferum	B-	Has been cultured from the mouth and feces, from abscesses of the liver and rectum, and from persons with septicemia, emptema (pus in body cavity, esp the pleural cavity (membranes enveloping lungs, and linings of the wall of the chest cavity) and urinary tract infections.
Fusobacterium nucleatum	B-	Has been recovered from human wounds, the mouth, and infected upper respiratory tract and pleural cavity where it caused empyema.
Lactobacillus acidophilus	B+	Present in milk and buttermilk, and increases in numbers as milk becomes acidic. Part of the normal oral and vaginal flora. Has been isolated from decaying tooth dentine (hard tissue forming main substance of teeth). Also isolated from the stool of bottle-fed infants and from adults on diets high in milk content.
Mycobacterium smegmatis	B+	Rapidly growing organism frequently present in human spegma, and in soil, dust, and water.
Peptococcus assacharolyticus	B+	Isolated from clinical specimens in cases of puerperal (period of confinement after childbirth) sepsis, tonsillitis, colitis, acute appenicitis, cystitis, and pleurisy. Also from the gums, and occesionally from normal skin and the female genital tract.
Propionibacterium acnes	B+	Part of normal skin and intestinal flora. Originally and commonly isolated from acne pustules (abscesses on the skin). Has been cultured from clinical specimens in cases of conjunctivitis (infection of conjunctiva (delicate membrane that lines the eyelids and covers exposed surfeace of the eyeball), septicemia, endocarditis, and lung infections, and from absceses and wounds. Persons with immune deficiencies appear to be predisposed to infection.
Pseudomonas aeruginosa	B-	World-wide distribution. Common inhabitant of the soil. Typically and iridescent in appearance. Frequently present as part of the normal intestinal flora and skin flora. The bacteria acts as a pathogen when out of its normal habitat, especially after instrumentation (instruments used in medical treatment) or catheterization (introducing a catheter (slender, flexible tube) into a bodily channel to induce/remove fluids). May infect wounds, and produce a blue-green pus. Often contaminates burns, draining sinuses and ulcers. Infections are more inclined to develop in patients taking antibiotics.

Organism	Type	Infection
Streptococcus mutans	B+	Indicated as a cause of dental caries (breakdown of bone) and, less frequently, of bacterial endocarditis.
Serratia marcescens	B-	Widely distributed in soil and water. Formerly thought to be harmless, but may produce serious pulmonary infection, empyema, septicemia, urinary tract infections, meningitis, post-operative wound infections, sinusitis, arthritis, eye infections, chronic skin granulomas (tumours composed of a granular mass of tissue) allergic reactions. May cause hospital epidemics.
Streptococcus faecalis	B+	Part of a normal flora in intestinal tract. Produces urinary tract infections, subacute bacterial endocarditis, meningitis, and opportunistic infections. Occasionally associated with food poisoning: has been isolated from dairy products.
Staphylococcus aureus	B+	Characteristically produces pimples, abscesses or boils. Also the cause of carbuncles (similar to boils, but more severe), impetigo (contagious skin disease identified by visible pustules), wound infections, brain abscesses, and suppuration (formation or discharge of pus) in almost any organ. A great many resistant strains exist in this genus; all staphylococcal infections require antimicrobial susceptibility tests on isolates.
Streptococcus pyogenes	B+	Most common species of the strep genus. Capable of producing innumerable infections in humans: scarlet fever, rheumatic fever, suppurative infections of throat, ear, and sinuses. Also mastoids, tonsillitis, peritonsillar abscesses, Ludwig's angina, impetigo, pneumonia, septicemia.
Chaetomonium Globosum	F	An organism that is present on walls and buildings, it breaks down and assists the decay of wallpaper, bitumen roof tiles etc.
Trichophyton mentogrophytes	F	Ectothrix infections, chronic athlete's foot, and skin abrasions.
Trichophyton Spp *Microsporum Spp* *Epidermophyton floccosum*	F F F	Filamentous fungi, the principal causes of infection to the skin, nail and hair. "Ringworm".
Trichomonas vaginalis		A protozoan of the species group Flagellates (Trypanosomes), which causes vaginitis.

Key

B+ = Bacteria (Gram positive)
B- = Bacteria (Gram negative)
F = Fungi

Information obtained from;

Antimicrobial Chemotherapy, 3rd Edition - D. Greenwood, University Hospital, Queens Medical Centre, Nottingham, UK. 1995.

Principles and Practice of Infectious Diseases - Antimicrobial Therapy, 1992. Mandell, G.L., Douglas, R.C. Bennett, J.E. Churchill Livingstone, Inc 1992.

A Clinician's Dictionary Guide to Bacteria and Fungi (4th Edition). Mikat, D.M., Mikat, K.W.

Control of Communicable Diseases in Man (15th Edition). Benson, A.S., 1990. An Official Report of the American Public Health Association.

The Healing Wonder From Down Under - Turpin, N. 1995. USA.

Chapter Five

Home & Away Applications

HOME AND AWAY APPLICATIONS

Tea Tree oil can replace a large proportion of chemicals and toxins within the home. It is anti-bacterial, anti-fungal and insecticidal, yet safe and natural. It is perfect for the home environment.

This chapter shows you how to effectively replace many chemical products, with a safer, natural alternative and how to use Tea Tree oil to its best effect, in room by room alphabetically ordered applications.

Always do a patch test initially, on a hidden area, especially on furniture and soft furnishings, before cleaning the whole object.

PLEASE READ NOTES ON PAGE 8 BEFORE USING THIS CHAPTER

1ml Tea Tree Oil/Essential Oil = 20 drops
5ml Tea Tree Oil/Essential Oil = 1 Teaspoon

SECTION 1 / ALL AROUND THE HOME

AIR FRESHENERS

See ATOMISER
See ASHTRAYS
See TEA TREE OIL POT POURRI CHAPTER 8

ASHTRAYS

Empty the ashtray. Wipe around with neat Tea Tree oil. Fill it with Fullers Earth or pumice stone pieces. Both can be dyed using natural food colouring and allow to dry overnight on kitchen paper. (Keep out of reach of young children). Sprinkle on 3 drops Tea Tree oil and 3 drops lavender oil.

ATOMISER

In an all purpose mist sprayer put 250ml warm/hot water. Add 2ml Tea Tree oil, (dissolved in one teaspoon vodka) shake well before using and spray around the house as an air freshener and as a germicide when family have colds or flu etc.

BRASS

Rub a few drops of Tea Tree oil into brass ornaments. For stubborn stains add salt to Tea Tree oil and rub onto ornament. Polish with soft dry cloth. **This should not be used for varnished or coated brass.**

CARPETS

Add to carpet cleaning water 8ml to 1 litre to eradicate parasites from carpets and to disinfect carpet after soiling by pets, etc.

See VACUUM CLEANER.

COPPER

See BRASS

DEODORISER

Tea Tree oil is an effective room deodoriser and it can be used in several ways.

*For a quick room deodoriser, soak a flannel in warm water, add a few drops of Tea Tree oil and place over radiator only (never place near to a naked flame). *Or mist area with atomiser filled with 100ml hot water 10 drops Tea Tree oil (and 5 drops lavender oil) shake well before use.

*Add a bowl of steaming water to room, **place safely out of reach of children,** and add 5-10 drops of Tea Tree oil to bowl, or use an aromatherapy lamp/candle.

*Add a few drops of Tea Tree oil to tissues/kitchen towel and place under radiator on the floor.

* On a table lamp base, china or glass. Put 2-4 drops of Tea Tree oil on tissue and wipe around the lamp base, away from electric parts. Patch test first, do not continue if discoloration occurs.

DOOR HANDLES

Clean and disinfect door handles especially bathroom and cloakroom. Apply a few drops of Tea Tree oil to damp cloth and wipe over.

DOORS

The tops of doors are usually left unpainted and uncleaned. They can harbour dust and dustmites.

Wipe over with Tea Tree oil solution 8ml Tea Tree oil to 1 litre hot water. See top of page 53.

DRAWERS

Wipe out drawers with a Tea Tree oil solution (see above), apply liberally to wood inside drawers and furniture to repel wood beetles etc. (remember to allow drawers to dry before use) Use Tea Tree oil furniture polish on outside of wooden furniture. See Wood Polish.

See MISCELLANEOUS CHAPTER 6

DUSTER

See WOOD POLISHING DUSTER

DUSTMITES

Dustmites are known allergens to susceptible people. They can live happily in the home environment. Tea Tree oil is effective in their eradication without adding toxins to the home. Tea Tree oil solution - 8ml Tea Tree oil to 10ml alcohol (Approx. 2 teaspoons ie Vodka or alcohol, available from chemists). Dissolve Tea Tree oil to make water soluble then add to 1 litre of hot water, stir well. (Keep out reach of children).

Or make up a Tea Tree oil solution with 8ml Tea Tree oil to every 1 litre of hot water, use a small squirt of organic washing up liquid to emulsify.

Wash down everything where dust can collect, tops of doors, skirting boards, carpets, upholstery, dry-clean or wash soft furnishings.

For soft furnishings, always check on label before washing; add 5ml Tea Tree oil and 1 teaspoon salt to rinse water, soak for 1 hour and rinse well. Initially remember to do a small patch test before washing anything.

How to make Tea Tree oil anti-dustmite wood polish is listed in chapter 6.

See WOOD POLISHING DUSTER

FLEAS

Just 2 fleas entering your home and given the right conditions can generate over 200 trillion offspring within 9 months!!. They can each live for up to 2 years and survive months without eating. Anyone buying a new house with carpets should take steps to ensure their house is free of parasites, before they move in with their furniture..

For dealing with an infestation without using poison:

Fleas love woollen carpets but can survive happily in manmade fibres too. Shampoo all carpets with an organic carpet shampoo (low lather) add 8 ml of Tea Tree oil to every 1 litre of solution, before shampooing.

FLEAS (Cont.)

Add 8ml Tea Tree oil per litre of hot water and 1 tablespoon salt, stir vigorously, often, to disperse. (Do a small patch test first). Apply to skirting boards and liberally to small cracks and crevices in woodwork.

For furnishings and soft furnishings make a solution of 5ml Tea Tree oil to every 250ml alcohol, - alcohol is available from large chemists, and 'dry' wipe down mattress, pillows and headboard, upholstery. (Do a small patch test initially for each item). Always work in a well ventilated room, and wear rubber gloves when applying. Apply with small sponge.
Keep out of the reach of children.

See VETERINARY SECTION 17

FLOOR CLEANER

Add 3ml of Tea Tree oil to floor mopping water, in bucket, to ensure safer fragrant floors.

FLOOR MOP

After cleaning floors, wash and rinse out. Add a few drops Tea Tree oil, to rinse water. Rub through as this will help to prevent them going musty.

HINGES

In an emergency a few drops of Tea Tree oil & olive oil 50/50 on creaking hinges can help to lubricate them.

HUMIDIFIER

Tea Tree oil is perfect for humidifiers. The warm moist conditions of some humidifiers are a breeding ground for germs, apply a few drops of Tea Tree oil to water reservoir of humidifier.

INSECT REPELLENT

Tea Tree oil makes an effective household insect repellent. Mixed with a few drops geranium or citrus oil makes it even more effective.

If you have ever owned a rope door curtain you will realise that it is not an effective insect repellent. But spraying or dipping it in a solution of Tea Tree oil mixed with either geranium or citrus oils will make your rope curtain a lot more effective and will help to fragrance your home at the same time.

A steaming cup/container of hot water on a window ledge sprinkled with a few drops of Tea Tree oil and geranium oils will also be quite effective. (Keep out of reach of children). **Also label cup/jar so everyone knows what it contains.**

JEWELLERY

See MISCELLANEOUS SECTION 16

KEYS

Smear a few drops of Tea Tree oil & olive oil 50/50 onto your keys before you put then into the lock, to lubricate and make them easier to turn. It will also guard against the lock freezing up in winter.

LABEL REMOVER

See STICKY STUFF REMOVER
See LABEL REMOVER ON FRUIT / KITCHEN SECTION 2

LIGHT SWITCHES

Grubby marks on light switches can be removed with a few drops of Tea Tree oil on a dry duster. Remember to switch off the light before you clean.

PARASITES

See DUSTMITES
See FLEAS
See INSECT REPELLENT
See VETERINARY SECTION 17

PLASTERS

The adhesive left by plasters can be unsightly and very hard to remove. Rub in a drop of Tea Tree oil and wash area.

PEN MARKS

Try a patch test first to avoid discoloration. Stubborn pen marks on washable fabrics may be removed (depending on type of ink used), rub in neat Tea Tree oil and a drop of organic washing up liquid and wash. *Pen marks on hard surfaces can generally be removed using a few drops Tea Tree oil on a clean damp cloth. Always patch test item first.

PET SOILING

Remove any surface matter, mop up liquid, wash area with solution of organic cleaner (depending on surface type) with 1ml (20 drops) Tea Tree oil to every 100ml water and cleaner. This will effectively kill germs and deodorise area. Pets can sometimes re-soil area if scent is left.

POLISH

See CHAPTER 6
See WOOD POLISHING DUSTER

POT POURRI

See CHAPTER 6

ROPE DOOR CURTAINS

See INSECT REPELLENT

RUSH MATTING

To keep new rush matting fresh and prolong its life spray twice a week with solution of Tea Tree oil. Add 10-20 drops Tea Tree oil to every 50ml hot water and a small squirt of organic washing up liquid, shake well before use and spray. (An old mat should be thoroughly cleaned first).

SILVER

Tea Tree oil is very effective for cleaning silver. Apply a few drops with a clean duster. Rub in well and buff with clean cloth.

STICKY STUFF REMOVER

Tea Tree oil is also an effective solvent. Dab onto the glue residue left by labels, price stickers etc; on china, glass, jars etc. and just wipe off sticky stuff. Stubborn marks may need a couple of applications and leave to stand before removing.

See LABEL REMOVER ON FRUIT / SECTION 2 / KITCHENS

VACUUM CLEANER

Tea Tree oil can be used to refresh air freshener in vacuum cleaners or try dropping a tissue in the dustbag which has been soaked in a few drops of Tea Tree oil and lavender oil.

WOOD POLISHING DUSTER

To impregnate a duster for easy dusting, take a clean fresh duster square approx 12"x 12" and sprinkle on mixture of: 20 drops Tea Tree oil, 10ml almond oil and 10 drops Lavender oil.

Leave to stand 24 hours in small air tight container or plastic bag. Use as duster whenever required for wood/polished surfaces (not glass). Return to airtight container when not in use. Wash and re-oil when necessary.

See WOOD POLISH CHAPTER 6

WHITE RING REMOVER

White rings left from hot liquids on polished surfaces can be removed with a little elbow grease. mix 10 drops of Tea Tree oil and 10 drops of linseed oil and apply to a dry, soft duster. Rub round and round the ring with the Tea Tree oil and linseed oil mixture, pressing down with your fingertips from beneath the duster. Dipping duster into 2 lots of oil may be required.

Depending on severity of ring it could take a couple of applications of 5-10 minutes. Use more of the above oil each time.

See JAPANNED TRAYS / SECTION 7 DINING ROOM

SECTION 2 / KITCHEN APPLICATIONS

The kitchen can be a breeding ground for germs and bacteria. Make a solution of 8ml Tea Tree oil to 1 litre hot water and one teaspoon of organic washing up liquid - this will also act as an emulsifier. OR

To make Tea Tree oil water soluble, mix with equal quantities of alcohol - vodka or alcohol from chemists - and follow instructions on label. Mix 8ml Tea Tree oil, 8ml alcohol and add to 1 litre of water. This can help to eradicate germs, deodorise and have an insecticidal action.

BINS

Wipe over with the above solution.
*Freshener - shake 2 drops of Tea Tree oil and 2 drops lavender oil into pedal/swing bin to deodorise.

CAN OPENERS

Wipe over with the above solution.

CHOPPING BOARDS

Soak in a solution as above with 2 teaspoons salt added, rinse well.

CUPBOARDS

Wipe all around cupboards with Tea Tree oil solution. Allow to seep into cracks and crevices. Pay special attention to surfaces and doors and tops of cupboards.

CUPS

Tea stains on cups can be easily removed by making a paste of 1 teaspoon bicarbonate of soda and a few drops of Tea Tree oil. Mix together with water, apply by dishcloth or small brush, rinse well and dry.

See TEAPOTS

CUTLERY

Apply a few drops to edge of dishcloth and rub into silver, cutlery etc. This will clean and guard against tarnishing. Wipe over with clean cloth before use.

DISHCLOTHS

Rinse dishcloth often in Tea Tree oil solution to keep fresh.

DISHWASHER

Add 1-2 tablespoons sodium bicarbonate (available from chemists) and 5-10 drops Tea Tree oil to the dishwasher dispenser. It will clean just as well as an expensive dishwashing detergent.

DISH WASHING WATER

Add a few drops of Tea Tree oil to dish washing water to kill germs and ensure germ free dishes. Add 1 teaspoon sodium bicarbonate for dried on food. (This will not make dishes sterile at this potency).

FRIDGE CLEANER

Clean a defrosted fridge with 1/2 a litre of the Tea Tree oil solution, with 2 teaspoons of salt added, to kill germs and inhibit mould growth.

FRIDGE SEAL CLEANER

Apply a few drops of neat Tea Tree oil to damp dishcloth and apply to the door seal, in-between the rubber layers and right around the edge.

FRUIT WASH

Fill a bowl with 2 litres of warm/hot water, add a few drops of Tea Tree oil, two tablespoons of white wine vinegar and a squirt of organic bio-degradable washing up liquid. Stir well. Wash and scrub fruit and non-peeled (root) vegetables. Rinse well.

See LABEL REMOVER ON FRUIT

GARLIC ODOUR

See ONION AND GARLIC ODOUR ON HANDS
See BAD BREATH CHAPTER 7
See TEETH PASTE CHAPTER 6

LABEL REMOVER

Tea Tree oil is remarkable for removing sticky residue left behind from labels or price/special offer stickers. Soak jars/plates etc. in hot water and washing up liquid remove as much of the label as possible - dry and apply neat Tea Tree oil to glue residue left by labels and rub in, remove with a soft moist cloth. Instant removal.

LABEL REMOVER ON FRUIT

Remove the label, apply a couple of drops of Tea Tree oil to sticky stuff rub with a kitchen towel and wash well. See Fruit Wash.

ONION AND GARLIC ON HANDS

Begin by wetting hands under tap (water tepid) with stainless steel tablespoon. Rub the back of the spoon, everywhere the garlic has touched, over the skin on both hands, between the fingers, always under the running water. Dry hands, apply soap and 1 drop of Tea Tree oil (and 1 drop lemon oil - optional) to fumigate and rub in well, wash in warm water and dry.

RAW MEATS

Handling raw meat in the kitchen can transfer bacteria to other foods especially salads. Wash chopping boards, scissors, knives and tops etc. and everything that came into contact with the raw meat in the Tea Tree oil solution (see page 53). Wash and scrub your hands especially under the nails with soap and a few drops of Tea Tree oil.

SCOURERS, SCRUBBING BRUSHES

These items can all harbour germs if left damp on the edge of the sink. Rinse thoroughly with Tea Tree oil solution, (page 53).

SINK FRESHENER

Apply 10 drops Tea Tree oil to the plug hole. Wait 5 minutes, pour boiling water down the sink. Clean sink plug (stopper), top and underneath with neat Tea Tree oil. For a quick freshener a couple of drops works wonders.

TAPS

Clean around taps and the taps themselves with a few drops of Tea Tree oil on dishcloth. Cleans and helps to guard against limescale. For light limescale deposits around taps, make a paste of salt, bicarbonate of soda and a few drops Tea Tree oil, using an old toothbrush scrub the limescale with the paste. Leave to soak in for 5 minutes then scrub again to remove.

TEAPOTS

Clean stained teapots as cups. Or use the light limescale cleaner above, for stubborn stains.

WORK SURFACES

Wash down with Tea Tree oil solution, (page 53).

SECTION 3 / UTILITY ROOM

BEDDING WASH

For clean bedding, especially nylon that cannot be boiled, put 2.5ml (50 drops) Tea Tree oil in final rinse water. Boil wash all cotton bedding. (Never use a hotter temperature than stated on laundering label).

CLOTHES WASH

To prevent re-infection of contagious conditions from clothes ie. Impetigo, Ringworm (Tinea), Thrush etc. soak clothes, in 5 - 8ml Tea Tree oil and 2 teaspoons salt to every 1 litre of hot water, for 30 minutes before washing (for small areas, apply a few drops to area and wash as normal) rinse well. (TTO can be dissolved in alcohol - SEE KITCHEN APPLICATIONS, page 53)

DISHCLOTHS AND DUSTERS

Rinse in solution of Tea Tree oil and dry. (5ml Tea Tree oil mixed with 1 tablespoon white vinegar stir well and add to 1 litre of hot water and a squirt of organic washing up liquid).

FLANNEL WASH

Boil wash, if applicable, and rinse in a solution of Tea Tree oil (see above-dishcloths & dusters).

NAPPY WASH

Boil wash nappies. In the case of infected nappy rash rinse in 8ml solution per litre of hot water (and stand for at least 30 minutes) to prevent re-infection.

SHOE CLEANER

For patent and crocodile skin shoes and accessories clean with a few drops of Tea Tree oil on a clean duster.

SHOE FRESHENERS

Make your own shoe trees, which also acts as a good shoe freshener.
Take a pair of old socks, darn holes, line with feet from a pair of stockings, and a clear polythene bag, fill with dry sawdust or even dry, fresh cat litter (Fullers Earth), pack tightly, sprinkle with Tea Tree oil - use shoes as guide. Sew, press stud or clip tops 1/2" above shoe tops. Keep in shoes when not in use. Refresh often with few drops of Tea Tree oil and lavender or geranium oil. For shoes in need of a stronger freshener add a few drops of Tea Tree oil to sides of shoes, these are usually the most porous areas.

SHOE INSERTS

Partly fill undamaged stocking 'feet' with a little home made pot pourri (or Fullers earth in a polythene bag - chapter 6), sprinkle with geranium oil and Tea Tree oil, tie top with ribbon and keep in shoes stored in a wardrobe/ cupboard, this is an excellent shoe freshener and wardrobe moth repellent.

STAIN REMOVER

Tea Tree oil is an effective solvent, when added to other ingredients it can help to remove some stubborn stains.

As a general guide - do not use on non-washable fabrics

Always do a patch test first where it cannot ruin the garment if adverse re-action occurs.

5ml glycerine and 2 drops of Tea Tree oil.
Stain: chocolate/coffee/grass/fruit /wine stains

1 teaspoon salt, 2 drops Tea Tree oil and mix with lemon juice.
Stain: perspiration/rust/tea.

* Mix 1 teaspoon surgical spirit with 3-4 drops Tea Tree oil
Stain: **For stubborn stains of the above, and** chewing gum (surface matter removed)/pen marks/grease/old stains/deodorant stains etc.

*** Be careful it may damage delicate fabrics. Always do a patch test
initially.**

Work stains from the outside in with a pad of cotton wool or gauze. Rub in organic (biodegradable) washing up liquid and launder.

STAIN REMOVER (CONT.)

For organic stains (blood/milk etc) or as a general stain remover before washing dab stain with a solution made from 1 cup tepid water, a squirt of organic (biodegradable) washing up liquid and 4 drops of Tea Tree oil. Wash as normal.

See WASHING

TOWEL WASH

See BEDDING WASH
See FLANNEL WASH
See NAPPY WASH

UNDERWEAR WASH

See CLOTHES WASH

VACUUM CLEANER

See ALL AROUND THE HOUSE / SECTION 1.

WASHING

To save money when doing the weekly wash, add half a tablespoon of sodium bicarbonate (available from chemists) to your washing machine powder dispenser and only half the powder you would normally add, wash as per washing instructions.

WASHING MACHINE FRESHENER

When going away on holiday etc. and the washing machine is inactive for more than a week, it is advisable to make sure that it is clean, or when you next use your machine you will find that it may smell musty.

Clean out all the filters, the soap dispenser, and wipe around all the surfaces with a solution of Tea Tree Oil, made with 1 litre hot water, a squirt of organic washing up liquid and 1 ml (20 drops) Tea Tree oil. When finished add a few drops of Tea Tree oil to the drum, remember to leave the door open for the air to circulate.

SECTION 4 / THE BATHROOM

To make a solution of Tea Tree oil, add 5ml (1 teaspoon) to the same of alcohol, either vodka or alcohol from the chemists, mix well and add to 750ml hot water.

A substitute for washing purposes can be made by adding 5ml (1 teaspoon) Tea Tree oil to 1 tablespoon of white vinegar, stir well, add 750ml (approx. 1½ pints) of hot water and a squirt of organic washing up liquid, stir well and use as required.

BIN FRESHENER

Wipe around bin with a solution of Tea Tree oil and hot water (as above). Shake a couple of drops of Tea Tree oil into base of bin before putting in plastic liner.

BREATH FRESHENER

Add 2 drops of Tea Tree oil to normal toothpaste on toothbrush when cleaning teeth, rinse well. Or add 2 drops of Tea Tree oil to a small glass of warm water and rinse mouth. For an emergency breath freshener, wash hands thoroughly, add 1 drop Tea Tree oil to finger and apply to teeth.

See TEETH PASTE CHAPTER 6

DENTURE CLEAN

See preparation in CHAPTER 6

DEODORANT

Tea Tree oil is an effective deodorant, apply a few drops under arm area after bathing or hair removal. For a more feminine fragrance add a few drops lavender oil and apply.

Add a few drops to bath or sitz bath and apply as above.

See FOOT CARE CHAPTER 7
See FEET CHAPTER 6

LIMESCALE PREVENTER

Wipe around taps with a few drops of Tea Tree oil. For minor limescale build up, combine 5 drops of citrus oil, 5 drops of Tea Tree oil, 2 teaspoons each of bicarbonate of soda and cooking salt, mix to a paste with a little vinegar and apply to limescale with old toothbrush. Do not leave on too long especially on plastic baths and do not scour plastic baths. (If in doubt of the quality of your plastic bath do not use Tea Tree oil paste).

LOOFAH

To keep loofahs fresh, rinse in hot water with 1 dessertspoon white vinegar and 5 drops Tea Tree oil after use.

MIRRORS

To stop mirrors misting up in the bathroom mix 1 teaspoon glycerine to 2 drops of Tea Tree oil. Rub well into mirror surface after cleaning, repeat as necessary. (Can also be applied to windows).

MOULD

See SHOWER CURTAINS

NAIL BRUSHES

To keep nail brushes clean and infection free rub in a 2-3 drops of Tea Tree oil after using.

PLUGS

See SINK FRESHENERS.

SHOWER CURTAINS

To kill germs and inhibit mould growth on shower curtains between washing, spray curtain with a solution of: for every 500ml of hot water, add 2 tablespoons white vinegar, 2ml (40 drops) Tea Tree oil and a small squirt of organic washing up liquid. Shake well before use, spray/wipe tiles, especially grouting - clean with a soft brush or old nail brush dipped in the same solution. Also wipe down walls, behind toilet and washbasins to discourage mould growth.

See WOOD LICE

SPONGES

See LOOFAHS

TAPS

Wiping over taps with a couple of drops of Tea Tree oil on a clean, dry cloth will ensure that they are kept sparkling clean.

See LIMESCALE PREVENTER.

TILES

Wipe over tiles with the solution of Tea Tree oil (on top of page 61) and buff to a shine using a clean, dry, soft cloth.

See SHOWER CURTAINS

TOILET HANDLE

Wipe handle with a couple of drops of neat Tea Tree oil to kill germs, or use the solution top of page 61.

TOILET SEATS

Wipe seat often with a few drops of neat Tea Tree oil or use the solution on top of page 61.

TOOTHBRUSH

A bathroom with toilet is not the most hygienic place to keep your uncovered toothbrush. After using rub in 2 drops of Tea Tree oil to keep germ free and rinse under hot tap before using. Store in Cupboard.

See TEETHPASTE CHAPTER 6.

WOOD LICE

Wood lice love dark, damp conditions especially with decaying matter. Keep bathroom scrupulously clean, even under the bath if possible. Wiping behind the toilet, sink and bath every week with a solution of Tea Tree oil (as described under shower curtains or top of page 61) this will effectively inhibit mould growth and help to discourage wood lice.

See SHOWER CURTAINS.

SECTION 5 / THE SITTING ROOM

AIR FRESHENER

See SECTION 1 ALL AROUND THE HOUSE

COASTERS

To clean the stains from coasters clean with a damp cloth and add 2 drops of Tea Tree oil, rub well in and polish with a soft dry cloth.

LAMP BASES

For glass or ceramic lamp bases wipe with 2 drops of Tea Tree oil on a tissue for a pleasant fragrance.

OIL PAINTINGS

I have found that a few drops of Tea Tree oil on a little cotton wool will effectively clean my (new, inexpensive) oil paintings, without damaging the surface. For very old paintings it is advisable to consult a specialist before attempting this.
Always do a patch test initially.

T.V. CONTROLS

To stop the gunge build up on T.V. controls wipe with a solution of 1/2 a cup of clean washing up water - 3 drops of Tea Tree oil. (Avoid washing the writing as it may remove/fade it)

WHITE RING REMOVER ON FURNITURE/POLISHED SURFACES

See same SECTION 1 / ALL AROUND THE HOUSE.

For further applications ie. furniture, silver, brass, light switches etc.
See SECTION 1 / ALL AROUND THE HOUSE.

SECTION 6 / THE STUDY

BOOK COVERS

To remove stains from book covers (NOT CLOTH ONES) apply a few drops of Tea Tree oil, to a damp cloth. (Remember to do a patch test first).

To wipe over book covers and shelves with Tea Tree oil solution (put 1 litre of hot water into a bowl, add 5 ml Tea Tree oil and a squirt of organic washing up liquid) this will also guard against book lice. Always patch test initially.

GLUE RESIDUE REMOVER

Glues, pastes, sellotape etc. all leave a residue on objects, desks and on fingers. Wipe over area with a few drops of Tea Tree oil on a soft cloth. (Do not forget to initially do a patch test.)

GUNGE GONE

Apply as glue residue remover.

KEYBOARD CLEANER

Wipe over with a few drops of Tea Tree oil on a soft cloth to remove grease from keyboard. This will also remove pen/sellotape marks from the surfaces of other office equipment too. Always abide by manufacturers cleaning instructions.

PEN CLEANER

Tea Tree oil cleans pens when finger grease has built up on the casing. Use a solution of 1 tablespoon hot water, 2 drops Tea Tree oil and a drop of washing up liquid.

(Be careful when cleaning delicate finishes. Read and abide by instructions enclosed with your pen, patch test first).

PEN MARKS

See KEYBOARDS

For pen marks on clothes, rub a few drops of Tea Tree oil onto mark and launder as normal, for stubborn stains see STAIN REMOVER, UTILITY SECTION 3. Always patch test first.

SELLOTAPE RESIDUE CLEANER

See GLUE RESIDUE REMOVER.

STICKY STUFF REMOVER

See GLUE RESIDUE REMOVER.

TELEPHONES

Clean all telephones and fax machines as pens (See PEN CLEANER). If any member of the family has a cold or flu - clean mouthpiece with neat Tea Tree oil on soft cloth to kill germs.

See PUBLIC TELEPHONES TRAVELLING SECTION 14.

SECTION 7 / THE DINING ROOM

COASTERS

Clean stubborn marks with neat Tea Tree oil on a soft, damp cloth or wash over with a solution of; 1 cup hot water, a squirt organic washing up liquid and 5 drops of Tea Tree oil, polish with a soft, dry cloth.

CONDIMENT TRAYS

See COASTERS.

CUTLERY

See COASTERS
Or
See SILVER - ALL AROUND THE HOUSE / SECTION 1

DECANTERS

To remove old wine stains or to freshen decanters, fill with a solution of 500ml hot water (not too hot), 1 tablespoon white vinegar, a squirt of organic washing up liquid and 20 drops of Tea Tree oil. Shake well (a bottle cleaning brush is very useful for stubborn stains) and top up to the brim with hot water, soak until cold, shake and rinse well.

To dry: Fill decanter to brim with warm to hot water - empty out and turn upside down and allow to empty whilst the hot tap (but not too hot) runs at full force over the upturned base. This will dispose of most of the water. Still upturned, dry outside. Apply gentle heat with hairdryer, not too hot or may crack decanter. Replace stopper only when dry.

JAPANNED TRAYS

To remove heat marks from Japanned trays rub in a mixture of 1 teaspoon almond oil, 10 drops Tea Tree oil. Rub in until mark disappears. Depending on age or depth of stain it may take 5-10 minutes.

68

TABLE MATS

See COASTERS.

TRAYS

See JAPANNED TRAYS.
See COASTERS.

VASES

See DECANTERS and ALLOW TO AIR DRY.

WOODWORK

See WOOD POLISHING DUSTER
See WOOD POLISH MISCELLANEOUS CHAPTER 6

See ALL AROUND THE HOUSE / SECTION 1 for further applications in the dining room.

SECTION 8 / THE BEDROOM

BEDS

To keep headboards, mattresses and bases germ free and dustmite free, wipe over every 6 months or so with a solution of 50 drops Tea Tree oil to every 100ml of alcohol - (use vodka or alcohol available from chemists). Keep out of reach of children. Work in a well ventilated room, do not smoke, and always wear rubber gloves.

BEDDING

See BEDDING. UTILITY SECTION 3.

BEDSIDE LAMPS

Polish base of lamps with 1 drop Tea Tree oil to 2 drops of lavender oil for a restful night.

CLOTHES

See CLOTHES WASH UTILITY SECTION 3.

COAT HANGERS

To freshen a covered coat hanger open the seam and sprinkle on 5 drops of Tea Tree oil and 5 drops of rosemary oil, re-sew. This will freshen a wardrobe and guard against moths.

CUPBOARD AND DRAWER FRESHENERS

See FRAGRANCE SACS
See MISCELLANEOUS / CHAPTER 6

FRAGRANCE SACS

To guard against moths and to freshen the cupboards, wardrobes or drawers, pot pourri sacs are inexpensive and simple to make.

QUICK NO SEW METHOD.

For each pot pourri sac you will need;

    2 tablespoons granulated FULLER'S EARTH
    (the least expensive is cat litter) See CHAPTER 6
    25 drops of your favourite 'moth repellent' quality essential oils.
    Or see below for a recommended blend.

    Small plastic bag 6"x4" food quality
    A circular piece of lace (8") or coloured/dyed tights
    A length of ribbon

BLEND 1
15 drops Geranium oil
10 drops Tea Tree oil

BLEND 2
15 drops Lavender oil
10 drops Tea Tree oil.

BLEND 3
15 drops Rosemary oil
10 drops Tea Tree oil

BLEND 4
10 drops Moroccan Cedarwood oil
5 drops Rosemary oil
5 drops Tea Tree oil

BLEND 5
10 drops Lemon oil
10 drops Tea Tree oil

In a small plastic bag put 2 tablespoons of granulated Fuller's Earth.
Sprinkle on the essential oils, shaking bag every 3-5 drops. Knot the bag.
Plastic bags are ideal as they are air tight, but they let the fragrance through.
Cut off the surplus plastic from top of the bag.

Place into one of the feet of an old pair of clean, coloured tights (white, red,
etc) or in the middle of an 8" circle of a net curtain or lace, put edges
together, drape around a bright contrasting piece of ribbon, secure with a
knot - for hanging in a cupboard or wardrobe make a loop and knot again.
For putting into drawers tie and make a bow.

Refresh as necessary every few months, by opening the ribbon, transferring the Fuller's Earth to a new plastic bag and sprinkle on more essential oils, make up as before.

MELAMINE CLEANER

Wardrobes, dressing tables etc. can be washed with a solution of Tea Tree oil as for kitchen cupboards (section 2). Stubborn marks may be removed with a couple of drops of Tea Tree oil on a damp cloth.

SHOE FRESHENERS

See UTILITY SECTION 3

TABLE LAMPS

See BEDSIDE LAMPS

WARDROBE FRESHENERS

See FRAGRANCE SACS
See MISCELLANEOUS CHAPTER 6

See ALL AROUND THE HOME / SECTION 1 for other relevant applications.

SECTION 9 / THE NURSERY

Tea Tree oil is very good for ailments from cradle cap to nappy rash. See Chapter 7. It is a powerful, but gentle, antiseptic helping to keep the nursery germ free.

New-born babies should have the advice of a qualified Aromatherapist.

Do not apply more than 5% solution to a young baby's skin. See Midwife.
(5 - 10 drops - Tea Tree oil to every 10ml grapeseed oil)

Do not apply more than 10% solution to a baby's skin. (1 year old)
(10 - 20 drops - Tea Tree oil to every 10ml grapeseed oil).

READ PAGE 8.   ALWAYS DO A SENSITIVITY TEST FIRST.

FIRST AID KIT

See SECTION 10

NAPPY BAG

Tea Tree oil is a useful addition to the nappy bag especially when potty training. Taking a child outside the home can mean that the child comes into contact with unwelcome germs. A child using a public convenience is protected if you wipe the toilet seat over with neat Tea Tree oil, wipe hands over before washing too.

See TEA TREE OIL SUPER ANTISEPTIC HEALING CREAM / CHAPTER 6.

NAPPY RASH

See NAPPY RASH CHAPTER 7
See TEA TREE OIL SUPER ANTISEPTIC HEALING CREAM

NAPPY SOAK

See UTILITY SECTION 3

NIPPLES

See BREASTFEEDING CHAPTER 7
See BREAST TONING OIL CHAPTER 6

POTTY

Wipe over potty with neat Tea Tree oil on tissue or damp kitchen roll to keep germ free.

SURFACES

Keeping the nursery clean and germ free is easy using a solution of Tea Tree oil. Wipe over surfaces using a mix of 500ml hot water, 4ml Tea Tree oil and a squirt of organic washing up liquid.

See MELAMINE SECTION 8

TEETHING RINGS

Wipe over teething rings with mix of 20 drops extra virgin olive oil, 2 drops Tea Tree oil. Wipe with clean tea towel. This is especially useful when travelling and the teether could not be cleaned.

TOYS

Wipe over toys using solution of Tea Tree oil as for surfaces.

See SURFACES

TEA TREE OIL VAPOUR RUB

See CHAPTER 6

SECTION 10 / FIRST AID BOX

Tea Tree oil should be your first choice for the first aid box. Keep one bottle of Tea Tree oil at room temperature in each of your first aid boxes and one bottle in the refrigerator for emergencies that need cold Tea Tree oil, ie sprains, bruises etc.

See A-Z of First Aid Applications for a guide to the many ailments Tea Tree oil helps, prevents and cures.

You can make a first aid box from a biscuit tin or Tupperware container. I did both and keep one in the cupboard and one in the car. I have been very pleased that I did on several occasions.

I have found that this basic kit covers quite a few emergencies especially when travelling with children.

CONTENTS

1) One bottle of pure Tea Tree oil, *Melaleuca Alternifolia.*

2) One mixed bottle of 2ml Tea Tree oil and 20ml olive oil
   Mix together and keep in a small 30ml, labelled dark glass
   bottle.

3) Small tub of 'Tea Tree Oil Super Antiseptic Healing Cream',
   (Chapter 6)

4) Small tub of 'Tea Tree Oil Anti-fungal Cream', (Chapter 6)

5) Small tub of Tea Tree Oil Burn Ointment (Chapter 6)

6) Plasters (Assorted sizes)

7) Bandages (Assorted sizes)

8) Scissors (Small rounded tips)

9) Tweezers

10) Safety Pins

11) Surgical Tape

12) Needle (Stored in a case or with the sharp point stuck firmly into a cork)

13) Nail File

14) White Cotton Wool Balls.

15) Gauze

Lavender oil is very good for burns, I keep a bottle in my kitchen first aid box, after flooding the burn with water, I pat dry and put on a couple of drops.

This small First Aid box will cover a multitude of scrapes, burns, splinters etc. It will save a lot of tears and time trying to find items when an accident has occurred.

SECTION 11 / GARAGE AND TOOL BOX

CUTS

In an emergency, if it is just a superficial wound, flood with neat Tea Tree oil, cover, until you can clean the wound properly.

GRAZES

See Above
See ABRASIONS CHAPTER 6
See FIRST AID BOX SECTION 10

HAMMER

Hitting hands or fingers with a hammer is quite a common occurrence. Apply cold Tea Tree oil ice pack. A few drops of cold Tea Tree oil on a flannel that has been kept in a freezer, (see cold compress - chapter 6) or hold area under a cold running tap for a few minutes to stop the swelling. Pat dry and massage in Tea Tree oil.

HINGES

In an emergency, with nothing else to hand, a few drops of Tea Tree oil can help to ease grinding hinges, its solvent properties assists in cleaning the moving parts for a smoother action.

MASKING TAPE RESIDUE

Neat Tea Tree oil is very efficient at removing glue residue from surfaces. Wipe over with a soft cloth dipped in Tea Tree oil. For old, stubborn residues allow to soak for 10 minutes before removing with a clean soft cloth.

NUTS AND BOLTS

A few drops of Tea Tree oil on a stiff nut or bolt can work wonders, see hinges above.

PAINT

Paint specks on glass can be removed using Tea Tree oil and an old razor blade. Soak paint with neat Tea Tree oil and remove with blade.

(Be careful - the blade can still be quite sharp, KEEP OUT OF THE REACH OF CHILDREN).

SECTION 12 / IN THE CAR

AROMATHERAPY

Mix together 5-7 drops Tea Tree oil and 5-7 drops of geranium oil or lemon oil. It is a very good reviver when travelling. It will also help to repel insects from entering your car.

5 drops of mandarin oil, 2 drops of pine oil and 5 drops of Tea Tree oil is also a good reviver and can help to alleviate cold symptoms.

You can sprinkle them on to a tissue and put them into the open ashtray or you can use the ashtray freshener method below, which also acts on a similar principle.

ASHTRAY FRESHENER

Take 1 tablespoon of granulated 'Fullers earth' (a cheaper version is cat litter which works just as well), and dye with a natural food colouring - dry overnight on kitchen towel. Place the dyed 'Fullers earth' into the ashtray and sprinkle with essential oils as described in Aromatherapy (above and in chapter 8). It will freshen your car and help to revive you on a long journey. Refresh with a few drops of essential oils when necessary.

See AROMATHERAPY ABOVE.

DE-MISTER

Mix together 25ml glycerine, 5 drops of Tea Tree oil - stir well. Using a clean, lint free cloth, apply to inside of the clean windows all round the car. Rub well in until the windows are smear free.

This will guard against misting up and help to prevent frosting. Do not use on outside of windscreen. Repeat as necessary.

FIRST AID KIT

See FIRST AID BOX   SECTION 10

FRAGRANCE CUSHION

To make a no-sew fragrance cushion see CHAPTER 6.

INSECT REPELLENT

See AROMATHERAPY.

KEYS

Smear 2 drops of Tea Tree oil onto car keys. It will keep locks smooth and guard against them freezing up in the winter.

MOTION SICKNESS

5 drops of Tea Tree oil sprinkled onto a tissue can guard against nausea caused by the rocking motion of the car and by the petrol fumes. It is also invaluable when driving with a cold or blocked sinuses.

PETS

See FLEAS - SECTION 1 ALL AROUND THE HOME
See VETERINARY   SECTION 17
See TEA TREE VETERINARY PRODUCTS IN USEFUL ADDRESSES

PUBLIC CONVENIENCES

See TRAVELLING   SECTION 14

PUBLIC TELEPHONES

See TRAVELLING   SECTION 14

SECTION 13 / IN THE GARDEN

BARBECUE INSECT REPELLENT

30 minutes before a barbecue light half a dozen aromatherapy lamps, sprinkled with a few drops of Tea Tree oil and geranium oil/citronella oil or light home-made aromatherapy candles.
(Keep out of reach of young children)

See KITCHEN SECTION 2 RAW MEAT
See MISCELLANEOUS - CHAPTER 6 AROMATIC FIRELIGHTERS
See CHAPTER 6 - AROMATHERAPY CANDLES

FUNGICIDE AND INSECTICIDE SPRAY

Spray plants with solution of:
3ml Tea Tree oil to every litre of tepid onion & chrysanthemum water, and 1 teaspoon of organic (biodegradable) washing up liquid.

Take 100g chrysanthemum heads, stems or leaves, 2 onions (and garlic, optional) chop, put in liquidiser with nearly 1 pint water, blend until smooth, sieve through a fine mesh sieve (muslin is the best, squeeze every drop of liquid - wear rubber gloves), make up with tepid (boiled) water to 1 litre. Soak and wash liquidiser well before use.
Add the Tea Tree oil, washing up liquid and pour into a plant/garden sprayer.
IF STORING, LABEL AND DATE THE LIQUID, KEEP OUT OF THE REACH OF CHILDREN. IDEALLY STORE IN BOTTLE WITH CHILDPROOF CAP.

Shake contents well and spray making sure every part of the plant gets a good soaking, especially on the underside of leaves - spray once or twice a week during May-June-July-August-September on a dry, cool evening.

GREENHOUSE

Tea Tree oil can be used as an insect repellent inside the greenhouse.
1) On the greenhouse door hang a large plain net curtain, making sure the curtain has a large hem to hold stones. Un-pick 2" of the hem, fill and sew with stones into the bottom of the curtain. This will weigh it down. Spray the hem and stones with a solution of 1ml Tea Tree oil, 1ml geranium oil or

citronella oil to 20ml alcohol (available from chemists) and 100 ml water. Shake well before use.
Put into the garden sprayer and shake well. Refresh stones every morning during season.

2) Fill the feet of tights with Fullers earth (cat litter). Spray with solution and hang in the greenhouse - quite close to the open windows or place under plants.

NB. The 'Fungicide and insecticide spray' can also be used as a spray deterrent in the greenhouse, as above.

PLANT POTS

Used plant pots can harbour germs and fungi from previous plants. Soak and wash well in a bowl of hot water with 20 drops of Tea Tree oil, 1 tablespoon vinegar and washing up liquid. Scrub pots and allow to dry naturally.

SECTION 14 / TRAVELLING

In Australia Tea Tree oil has been known affectionately as "A medicine kit in a bottle" for many years.
It is perfect for popping into your handbag/suitcase when travelling at home or abroad.

FIRST AID KIT

For a (handbag sized) first aid kit put 1 X 10ml bottle Tea Tree oil, 10ml bottle geranium oil, 10ml bottle lavender oil, plasters (various sizes), gauze, surgical tape, tweezers and small pair of scissors into a make-up bag.

HAND WASHING

If you have ever tried to wash your hands in unfamiliar surroundings with no soap you will be pleased to hear that Tea Tree oil is an effective bactericide. Put 4 drops on your hands. 'Dry' wash them, rinse under tap and dry.

MOTION SICKNESS

Apply 1 drop Tea Tree oil to each wrist, apply pressure to inside of each wrist with finger tips, either constant pressure or slight rubbing movements, whichever you feel comfortable with. Try to keep eyes firmly fixed ahead and relax. Count backwards from 100.
The rubbing motion together with the pleasant aroma really does help to conquer nausea. Lavender oil can be used instead, whichever you prefer.

PUBLIC CONVENIENCES

When travelling and having to use public conveniences, I cringe at the condition I usually find them in!. Thank goodness for Tea Tree oil!.

First, dry the seat with tissue, then sprinkle a few drops on to the seat and wipe round with a tissue. I also do this in the cleaner hotel powder rooms too.

PUBLIC TELEPHONES

Before using a public telephone wipe the ear and mouth piece with a few drops of Tea Tree oil sprinkled onto a tissue.

You should also do this on your home telephone when a member of the family has a cold or flu.

REVIVER

When stopping for a rest and drink ask for a cup of hot water. Sprinkle on 2 drops geranium oil and 2 drops Tea Tree oil and relax with the reviving aroma. Aromatherapy in a cup.

If staying in an hotel hang damp cotton wool balls over the radiator with a few drops of Tea Tree oil and geranium oil sprinkled onto them, when the heating comes on in the morning you will wake up to a refreshing aroma.

SLEEPING

If staying overnight in a strange room, place your lavender oil into your suitcase. Either sprinkle 2 drops of lavender oil and 2 drops of Tea Tree oil onto your pillow or into a cup of hot water by your bed, it will help you to relax - it is an effective insect repellent too.

It seems that research has now found that foot odour can attract mosquitoes, rub a couple of drops of lavender oil and Tea Tree oil into your feet before going to bed, and before setting out in the morning.

TRAVEL SICKNESS

See MOTION SICKNESS

SECTION 15 / CAMPING AND HOLIDAYS

SEE ALSO TRAVELLING - SECTION 14.

FIRST AID KIT

See SAME, TRAVELLING - SECTION 14.
See FIRST AID BOX - SECTION 10.

EMERGENCY HAND CLEANER

Rub a few drops of Tea Tree oil into hands, rinse if possible and dry with a tissue.

INSECT BITES

Apply neat Tea Tree oil as soon as you notice you have been bitten. This will help to stop the itching. If abroad, medical attention should be sought as soon as possible. Have a description of the insect ready.

INSECT REPELLENT

Apply mixture of 2ml geranium oil and 2ml Tea Tree oil to every 40ml olive oil. Rub in well - neat oil can also be used, if you know they do not cause a skin reaction. Always remember to do a sensitivity test initially.

If camping at night and you have lit a fire, sprinkle a few drops of Tea Tree oil and geranium oil into a metal cup containing hot water, place near to the fire and/or sprinkle a few drops of the oils onto the warm stones around the fire for an effective insect repellent.

LEECHES

To repel leeches in marshy areas apply a few drops of Tea Tree oil to socks and lower legs or any exposed skin.

See TICKS

See INSECT REPELLENT

SANITARY WIPES

Pre-soak natural, unbleached, strong kitchen roll squares (enough to fill chosen box) in a solution of Tea Tree oil and hot, boiled water. (100ml water to 2 ml Tea Tree oil). Tip onto the kitchen roll in a small (sterilised) airtight "Tupperware" type box allow to cool, replace lid. Use as required.

TICKS

These nasty little creatures not only give a painful bite but can carry lymes disease. If you intend to walk through woodlands or fields, it is sensible to cover up, wherever possible, and use the right footwear. Tea Tree oil is also very effective as a tick repellent, apply to exposed skin before outing.

See INSECT REPELLENT
See LEECHES

WASHING WATER

If the dishwashing or personal washing water is cold (but looks clean), or you are unsure of quality, add 20 drops of Tea Tree oil to it, stir vigorously, add 'soap' and wash.

SECTION 16 / MISCELLANEOUS

EARPHONES

Wipe over plastic ear phones with a few drops Tea Tree oil and same of olive oil, on a tissue and dry with a soft cloth, this can help to avoid infection.

FRUIT WASH

See KITCHEN APPLICATIONS   SECTION 2

HEARING AID

Keep earpiece clean with a daily wipe over with a few drops of Tea Tree oil, and olive oil, sprinkled onto a tissue, dry with a soft cloth.

JEWELLERY

Amber - To keep amber clean and in good condition try wiping with 1 drop of neat Tea Tree oil on a soft dry cloth.

Wipe over gold and silver jewellery with a soft cloth sprinkled with a few drops of Tea Tree oil and polish to maintain brilliance.

For stubborn marks on silver, rub persistently with a few drops of neat Tea Tree oil on soft cloth.

MUSICAL INSTRUMENTS

To keep mouthpieces clean, wipe over with Tea Tree oil before and after use, buff with a soft, dry cloth.

STICKING PLASTER ADHESIVE

Sticking plaster adhesive is unsightly and makes hands look dirty. Rub in a few drops of Tea Tree oil and wash hands.
(Also removes adhesive left by price stickers on fruit, glass and crockery).

See LABEL REMOVER ON FRUIT SECTION 2
See LABEL REMOVER SECTION 2

THERMOMETER CLEANER

Wipe with neat Tea Tree oil after use. Store in its own case. Wipe before use with a CLEAN, dry cloth.

SECTION 17 / VETERINARY

INITIALLY A SENSITIVITY TEST <u>MUST BE</u> CARRIED OUT BEFORE USING TEA TREE OIL DIRECTLY ON PETS. *APPLY NEAT/DILUTED (AS BELOW) TO A SMALL AREA FOR 48 HOURS IF NO REACTION IT SHOULD BE SAFE TO USE.*
<u>ALWAYS KEEP ESSENTIAL OILS AWAY FROM THE EYE AREA.</u>

ABSCESS

Pets often get into fights, it is natural territorial trait, but if not very careful, when the skin is punctured by a tooth or claw, infection can set in and an abscess is the likely result.

At first signs of an abscess dab with appropriate mixture on cotton wool 4 times per day. When the abscess bursts drain and keep applying Tea Tree oil mixture for 10 days.
If abscess is large, if it is situated in the mouth, shows no sign of improvement or the animal is in obvious distress consult the vet.

LARGE DOG
Mix 20ml Tea Tree oil to every 20ml olive oil, keep in labelled glass jar/bottle. Apply to abscess at first signs, 4 times a day.

MEDIUM TO SMALL DOG
Mix 10ml Tea Tree oil to every 20ml olive oil, keep in labelled dark glass jar/bottle. Apply 4 times a day.

CAT
Mix 5ml Tea Tree oil to every 50ml olive oil. Keep in labelled dark glass jar/bottle. Apply 4 times a day.

ANTISEPTIC

Tea Tree oil is a natural antiseptic for your pet. Bathe wounds, bites, scratches etc. with a solution as detailed below in warm water with cotton wool. Apply a little of the tea tree and olive oil mix to wound (See listed below, strengths for type of pet). Dab onto wounds 2-3 times per day to help to stop infection. For large wounds or slow to heal, seek advice from the vet.
* Use less than 1% to 5% on small birds, rodents up to hens, (1-10 drops to every 10-15ml warm water) and 10 drops to 5ml per 100ml of olive oil
* Use 10% solution on small dogs and cats (20 drops to 10ml) and 10ml per 100ml olive oil.
* Use up to 50% solution on large dogs (1ml to 1ml) and 10ml Tea Tree oil per 10ml olive oil.
* Use from 50% as above, or neat Tea Tree oil on horses and cattle.

BAD BREATH

See GUMS

BATHING

Bathe dogs often to avoid infestation by fleas, add 20 drops of Tea Tree oil to bath, rinse coat, shampoo with organic pH balanced shampoo. Add 3ml-5ml of Tea Tree oil per 100ml of shampoo. Leave on coat for 10 minutes and rinse. Bath every day if animal is already infested with fleas, continue for 5 days. AVOID THE EYE AREA.

BEDDING

Wash bedding often, boil wash if possible. It is easy to make a bed that can be boil washed in your washing machine.

Depending on size of your dog/cat. Use 1, 2 or 3 pillow cases or ticking - For just 1 pillowcase do not open any seams. For 2 pillowcases, open 1 long side seam, on each pillow. (The middle seams for duvet style case). For 3 pillowcases, open one long seam on 2 out of the 3, the 3rd one - open both long seams, this is the middle case. Pin pillowcases together along opened seams until you have what resembles a small duvet cover, sew up. (for a very large bed use 4 or utilise a small duvet cover).

ANOTHER QUICKER METHOD IS TO FILL PILLOW CASES (1,2,3 OR 4 DEPENDING ON SIZE) WITH THE COTTON FILLING DETAILED BELOW AND SEW ALL SEAMS, JOINING THE PILLOWCASES TOGETHER AND END SEAMS TO SEAL EDGES.

Shred old sheets, old towels (anything that can be boiled) cutting them into approximately 6" squares. Fill pillowcases until padded then sew up the top seam. Every 2-4 weeks throw the whole bed into the washing machine. If you have made an additional, separate cover out of old towel or sheet, wash that too. Boil wash, put 2ml of Tea Tree oil into final rinse waster. Tumble dry. Wipe over the area that the bed was on, with solution of Tea Tree oil. In the winter you may find two beds are useful, you can wash one while using the other.

BIRDS & POULTRY

Tea tree oil is very effective for masking the scents that cause poultry cannibalism. Add 20-40 drops Tea Tree oil to a spray (atomiser) bottle of 500ml warm water (depending on size of the bird). Shake bottle well before each use, and either spray direct onto area (avoid eyes) or mist a piece of gauze and dab area. This is effective for stopping self-plucking and parasites. Wipe around cages too. See CAGES   See CAGE BIRDS

BITES

INSECT BITES: Apply a mixture of Tea Tree oil and olive oil to bite in 10% or 75% solution depending on size of animal. (See ANTISEPTIC)

INSECT STINGS: If in mouth dab with vinegar and ice to avert swelling. Consult vet as soon as possible. See STINGS,

ANIMAL BITES See ANTISEPTIC

BLANKETS

Some pet blankets you can wash but not boil wash. Follow the washing instructions on blanket and add 5ml of Tea Tree oil to final rinse water. Allow to stand for at least 30 minutes.

CAGE BIRDS

Tea Tree oil is effective for combating self-mutilation of parrots, budgerigars, etc. Add 10-20 drops Tea Tree oil to 500ml warm water in a spray (atomiser) bottle, shake well before each use. Either spray the area (avoid the eyes) or spray onto gauze and dab the area, it will also help to combat parasites.

CAGES   Hamsters, rodents, birds etc.

When cleaning out cage wipe around with a solution of 20-30 drops Tea Tree oil to a pint of warm water and a small squirt of organic washing up liquid, (stir well).

CAR ACCIDENT

Car accident victims must be seen by a vet. Either call a vet to the scene or get your pet to him as soon as possible. Small dogs and cats can be wrapped in a blanket and put into a large box to make travelling easier.

CAT LITTER

Apply 2-5 drops of Tea Tree oil to cat litter to deodorise. Apply only a small amount at first for your cat to get accustomed to it.
When changing litter it is often advisable to put an opened supermarket carrier bag, as a liner, onto the base of the tray - tuck edges under tray (or a couple of pages from a newspaper folded to fit) and fill with cat litter. This can then be scooped up and disposed of when the litter is very soiled.
Wipe out litter tray with piece of dampened kitchen towel soaked in a solution of 50ml hot water, washing up liquid, 10 drops Tea Tree oil before putting liner down.

COAT CONDITIONER

In between bathing your pet, keep coat healthy and pest free by mixing either a 10% solution to 50% depending on size, ie medium dog 1ml (20 drops) Tea Tree oil to every 5ml olive oil (1 teaspoon), mix and warm oil, sprinkle drops all over coat, around neck area especially, comb through. Or sprinkle drops onto a sponge and rub over coat. Always avoid the eye area.

COLLARS

For the felt variety of cat collar mix a little Tea Tree oil and olive oil, in equal quantities, add a few drops onto the outside of collar to deter fleas. For dog collars apply to outside of collar - it may discolour leather but it will keep it fresh and supple.

CUTS

See ANTISEPTIC APPLICATIONS
See TEA TREE OIL VETERINARY PRODUCTS USEFUL ADDRESSES

DEODORANT

If your dog needs a deodorant see BATHING and COAT CONDITION. Both applications work as a deodoriser too.

DEW CLAWS

For damaged dew claws treat as a wound. If persistently damaging dew claws see vet as soon as possible.

See ANTISEPTIC APPLICATIONS.

EARS

Dogs, cats and horses are often prone to ear infections, sometimes caused by parasites. When applying to ears, use a dropper and massage in - be careful of the animal shaking its head.
Apply a warm mixture of the following, twice per day if possible, until alleviated. Swab excess with cotton wool.

CAT/ &   1 small drop Tea Tree oil to 1ml (20 drops) olive oil, apply
Sml Dog: to each ear.

DOG: 10 drops Tea Tree oil to 10ml olive oil, apply to each ear.

HORSE: 30 drops Tea Tree oil to 25 ml olive oil, apply to each ear.

If infection persists see vet.

ECZEMA
(Sweet Itch in horses)

Apply solution twice per day:

CAT/&   Apply 10 drops Tea Tree oil to 10ml olive oil to infected area
Sml dog: with cotton wool.

DOG: Apply 2ml Tea Tree oil to 20ml olive oil to infected area with
cotton wool.

HORSE: For large areas make up a large (150ml) dark glass labelled
bottle of 30ml Tea Tree oil and 100ml olive oil and apply to
infected area with cotton wool. If no reaction, 50% or neat Tea
Tree oil can be applied to area also.

If condition persists consult vet.

FISH

For fungal diseases affecting fish consult vet. Either sprinkle on 50 drops of
Tea Tree oil onto a large pond or 2 drops of Tea Tree oil into tank every
other day for 7 days.

FLEAS

Did you know that in just 9 months, two fleas can multiply to over 200
trillion - they in turn have a lifespan of up to 2 years!. They can survive the
coldest conditions and can go months without eating.

Even if you have never owed a pet it is possible that fleas exist within your
home.
How to rid your home of fleas, mites and dustmites:
See ALL AROUND THE HOME / SECTION 1 for full instructions.
Shampoo carpets, upholstery and soft furnishings with Tea Tree oil in the
water reservoir, if using an electric shampooer, or add Tea Tree oil to the
washing water (8ml to 1 litre). Do not forget the car either.

Wipe over skirting boards with strong solution and into cracks and crevices.
Wipe all kitchen cupboards regularly. Let water drip into cracks and
crevices.

See TEA TREE OIL VETERINARY PRODUCTS USEFUL ADDRESSES

PETS

Do a small patch test on your pet to ensure that there is no allergic reaction.

As a preventative measure bath pet with *10 - 30 drops (*depending on size of pet) of Tea Tree oil in warm water, a dog every 2 weeks - a cat every month or use a coat conditioner.
 If your pet is already infested add 3-5ml Tea Tree oil to every 100ml of their regular organic shampoo and bathe every day for 5 days.   Remember to leave on coat for 10 minutes before rinsing. Repeat after 10 days.
It is possible to use a mild, organic washing up liquid instead of shampoo.

Collars - add a few drops of Tea Tree oil, allow to dry, rub into collar at either *full strength or at least 10%.
 Condition coat regularly with either a 10% or 50% solution of Tea Tree oil and olive oil, apply a few drops to a damp sponge or cloth and wipe all over pet, especially around neck, tummy and back at base of tail.

If infested boil wash pets bedding at least once a week, for a month, and then every 2-4 weeks to prevent re-infestation. Add 2 ml of Tea Tree oil to final rinse water, add 8ml and stand for 30 minutes, if unable to boil wash.

Make two pet beds, one can be used, whilst the other is put into the boil wash and then tumble dried. This will ensure a flea free pet bed.
See BEDDING for full instructions.

You may also like to add garlic and brewers yeast to your pets diet, fleas hate the taste. Many pet owners swear by it.

See BATHING
See COAT CONDITIONER

FOOD HYGIENE

Keep area clean by wiping with a solution of 1ml Tea Tree oil to 500ml hot water and a small squirt of organic (biodegradable) washing up liquid.

FUR CARE

Comb fur daily, especially on long haired breeds. If matted try wetting matt with warm water, sprinkle on a couple of drops Tea Tree oil and rub in. Try to ease matted fur a little at a time from top of matt with a comb.

FUR CARE (Cont.)

If you do have to cut the patch of fur off, try cutting down vertically instead of horizontally and ease with comb again. Cutting this way makes less of a bald patch. If skin is nicked apply a drop of tea tree oil to stop infection.

GUMS

Pets need to keep their teeth and gums clean, just as we do. Usually a "chew" given regularly can help. If discoloration or bad breath does occur you may need to clean their teeth for them.

If your cat or dog will not let you clean them with a toothbrush, try a gauze pad around your finger. (Read the signs; if pet angry do not try, if pet is volatile or showing signs of anger it may not be possible - consult your vet.)

When you have a new puppy or kitten it is best to rub gently around teeth and gums with a gauze pad soaked in water so that he gets used to his mouth being handled. Repeat every 2-3 days.

CAT: Mix 1 drop of Tea Tree oil 10ml warm water, shake well.

DOG: Mix 2 drops of Tea Tree oil to 10ml of warm water, shake well

Apply the above mixture, with a 'milk teeth' toothbrush if possible or a gauze pad, to gums and teeth twice per day until better. This will clean teeth and help alleviate any infection.

ON HEAT

Tea Tree oil can be safely used as a masking agent when bitch is on heat. Apply 1ml Tea Tree oil to 4ml olive oil. Dab around underside of dog, on fur, and down the tail. Blot excess with a tissue. If she still causes attention make a stronger 50% solution of 1ml Tea Tree oil to 2-3ml olive oil and apply as above application.

INFECTIONS OF THE MOUTH

See GUMS.

INFECTIONS OF THE SKIN

See ABSCESS
See ECZEMA
See BATHING
See COAT CONDITIONER
See FLEAS

ITCHING

See ECZEMA
See BATHING
see COAT CONDITIONER
See FLEAS

KENNEL HYGIENE

See BEDDING

If you have to keep your dog in a kennel wash it down every 3 months (but make sure it is not damp in winter) with a soapy solution of 1 litre of hot water, 5ml Tea Tree oil and approx. 1/2 a tablespoon washing up liquid.

LEECHES

If you live by marshy ground your dog or cat could pick up a leech. Dab leech with neat Tea Tree oil until it falls off. Treat wound as in ANTISEPTIC APPLICATIONS.

LICE

LARGE DOGS: Sprinkle coat all over with 20-30 drops Tea Tree oil to every 5ml (1 teaspoon) of olive oil and comb through. Bath often.

SMALL DOGS/ Mix 5-10 drops Tea Tree oil to every 5ml olive oil and
CATS: sprinkle all over coat, comb through. Bath Often

See BEDDING
see BATHING
See COAT CONDITIONER
See KENNEL HYGIENE
See CAGE BIRDS
See BIRDS AND POULTRY

LITTER TRAY

See CAT LITTER

MANGE

See ECZEMA

MOUTH INFECTIONS

See GUMS
See ABSCESS
See STINGS

NAIL (CLAW) CARE

Cutting dogs claws/nails usually needs to be done by a professional with a special claw/nail clipper.

Before your appointment soak claws in a solution of 5 drops Tea Tree oil and 10ml olive oil, 2 days before and for 2 days after they have been clipped to help to prevent splitting and infection.

NAIL (CLAW) INFECTIONS

Apply neat Tea Tree oil to claws/nails twice per day for 14-21 days. If infection persists or gets worse see Vet.

See NAIL (CLAW) CARE

OIL

See TAR

PARASITES

See FLEAS
See TICKS
See BATHING
See KENNEL HYGIENE
See LICE
See BIRDS AND POULTRY
See CAGE BIRDS

PARROTS

See CAGE BIRDS
See ANTISEPTIC

PAWS

A dog's and a cat's paws can become cracked and infected. Bathe paws in solution of 1ml Tea Tree oil to 100ml warm water - pat dry and apply Tea Tree oil as under ANTISEPTIC APPLICATIONS 2-3 times per day.
If the pet would wear little socks it would assist healing and help to keep wound clean.

See NAIL (CLAW) INFECTIONS
See NAIL (CLAW) CARE.
See SPLINTERS

POULTRY

See BIRDS AND POULTRY
See ANTISEPTIC

RASHES

See ECZEMA
See LICE

RODENTS

See ANTISEPTIC
For LICE - See as for CAGE BIRDS

SCENT MASKING

See ON HEAT
See SOILING

SHAMPOO

Add 3-5ml Tea Tree oil to every 100ml proprietary brand pet shampoo (plain/organic) for an effective skin conditioner and insecticide. A mild organic washing up liquid is a good shampoo substitute, add TTO as above.

See COAT CONDITIONER
See TEA TREE OIL VETERINARY PRODUCTS   USEFUL ADDRESSES

SKIN CONDITIONS

See ECZEMA
See BATHING

SOILING

To clean area, mask smells and so prevent re-soiling: clean matter from area, blot liquids with kitchen towel. Clean with a solution of 250ml hot water and a squirt of washing up liquid - depending on the type of soiling

SOILING (CONT.)

add 20 drops to 30 drops of Tea Tree oil to hot water and apply to area, clean and blot dry.

SPLINTERS

If your pet picks up a splinter or thorn, remove with a pair of tweezers and apply 1 drop of Tea Tree oil to the site, twice per day until healed.

SPRAYING

Spraying is a natural habit for Tomcats, they are marking their territory. Neutering the cat usually stops this annoying habit but when a cat feels insecure by the addition of another pet, even another family member, moving house etc. your Tomcat could revert to his old ways again.

Make your cat as secure as you can with lots of reassurance. Mask the area he sprays with a solution of 200ml hot water, squirt of organic washing up liquid and 5 drops of Tea Tree oil and 5 drops geranium oil.

If all else fails and your Tomcat is still spraying inside the home, purchase a plastic spray bottle from a garden centre. Fill with warm water and 2 drops of Tea Tree oil - when (**and only when**) you actually catch him spraying inside the house, give him 2-3 short bursts of water to his back (always avoid spraying head and eyes) and put him outside. Within a few days he should have got the message, and stopped spraying indoors.
Never allow children to do this.

STINGS

If stung by a bee and the sting is still evident, scrape out with thumb nail or flat card (old credit card is ideal). Blot area with a drop of cold Tea Tree oil and apply ice.

If stung by a wasp apply 2 drops of cold Tea Tree oil to area and ice if possible.

If stung in the mouth apply vinegar and ice and consult vet as soon as possible.

If animal shows any signs of abnormal swelling, wheezing, coughing, sneezing, panting or anything that you are worried about consult vet immediately. Your pet may be having an allergic reaction to the sting.

SWEET ITCH

See ECZEMA

TAR

If your pet is covered in tar - mix 1 tablespoon of organic washing up liquid, 1 teaspoon salt and 10 drops Tea Tree oil and rub well in to the tar. Rinse away with warm water and repeat if necessary, a shower attachment to the bath taps makes this job easier (make sure the water is just warm). If fur is very clogged it may need further applications.

Use the same method if your pet becomes covered in diesel oil.

TEETH

See GUMS

THORNS

See SPLINTERS
See ANTISEPTIC

TICKS

If you notice a small greyish white lump protruding from the skin, your pet may have picked up a tick. The head will be buried underneath the skin so do not try to pull out by force. With a cotton wool bud or a small piece of cotton wool, dab on neat Tea Tree oil directly onto the ticks body and around edge. Repeat every 10 mins.

If the tick has not dropped, after 6 applications grasp it with a pair of tweezers and gently rock backwards and forwards, to loosen, do not pull directly. Repeat Tea Tree oil treatment until it drops. When the tick has loosened it's grip and you pull it away dab area with neat Tea Tree oil then twice a day for 5 days with Tea Tree oil and olive oil solution see ANTISEPTIC APPLICATIONS

TOYS

Wash toys often. Soft toys can be washed in a solution of hot water and organic washing up liquid with 2-3 drops Tea Tree oil, rinse and dry.

Wipe over plastic and rubber toys with the same solution.

WOUNDS

See ANTISEPTIC

Videx Animal Health Ltd., do a comprehensive range of TEA TREE OIL pet products by mail order, for their address, please see Useful Addresses at the back of the book.

SECTION 18 / AT WORK

AIR CONDITIONING

If the company you work for has an air conditioning system, it may be worth your while to ask them to install Tea Tree oil into the system. Tea Tree oil is used in Australia by many companies and hospitals. Their findings have been encouraging.

Tea Tree oil not only keeps the air free from germs, and so reduces absenteeism, but it also helps to inhibit unsightly mould growth on walls and ceilings, cutting down on decorating bills in the process.

ASHTRAY FRESHENER

Most companies nowadays do not allow smoking in the workplace but will allow it in the rest room. To cut down on ashtray fumes fill ashtrays with granulated 'Fullers earth' (an inexpensive alternative is cat litter see CHAPTER 6). This can be dyed with natural food colouring and sprinkled with 5-7 drops of Tea Tree oil and 5-7 drops geranium oil. This is also a natural reviver blend.

ATOMISER

See HUMIDIFIER

BIN FRESHENER

Apply a few drops of Tea Tree oil to an empty bin. Wipe round with a tissue.

BREATH FRESHENER

For all day confidence apply 2 drops of Tea Tree oil to toothbrush and toothpaste, clean teeth as normal, or rinse mouth with 2 drops in a glass of water. In an emergency rub 1 drop Tea Tree oil onto teeth with a clean, washed fingertip.

CHEWING GUM

Chewing gum on floors or furniture can be removed by scraping with a plastic card (ie. an old credit card) remove as much surface chewing gum as possible. Sprinkle 2 drops of Tea Tree oil on top of the residue and rub with your fingertips covered by a duster or damp cloth. Repeat until removed. Always patch test first, especially on polished wood. Old chewing gum residue may leave a mark also, depending on surface type.

CLOAKROOMS

Tea Tree oil is an effective germicide. Sprinkle a few drops of Tea Tree oil onto toilet seat and wipe with tissue.

See HAND CLEANER

CUPBOARDS AND FILING CABINETS

These can be refreshed by washing with a solution of 500ml hot water, a squirt of washing up liquid and 10 drops Tea Tree oil.
For stubborn stains use neat Tea Tree oil on a damp cloth, rub until stain diminishes or disappears - (do a patch test first if on polished wood, or on any surface liable to damage).

CUPS

Brown stains on cups and mugs can be removed by applying 2 drops of Tea Tree oil to cup, dip damp dishcloth in salt and clean by rubbing directly on stained area.

DISHCLOTHS

Rinse through with 250ml hot water, 1 tablespoon white vinegar and 20 drops of Tea Tree oil. Hang over rail to dry.

DISHWASHING WATER

Cups and mugs washed in luke warm water in an office environment can be a breeding ground for germs.
Add 20-30 drops of Tea Tree oil to dishwashing water. Rinse well and dry on a teacloth that is changed daily.

See CUPS

FIRST AID KIT

See FIRST AID BOX SECTION 10

GLUE REMOVER

Glue residue left on desks and office equipment can be unsightly. Wipe over with a few drops of neat Tea Tree oil on a soft cloth or kitchen towel.

HAND CLEANER

One bar of soap between all the office staff can pass on germs. Sprinkle 2 drops of Tea Tree oil onto hands before applying soap, wash as normal.

Liquid soap can be made more efficient by adding 1ml Tea Tree oil to every 100ml and then shake well before using.

HUMIDIFIER

During the winter months, colds and flu are responsible for more lost productivity than any other single factor. A small humidifier in the office with 10-30 drops (depending on size of humidifier) can help kill germs and make the office more comfortable for people with colds.

INSECT REPELLENT

Tea Tree oil is an effective insect repellent. Mix 3-4 drops of Tea Tree oil to 3-4 drops of geranium oil. Apply to damp cotton wool ball, leave or hang by window, hang fragrance sac by the window or see 'Reviver'.

See MISCELLANEOUS   CHAPTER 6   FRAGRANCE SAC

KEYBOARD CLEANER

Apply neat Tea Tree oil to a soft cloth, rub to remove stains like pen, sellotape residue etc.

LUBRICANT

Tea Tree oil is an effective lubricant for squeaky chairs, hinges etc. Apply 1 drop to problem area.

PEN CLEANER

As a pen cleaner apply Tea Tree oil on soft cloth and rub clean.

PEN/PENCIL MARKS

See KEYBOARD CLEANER

REPETITIVE STRAIN INJURY

See A-Z OF FIRST AID APPLICATIONS CHAPTER 7

REVIVER

In a cup of hot water sprinkle 3 drops Tea Tree oil and 3 drops of geranium oil - inhale aroma - label cup "Aromatherapy cup". Also a useful insect repellent if left by an open window.

RUBBER/ERASER MARKS

Rubber marks on floors and eraser marks on desks can be removed with a few drops of Tea Tree oil, on a soft cloth, rubbed into the mark.

SELLOTAPE RESIDUE REMOVER

See GLUE REMOVER.

SPONGE (FINGER/ENVELOPE) MOISTENER

The sponge is an ideal place for germs to breed. Rinse through with solution for dish clothes. Wipe inside holder with neat Tea Tree oil.

TELEPHONE FRESHENER

Wipe over the telephone receiver with a few drops of Tea Tree oil on a soft cloth, to eradicate germs.

TOILETS

See CLOAKROOMS

Chapter Six

Make Your Own Toiletries

HEALING PREPARATIONS

BEFORE USING ANY PREPARATIONS A SENSITIVITY TEST MUST BE DONE

TEA TREE OIL ANTI-FUNGAL OINTMENT

See PAGE 127

TEA TREE OIL SUPER ANTISEPTIC HEALING CREAM

25gms WHITE BEESWAX		2 ml	MANUKA OIL
40ml	OLIVE OIL	3 ml	ELEMI OIL
30ml	WHEATGERM OIL	10ml	TEA TREE OIL
2 Dessertspoons CLEAR HONEY		5 ml	CALENDULA OIL

Sterilise 2 small glass pots, toiletry pots or small 'Tupperware' type airtight pots. Melt the beeswax in a double saucepan or a microwave. (To melt in a microwave use only a toughened Pyrex glass jug because of the high temperature of the melted wax). Use protection of an oven glove even for microwave melting. Keep children/pets out of the kitchen, hot wax can burn.

Warm the olive oil, wheatgerm oil and honey until honey is melted. Dribble into hot wax and stir as it cools. Add Tea Tree, manuka, calendula and elemi oil when just warm and stir well. Pour into pots, replace lid, label and date. Store in a cool, dark place and use within six months. This cream promotes healing and helps to prevent scarring.

FOR AN EASIER VERSION: 75gms of emulsifying ointment can be used (available large chemists) melt over a low heat with the honey, stir until just warm, add only the essential oils, manuka, elemi, calendula and Tea Tree oil, stir until cool and store in sterilised jar.

BODY BRUSHING TO IMPROVE CIRCULATION

Body brushing can be very beneficial. Brushing actually encourages the body to release toxins. In the case of oedema, athritis etc body brush every day for seven days and then every other day.

Use a natural bristle, body brush or a coarse flannel. Using firm but comfortable, even strokes brush the body from the shoulders, back, chest down to waist, brushing every part of body UP from the feet, ankles, calves, thighs, buttocks, stomach to diaphragm. Then brush the diaphragm clockwise in a circular motion. This will not only release toxins but it will help circulation. Step into warm bath with 20 drops added of Tea Tree oil to water. Pat dry and apply body lotion.

To maintain healthy body brush 1-2 times per week.

See SPA BATH PAGE 124

__BRUISE BAN 1__   For unbroken skin.

Mix 1 dessertspoon Witch Hazel.
Add 5 drops of Tea Tree oil.
Apply lightly onto area as soon as possible after knock occurs. Apply cold compress.

__BRUISE BAN 2__   For broken skin

Mix 1 dessertspoon glycerine oil with 10 drops Tea Tree oil and 5 drops elemi oil. Mix well, chill and apply to wound, cover with gauze. Wrap in cling film. Apply cold compress. Keep elevated if possible.

__BURN CREAM__

75gms Cocoa Butter	5ml Lavender Oil
25ml Wheatgerm Oil	5ml Tea Tree Oil
25ml Aloe Vera Gel	

Melt the cocoa butter in a double saucepan or in the microwave. Warm the wheatgerm oil and beat into the cocoa butter. When just warm beat in the aloe vera gel and the essential oils, continue to beat until cool. Store in an airtight, sterilised wide necked jar in a cool, dark place. Use within 3 months. Apply liberally to burn 2-3 times per day, cover with gauze, so that the air can get to the area and promote healing. **See TTO Burn ointment page 112**.

A Burn Ointment can be made by purchasing a 50ml emulsifying ointment, (available chemists) warming it in a double saucepan and adding the above essential oils + 1 teaspoon warmed honey and stir until cool, bottle as above. PLEASE NOTE: All but minor burns must have medical attention.

__CHEST VAPOUR RUB__

ADULT:	1 Dessertspoon petroleum jelly, for every 15 drops of Tea Tree oil and 5 drops of oregano oil.
CHILD:	1 Teaspn petroleum jelly, for every 5 - 10 drops Tea Tree oil and 1 drop oregano oil. Mix well and rub on chest.
BABIES:	1/2 a teaspoon petroleum jelly, for every 1 - 2 drops of Tea Tree oil and 1 small drop of oregano oil.

Mix by warming the jelly and adding 1 drop of oil at a time. Mix well, store in a sterilised jar, use by rubbing onto chest, when required.

COMPRESS COLD

To make a cold compress soak a flannel, a small hand towel, or gauze wrapped cotton wool, in water and ice cubes with a few drops of Tea Tree oil in water. Wring out and apply to area as directed (replace when warmed up) or keep a couple of flannels in the ice box - rinse flannel in cold water, store in a plastic bag in the freezer, use as required.
In the case of heart disease or diabetes consult your doctor initially before using a cold compress or ice pack.

COMPRESS HOT

Soak flannel, small hand towel or gauze wrapped cotton wool in hot water and 2-3 drops of Tea Tree oil. Apply to area as directed. (replace when cool)

See HEAT PAD.

CUCUMBER EYE POULTICE

For tired, gritty eyes or for those that are puffy and sore-the CUCUMBER EYE POULTICE offers relief.

Peel approx. 2" of cucumber, blend to a pulp, cut two muslin squares 6" to 8" squares. Apply half of pulp to each square, fold corners 'in' to make a sack, tie. Place one sack on each eye, and put a small piece of cotton wool along each cheek to catch drips.
*Adding 1 teaspoon of chopped chamomile leaves or dried marigold petals (Calendula Officinalis) helps to guard against infections.
Never use essential oils on or near the eyes.

DEEP HEAT RUB. - For aching muscles etc.

1 DESSERTSPOON PETROLEUM JELLY	2-3 DROPS GINGER OIL
2-3 DROPS WINTERGREEN OIL	5 DROPS KANUKA OIL
5 DROPS TEA TREE OIL	3 DROPS OREGANO OIL

Add a drop of oil at a time to warmed jelly. Mix well and rub into affected area. (For children - cut essential oils down by half).
Never use neat ginger oil on the skin or in the bath

HAEMORRHOID CREAM 1

Mix together 2 drops geranium oil and 2 drops Tea Tree oil and 1/2 a teaspoon cold cream. Apply on gauze twice per day.

HAEMORRHOID JELLY 2

Mix together 2 drops geranium oil, 2 drops Tea Tree oil, 2 drops myrtle oil, 10 drops Wheatgerm or vitamin E oil, 1/2 a teaspoon petroleum jelly or water based jelly such as K.Y., by adding the oil drop by drop and mixing well each time. You may find it easier to warm jelly first, and stir until cool. Apply as cold as possible (even refrigerated) to area 2-3 times per day.

HAEMORRHOID OINTMENT 3

Heat 50gms Lesser Celandine leaves (Ranunculus Ficaria) in 100ml soya oil, leave overnight, liquidise and strain through muslin. Heat 15gms bees wax and 15gms anhydrous lanolin over a low heat in a saucepan or in the microwave - you must use a pyrex glass jug, oven gloves and keep children/pets away. Add the soya oil and stir until just warm add 1ml Tea Tree oil and 10 drops myrtle oil, store in a sterilised jar. Apply cold twice per day. (An emulsifying ointment may be used in place of the wax and lanolin, and use only 50ml of soya oil and make up as above).

Cold Witch Hazel with 2 drops Tea Tree oil can be applied with cotton wool to the affected area, instead, if irritation and bleeding are evident.

HEAT PACK

Half fill hot water bottle, Wrap in hand towel or put cover on and apply to area or use a commercial heat pad. For moist heat wrap in a damp towel.

ICE PACK

For an emergency ice pack a pack of frozen peas is very effective (do not re-freeze afterwards for culinary use) or keep a bag of crushed ice in the freezer, break up granules and put in large plastic bag (depending on injury). Knot the end and wrap in a towel and apply to area.

Please consult doctor - if you have heart disease or diabetes, to ensure that you are able to use ice packs with your condition.

MINERAL SPA BATH

As you are running the bath dissolve 1 tablespoon of honey under the hot tap - (be very careful if you have young children - you should not run all hot water into a bath first). Add a handful of sea salt, 20 drops Tea Tree oil and a bouquet garni of Herbs, either home made or 'tea bag' style from your supermarket. If you have dry skin or suffering from sunburn, a tablespoon of powdered milk or oat 'milk' and 10 drops of lavender oil, can be added too. Relax in the mineral spa bath for 10-20 minutes.

OATMEAL'MILK' SOOTHER

For over dry skin, sunburn, burns or eczema apply the soother twice per day. Grind 1 cup whole oats to powder, tip into large bowl, add 2 1/2 cups of hot water and stir - leave for 5 minutes. Pour into a fine plastic sieve or muslin and strain until liquid has drained through. (Push through with spoon until you have about 3/4 of a cup). Put liquid into a small blender and turn to fastest setting, dribble in 35ml grapeseed oil, 10ml wheatgerm oil and 1 dessertspoon clear (warmed) honey. Add 2ml of Tea Tree oil. Pour into a dark glass jar, label and date. Keep in the refrigerator and use within 1 month. Do not apply too much as it 'coats' the skin. Ideal for overnight application, or as face pack. *Put oat pulp into small tupperware containers and use for hot oat poultice or oat face pack. Freeze or use within 5 days.

POULTICE HOT 'OATMEAL'

Poultices are useful for drawing out impurities and relieving aches and pains. Depending on the size of area put 1 to 2 cups of ground whole oats into a large bowl, pour on 3 to 6 cups of hot water, stir and leave for 5 minutes. Drain and retain liquid in separate container to make "oatmeal 'milk' soother." (or use in your bath to nourish skin). Use the 'pulp' for the poultice. For every cup of oat pulp add 1 - 2 teaspoons of English mustard powder (less if too hot for your skin or if you have sensitive skin). Add 5-10 drops of Tea Tree oil, mix well. Place gauze over infected area, warm the poultice, if cool to the touch, (either in microwave or double saucepan. Not too hot or you will destroy heat from the mustard). Spread over the gauze and apply a second layer of gauze on top. If this is to be used on the face use a 1/4 of a teaspoon of mustard powder per cup and 2-5 drops of Tea Tree oil. Leave until cold to the touch. DO NOT use on sore or broken skin or for eczema, psoriasis etc.

POULTICE HOT LINSEED

Crush 3 to 6 tablespoons of Linseed seeds, add enough boiling water to make a smooth paste. Add 5-10 drops of Tea Tree oil, 5 drops of juniper oil and 3 drops of ginger oil, mix well. Apply gauze to area and spread over the gauze. Cover with a second piece of gauze and allow to go cold before removing. DO NOT use on the face, on sore or broken skin or for eczema, psoriasis etc.

RINGWORM TREATMENT

See ANTI-FUNGAL CREAM PAGE 127

SPLINTER/THORN STEAM EXTRACTOR

If you do not like digging out splinters or thorns this extractor may help. Place a heat-proof container with a narrow neck on a firm surface. Fill with near boiling water and 10 drops of Tea Tree oil, hold area (only if on limbs, hands or feet) over container so steam 'hits' the splinter/thorn perforation. Hold over for as long as possible. Repeat until splinter/thorn can be removed. For splinters on the body use a hot poultice to draw it out.

STEAM INHALATION

For colds, flu etc. a Tea Tree oil steam inhalation can be very beneficial. In a bowl or washbasin pour in 2 litres of steaming water. (Be very careful of small children. Keep out of their reach). Sprinkle on 10 drops of Tea Tree oil, bend over the bowl and drape a large towel over your head and over the bowl to make a steam 'tent', close eyes and inhale through the nose and exhale through the mouth for 5-10 minutes. If too hot raise head and open towel a little until cooler. This will also give you a steam facial. Take advantage by rinsing face, pat dry and apply moisturiser.
Do not use a steam inhalation if suffering from asthma.

TEA TREE OIL MINOR BURN OINTMENT II

All but minor burns should have medical attention. Melt 50gms of paraffin wax with 2 teaspoons honey over a moderate heat in a double saucepan, or in a glass jug in the microwave, keep children away. Stir to cool, add 20 drops lavender oil, 20 drops Tea Tree oil, 10 drops carrot oil, 5ml vitamin E oil, and 10 drops palmarosa oil. Store in a sterilised glass jar, use as required. Apply 2-3 times per day to burn and cover with a gauze dressing. Never cover with a plaster or a waterproof/air proof dressing. See BURN CREAM PAGE 108.

TEA TREE OIL EAR PLUGS

An infection after swimming is quite common, if possible make your own ear plugs. Use one teaspoon of petroleum jelly, 2 drops of tea tree oil and two small wads of cotton wool (each about the size of a large hazelnut). Mix the warmed petroleum jelly and the tea tree oil together, apply to both pieces of cotton wool. Gently apply cotton wool like a 'plug' to each ear.

TEA TREE OIL SALVE

Mix together 1 dessertspoon of water based gel, available from chemist, (or 'Sylk' a natural gel made from kiwi fruit) to 10 drops of Tea Tree oil. Apply to area as necessary.

HAIR

CREAM CONDITIONER NORMAL/DRY HAIR

To condition dry hair there is nothing better than a "Mayonnaise" type conditioner.

Put 1 egg yolk in a blender (save white for other preparations). Blend on high, dribble in 10ml Wheatgerm oil, 20ml olive oil, 1ml Tea Tree oil and 10 drops of rosemary oil (* if you are prone to high blood pressure, use clary sage oil instead). Blend until creamy.

Apply to hair and rub well into scalp, wrap in cling film (low in plasticisers), a supermarket carrier bag or a shower cap. Put large towel on top of covering, around head and leave on for 20-30 minutes. Rinse well in tepid to warm water. It is better to let hair dry naturally.

For normal hair leave on for 10-15 minutes. Rinse hair well in warm water. add 2 tablespoons of cider vinegar to 1 litre of water for final rinse. Dry as normal.

GREASY HAIR CONDITIONER

Beat 1 egg white until frothy. Beat in 10 drops Tea Tree oil, 10 drops rosemary oil (* see above) juice of 1/2 a lemon and apply to wet hair and massage into scalp for 5 minutes. Rinse out with warm water, dry as normal.

DANDRUFF TREATMENT

Mix 1ml Tea Tree oil with 1 tablespoon olive oil. Rub into scalp, massage for 3-5 minutes. Wrap towel around head for 15 minutes, rinse well. Shampoo (see below) and rinse. Add 1 tablespoon cider vinegar and 10 drops Tea Tree oil to final rinse water. Repeat twice a week for 2 weeks then once a week.

WASH COMBS, BRUSHES, SLIDES ETC. IN A SOLUTION OF TEA TREE OIL.

To make a 'natural' dandruff shampoo, purchase an unperfumed pH balanced shampoo, (Health shops). Add 3-5ml Tea Tree oil per 100ml of shampoo. Shampoo as normal but leave on hair for 5-10 minutes before rinsing.

See HAIR CARE CHAPTER 7
See DANDRUFF CHAPTER 7

HEADLICE SHAMPOO

Proprietary branded headlice shampoo has been reported to be linked to cancer. To make a 'natural headlice shampoo' purchase an unperfumed, pH balanced organic shampoo from health shops and add 5-10ml of Tea Tree oil per 100ml of shampoo. Add enough to make a lather, massage into scalp, leave on for 10 minutes, rinse and repeat, rinse well and in final rinse water add 1 dessertspoon of cider vinegar.

HEADLICE TREATMENT
See CHAPTER 7

SCALP RUB - FOR GENERAL HAIR CARE

To keep your hair in tip top condition apply scalp rub once a week.

DRY/NORMAL HAIR.

Beat together 1 tablespoon olive oil, 5 drops of Tea Tree oil, 1ml Wheatgerm oil and 10 drops of clary sage (do not substitute with sage oil, it is completely different and can be dangerous if used neat on the skin).

Massage into scalp then rub in vigorously. Put on shower cap or cling film (low in Plasticisers). Wrap towel around head and leave on for 25 minutes if possible. Shampoo and condition hair as you normally do, remember that dry hair does not like dry heat.

GREASY HAIR.

Mix together 1 tablespoon of Soya oil, 1ml Wheatgerm oil or Vitamin E oil, 5 drops of Tea Tree oil, 5 drops of Rosemary oil (If prone to high blood pressure use clary sage oil and a couple of drops juniper oil, instead0), 3 drops of lemon oil. Apply as above- in final rinse water add 2 teaspoons of lemon juice. Dry as you normally do.

EXCESSIVELY GREASY HAIR

Mix together 2 teaspoons of Witch Hazel, 2 teaspoons of lemon juice, 10 drops of Tea Tree oil, 1 beaten egg white. Beat together and apply to scalp. use as above.

SHAMPOO - FOR GENERAL HAIR CARE

Add 10-20 drops Tea Tree oil to every 100ml of ordinary organic pH balanced (preferably un-perfumed) shampoo (from health shops). This will keep your hair in tip top condition.
*You can add 10 drops to every 100ml of Baby Shampoo for shining, manageable hair.

114

FACE

ACNE TREATMENT

A facial sauna 2 - 3 times a week can be very beneficial, put 1-2 litres of steaming water into the bathroom basin, (out of the reach of children). Throw in 1 tablespoon each of the following: dried lavender flowers, dried chervil, dried elder flowers, (3-5 drops each of lavender and calendula oil can be used instead). Stir and hold face comfortably over the steam for 7-10 mins.
Apply the following lotion: Mix 1 tablespoon distilled Witch Hazel, 50ml lavender water, 3 drops Tea Tree oil and 3 drops manuka oil, shake well. Cleanse the skin 1-2 times per day depending on severity of condition.
Apply acne treatment oil twice per day, on cotton wool. To make: mix 25ml sweet almond oil, 10ml vitamin E oil, 25ml grapeseed oil, 2ml Tea Tree oil, 2ml lavender oil, 2ml palmarosa oil and 10 drops myrtle oil.

AFTERSHAVE BALM

For a soothing aftershave balm, add 3 drops of Tea Tree oil to a half teaspn of water soluble gel (from chemists), or "Sylk" a water soluble gel made from Kiwi fruit.

AFTERSHAVE OIL

Add 2 drops of Tea Tree oil, 1 drop of peppermint, 1 teaspoon grapeseed oil. This is cooling and easily absorbed. (Never use any type of mint oil neat on the skin, over a large area, or in the bath).

CLEANSING OATMEAL MILK   ALL SKIN TYPES

Grind 1 dessertspoon of whole oats, tip into a jug, add 250ml cold water and stand for 5 minutes-stirring often. Strain through fine mesh sieve. Collect the 'milk' and add 5 drops of Tea Tree oil to every 100ml milk and 1 teaspoon of Wheatgerm oil. Keep in the refrigerator until needed - use within 7-14 days.
To use - stir/shake well and pour 30ml into small basin. Using fresh piece of cotton wool each time, smooth over the face with firm strokes. Avoid getting into eyes-wring cotton wool out well before doing eye area.

LEMON CLEANSER   FOR GREASY SKIN

Use 1 egg white, beaten until frothy, then beat in 2 tablespoons of lemon juice, 1 tablespoon of glycerine and 5 drops of Tea Tree oil.

Use or discard cleanser within five days, cleanse skin. Keep in fridge but allow to rise to room temperature, naturally and beat well before use.

FRESH CLEANSING CREAM   FOR GREASY SKIN

Put 1 egg white into blender and add 1 tablespoon of cider vinegar. Blend on high, dribble in a mixture of the following oils; 25ml Grapeseed oil, 5ml Vitamin E oil, 5 drops Tea Tree oil and 5 drops of rosemary oil. Pour into sterilised airtight jar, label, date and use within 1 week. Store in a refrigerator. Use at room temperature.

RICH CLEANSING CREAM   FOR DRY AND VERY DRY SKIN

Put 1 egg in a blender, blend on high. Add 1dessertspoon of lemon juice, mix together oils as follows; 25ml olive oil, 20ml Soya oil, 20ml vitamin E oil and 5 drops of Tea Tree oil. Stir well and dribble into egg and lemon mixture while blending on high. Pour into a sterilised, airtight jar, label, date and use within 1 week, shake well before use. Store in a refrigerator, use at room temperature.

QUICK CLEANSER   FOR ALL SKIN TYPES

Mix 1 tablespoon liquid paraffin and 3 drops of Tea Tree oil, shake well and cleanse skin by; taking a clean piece of cotton wool, dip in mixture and clean face and neck, avoiding eye area. Then splash area with cool water. NB: Baby oil is very good for removing eye make-up.

FACE PACK   EXTRA DRY - MATURE SKINS

Mix 100ml olive oil, 20ml Wheatgerm oil and 5 drops Tea Tree oil, 5 drops palmarosa oil. Pour into a large bowl, warm to just above hand hot. Take a piece of cotton wool 6" by 12", soak in the oil mixture. Lie back with head on a couple of large towels. Protect eyes with 2 cucumber eye poultices (Section 1) or two pieces of cucumber and dry cotton wool. Put cotton wool pad over face, cut out holes for eye and nasal area and relax for 20 mins, or until cold. Cleanse and moisturise as normal.

FACE PACK   DRY AND NORMAL SKINS

Crack 1 egg yolk into a bowl, (save the egg white for other preparations). Add 1 tablespoon strained orange juice. Whisk with a hand held whisk or in a liquidiser, dribble in warmed 30ml Soya oil, 5ml vitamin E oil, 5 drops of Tea Tree oil, while still whisking, apply to face and neck. Leave on for 15 minutes. Remove with warm water. Avoid eye area.

LEMON AND CLAY FACE PACK   GREASY SKIN (ONLY)

Purchase some powdered green clay from the chemist. Put 2 tablespoons in bowl, add 1 tablespoon lemon juice, 5 drops of Tea Tree oil and 1 drop of lemon oil. Add enough warm water to make a soft paste. Apply to face and neck, leave 10-15 mins. Wash off with chamomile skin freshener.
NB: substitute cornflour for clay, not as effective, but would replace in an emergency.

FACIAL EXFOLIATING CREAM   ALL SKIN TYPES

Add 1 teaspoon ground whole oatmeal to every dessertspoon of cleanser. Rub into face and/or hands to remove dead skin cells. Avoid eye area.

FACIAL SAUNA   NOT FOR PEOPLE WITH BROKEN VEINS (ROSACEA)

In a bowl or bathroom basin, half fill with steaming hot water. Sprinkle on 5 drops of Tea Tree oil. Place a large towel over your head and around bowl to make a steam 'tent'. Close your eyes and let vapours drift up onto face, opening clogged pores.

CHAMOMILE SKIN FRESHENER   FOR GREASY SKIN

Put 1 chamomile tea bag into 8 fl. oz. of hot water, leave until cold. Add 1 tablespoon of cider vinegar. Use to remove face pack from greasy skin.

SKIN FRESHENER   FOR NORMAL SKIN

Take 6-8 sprigs of fresh rosemary or 1 rosemary 'tea (Herb) bag' and steep in 250ml boiling water until cold. Strain and add 3 tablespoons of fresh lemon juice and 5 drops of Tea Tree oil. Pour into sterilised bottle, cork, label and date and use within 2 weeks. Shake before use.
Apply to skin with cotton wool to remove traces of cleanser and tone up skin. Avoid eye area.

THERAPEUTIC SKIN FRESHENER   FOR DRY/NORMAL SKIN

Blend 2 teaspoons of fresh carrot juice, 1 tablespoon fresh orange juice, 1 teaspoon white wine vinegar and 3 drops of Tea Tree oil. Strain and use to remove make-up. Avoid eye area, baby oil is a good eye make-up remover.

LIP BALM

25gms Bees Wax	5ml Vitamin E Oil
30ml Olive Oil	20 drops Tea Tree Oil

In a large glass Pyrex jug (must be oven proof). Melt the Beeswax in microwave (Keep children/pets well away. Hot wax can be dangerous). Melt for 3 minutes on high. If not melted, melt for another 2 minutes on high. Then give 1 minute bursts until all melted (or melt in a double saucepan). The wax does get very hot and also the handle of the jug, so use oven gloves when removing jug from the microwave oven.

Stand on folded tea cloth. Hold handle with ovengloves and carefully stir with a wooden spoon. Dribble in (warmed) oils and stir well. Stir until nearly cool. Pour into small clean (sterilised) pots (ie. small plastic paracetamol pots), label, date and use within 6 months.

*Add 2 drops of natural red food colouring for tinted lip balm.

LIP SALVE

Mix together 1/4 of teaspoon of warmed petroleum jelly and 2 drops of Tea Tree oil. Rub onto cracked and/or bleeding lips. Rub well in. Repeat as necessary.

MOUTH WASH

Add 2 drops Tea Tree oil to 50ml warm water and rinse mouth when necessary, guards against infection and keeps breath sweet.

SKIN TONER
See SKIN FRESHENER.

SOAP

When you have about 6-8 pieces of 'end of soap bars' place them all in a large bowl, add 15ml olive oil and either melt in a microwave or in a double saucepan. When melted and hot take from heat and stir well until just above blood heat. Add 2 ml Tea Tree oil, drop by drop and continue stirring - pour into mould - (a clay modelling mould, small jelly mould or even a cup). Allow to cool, turn out and use as necessary.

* Add 2-5ml per 100ml pure liquid soap, for an anti-bacterial hand wash.

SUNBURN TREATMENT

Excessive damage, should have medical treatment, red and/or flaky skin, due to the drying effect of the sun, can be helped by applying a mixture of the following: 1 teaspn Aloe vera gel, 1 drop lavender oil, 1 drop Tea Tree oil, twice per day. Use Aloe gel only in eye area. Do not go out in sun until healed. ***Prevention* - wear a sun hat or use total sun block for the face.**

TEETHPASTE

FOR WHITER TEETH

Add two drops of Tea Tree oil on top of a pea-sized amount of your normal toothpaste, clean and rinse as normal. Use for 7 days then once per week to maintain whiteness.

FOR STAINED TEETH

Mix together 1/2 teaspoon bicarbonate of soda, a small pinch of salt, 2 drops of Tea Tree oil and enough water to make paste - clean and rinse teeth as normal.

DENTURE PASTE

Mix together 1 teaspoon bicarbonate of soda, 1 teaspoon salt, 10 drops Tea Tree oil, mix to a paste with lemon juice. Rub into dentures leave for at least 30 minutes or over night, scrub with a toothbrush and rinse well, before wearing.

*

Mrs Kate Baron of Bath, who helped to test the Tea Tree Oil and some of the preparations writes:

> *"My hands were always chapped, especially in the winter months. The TTO Barrier Cream was a Godsend."*........

> *" The lip balm has so far kept my lips moist and free from the usual dryness and peeling"*........

> *"For months I have had some very nasty spots on my face, the doctor prescribed a low dose antibiotic for 3 months, but it had no effect whatsoever. I tried Tea Tree Oil, which I applied twice per day on a cotton bud, after three weeks, they are beginning to fade, I'm very hopeful of a clear complexion."*

HANDS

BARRIER CREAM

This is an ideal cream for people who do not like rubber gloves. It will protect hands while in water - keep re-applying if hands in water for any length of time.

25gms Bees Wax	2ml Tea Tree oil
25ml Olive oil	1ml Lavender oil
20ml Wheatgerm oil	20ml Lavender water.

In a large glass pyrex jug, melt the bees wax in microwave (or melt in a double saucepan). Keep children away because wax gets very hot and can burn. Melt for 3 minutes on high, then if not melted, another 3 minutes on high then 1 minute bursts until melted. Remove from heat (using oven gloves or tea towel around handle of jug or saucepan).
Stand on a heatproof non slip mat and stir constantly with a wooden spoon. Dribble in the carrier oils whilst stirring, then dribble in the lavender water drop by drop still stirring constantly. If curdles, heat again and repeat procedure from the beginning. Finally, when cooler add the Tea Tree oil and lavender oil. Pour into a sterilised pot and leave by the sink.
 Before you do the washing up rub in a generous teaspoon of the cream. repeat after you have finished the washing up. Also beneficial after gardening. Use within 6 months.

GRANDMA'S BARRIER CREAM

Melt 75gms pure lard in the microwave or in a double saucepan, add 25ml warm olive oil, beat well to cool, if curdles reheat the ingredients and start again. Still beating add 2ml Tea Tree oil and 2ml lavender oil, continue beating until cool and a cream forms, spoon into a sterilised wide neck jar and use as above. Use within 2 months.

DRY SKIN REMOVER

Grind 1 tablespoon of whole oats until it resembles fine meal. Add 1 dessertspoonful to some cleansing cream or liquid soap. Rub into hands as if washing them. Rub in for at least 1 minute. rinse with tepid water and apply hand cream.

HAND AND BODY CARE CREAM

25gms Bees Wax   50ml Almond Oil.
25gms Anhydrous Lanolin   50ml Lavender Water.
30ml Wheatgerm Oil   2ml Palmarosa Oil
2ml Tea Tree Oil

In a large glass Pyrex (ovenproof) jug melt the bees wax and lanolin in a microwave, 3 mins on high, then another 3 mins, if still not melted then give 1 min bursts until they are fully liquid, (or use a double saucepan). Keep children and pets out of kitchen. Remove from the heat, using oven gloves. Stand on a heatproof, non slip mat, add the warmed wheatgerm and almond oil and stir consistently until just warm, but not beginning to set, dribble in the warmed lavender water, stirring all the time. If the mixture separates go back to the beginning and melt then keep stirring with wooden spoon. Finally add the Tea Tree oil and palmarosa oil drop by drop, beat until cool, store in sterilised glass jar, use within 6 months.
*If allergic to lanolin, use 50gms emulsifying wax, available from pharmacies.

NAIL CONDITIONING OIL

In a bowl add 60ml olive oil, 15ml wheatgerm oil, 10 drops tincture of myrrh, 2ml Tea Tree oil and 5 drops oil of galbanum. Stir well in a double saucepan until warm. Pour back into bowl and soak nails for 20 minutes. Pat dry with tissues or kitchen towel to remove surplus, try not to wash hands for at least 1 hour. Cover dish, save and repeat every 24 hours, for 7 days.

WARMING HAND OIL

50ml Grapeseed Oil   20ml Wheatgerm Oil.
10 drops Tea Tree Oil   10 drops Wintergreen Oil.
5 drops Lemon Oil.   5 drops Ginger Oil

Mix all oils together, pour into a sterilised bottle and cork, label and date. Always store in a cool dark place. Use within 2 months.
Shake well before use and apply a few drops and rub in well, just before going outside in winter. Remember to always wear gloves, a small pair of cotton gloves inside your normal pair would be beneficial, if possible.

Never use neat ginger oil directly on the skin or in the bath.

BODY

AFTER SUN SOOTHER

In a cup put 1 tea bag and 1 chamomile tea bag, pour on boiling water and allow to steep for 4 minutes. Discard tea bags. Pour into a blender, blend on high and add the following;

1 dessertspoon warmed Honey	25ml Glycerine.
2ml Tea Tree Oil	2ml Lavender Oil.

Dribble in 100ml olive oil and 10ml wheatgerm oil. Blend well.
If the blend separates warm mixture and blend until cool - pour into a bottle, label, date and store in cool dark place. Use within 2 months.

AFTER SUN SOOTHER DELUXE

Mix together 2 teaspoons hazelnut oil, 2 teaspoons avocado oil, 2 teaspoons seabuckthorn oil, 1 teaspoon vitamin E oil, 5 drops sweet orange oil, 5 drops Tea Tree oil and 8 drops lavender oil. Apply as required.

ANTI-CELLULITE CREAM

25gms Ivy (Leaves & Stems).	20gms Bees Wax
*20gms Anhydrous Lanolin	50ml Soya Oil.
25ml Avocado Oil	1ml Sweet Orange Oil.
15ml Wheatgerm Oil.	10 drops Tea Tree Oil
10 drops Cypress Oil	10 drops Lemon Oil.
10 drops Wintergreen Oil	10 drops Rosemary Oil
10 drops Geranium Oil.	10 drops Kanuka Oil
10 drops Lavender Oil	10 drops Oregano Oil

Boil The ivy in a cup of water until reduced by two thirds and steep. Melt wax and lanolin in a Pyrex jug in the microwave or in a double saucepan. (Keep out of reach of children). Warm the hazelnut, avocado, soya and wheatgerm oils. Stir into the melted wax. Strain the hot ivy (50ml) water drop by drop into the wax/oil mixture stirring constantly. Beat well, when just hand hot, stir in all the essential oils. Beat until nearly cool and pour into a wide necked sterilised jar (wipe around with 3 drops of Tea Tree oil). Label, date and use within 6 months. **See CHAPTER 7 Cellulite.**
*If allergic to lanolin, either increase beeswax to 40gms or use an emulsifying wax. Alternatively, You could purchase an over the counter base ointment (100ml) and add the ivy and the oils (omit soya & avocado oil).

ANTI-CELLULITE CREAM (CONT.)

Have a warm bath, pat dry, massage in cream vigorously to problem areas.
Wrap in cling film (low in plasticisers), not too tight and go to bed. Within
6 - 12 weeks, treating problem areas every or nearly every day, there should
be an improvement. Do not use on face, sensitive, sore or broken skin.
DIET CHANGE: Drink plenty of fluids, herb teas and filtered water, with
plenty of fresh, organic fruit and vegetables. Avoid caffeine and salt.

ANTI-CELLULITE OIL

Mix together: 75ml soya oil, 15ml evening primrose oil, 10 drops Tea Tree
oil, 10 drops wintergreen oil, 10 drops sweet orange oil, 10 drops lemon oil,
10 drops cypress oil, 1ml juniper oil, 10 drops lavender oil, and 10 drops
cumin oil (**never use cumin oil neat or in the bath**, if in contact with skin,
flood with a carrier oil such as soya or almond). Store in sterilised, airtight
bottle, use as above. Do not use on the face, sensitive, sore or broken skin. If
irritation occurs discontinue use.

BATH GEL OR SHOWER GEL   FOR NORMAL/OILY SKIN

100ml Glycerine   5ml Lemon Oil.
5ml Tea Tree Oil   5ml Rosemary Oil.

Beat in the oils slowly to the warmed glycerine. Store in a dark glass bottle
for baths or add to a cleaned shower gel tube and use as necessary in the
bath or shower. Shake well before use.

For dry skin: omit the Lemon and Rosemary oil and substitute 5ml
chamomile oil, 5ml sweet orange and 25ml Almond oil or Vitamin E oil.

CAUTION: Adding oils to the bath or shower will make them slippery.

BATH OIL   FOR DRY SKIN

100ml Almond Oil   25ml Wheatgerm Oil.
5ml Tea Tree Oil   5ml Geranium Oil.
5ml Sandalwood Oil   2ml Benzoin.
2ml Lavender Oil.

Beat oils together, pour into dark glass jar, label, date and use within 2
months. Use 15ml in warm bath water.

CAUTION: Adding oils to the bath or shower will make them slippery.

OATMEAL 'MILK' BATH

Grind 2-3 cups of whole oats into oatmeal (either make a bag of muslin 6"x 4" with a large tape to hang over cold bath tap or sew all four sides to make an oatmeal "sponge", to clean the body with - throw away after the bath).
Put the oatmeal into the muslin 'bag'. Hang over the cold tap so cold water runs through it, adding 'oat milk' to the water or put into a muslin bag and sew across top for use in the bath, as an 'oatmeal sponge'. Add 10-15 drops of Tea Tree oil to water or 15ml BATH OIL.

SPA BATH

Add a handful of sea salt, 10-15 drops Tea Tree oil, 5 drops of calendula oil and 2 drops of lemon oil. Relax in the refreshing spa.

BODY BRUSHING
See HEALING APPLICATIONS PAGE

BODY CREAM
See HAND AND BODY CARE CREAM.

BODY EXFOLIATING RUB

25gms Kelp Powder.
5gms Salt.
25gms Ground Whole Oats.

Mix together, store in a clean airtight jar. Before bath but standing in bath exfoliate all over body with firm rubbing motions. Bathe as normal.

BODY LOTION

Put a whole egg into blender and blend at high speed. Add 25ml Pure lemon juice, dribble in 50ml almond oil, 50ml soya oil, 10 ml wheatgerm oil and 3ml Tea Tree oil while still blending. Blend until smooth, bottle, label and date. Store in a dark cool place. Use within 2 weeks.

BODY OIL

Mix together 25ml sea buckthorn oil, 20ml wheatgerm oil, 2ml palmarosa oil, 1ml lavender oil, 1ml Tea Tree oil. Massage into skin after a bath or shower. Use within 3 months.

BREAST TONING OIL

50ml Soya Oil	20ml Wheatgerm Oil
15 drops Rose Oil	5 drops Tea Tree Oil
*(Rose oil is quite expensive and	10 drops Palmarosa Oil
often adulterated and sold cheaper)	5 drops Lemon Oil
10 drops Galbanum	*5 drops Neroli Oil

Mix together and massage the oil into each breast and into the stomach area - especially good for post natal skin care to encourage elasticity. Store in a dark, labelled bottle. Keep in the refrigerator, use cold and within 2 months. Pure rose oil can be very expensive, a small bottle is between £40-£50, as a substitute: use 5-7 drops YLANG YLANG OIL and 5-7 drops ROSEWOOD OIL

DEODORANT

Most deodorants contain aluminium in one form or another. It is far safer to use Tea Tree oil. For a quick deodorant just spread a few drops under each arm etc.
To make a deodorant that you could "re-fill" your existing, cleaned roll-on bottles with follow as detailed below; Shake well before use.
Mix 35ml "SYLK", a natural water based lubricating gel made from Kiwi fruit with 5ml Tea Tree oil and 5ml Lavender oil.

OATMEAL BODY PACK

To use the 'pulp' from all these oatmeal 'milk' preparations why not treat yourself to an 'oatmeal body pack'. It is a little sticky but a mud bath is too and this also is very therapeutic for your skin.

1-2 litres of 'oatmeal' pulp, either from the freezer or make fresh with 5 cups whole oats and one cup of wheatgerm, grind to a fine powder in a blender or coffee grinder attachment to the liquidiser. Put into a bowl, pour on 1 litre of boiling water, stir and cool slightly;

ADD:

3ml Tea Tree Oil	2ml Canadian Wintergreen Oil
3ml Sweet Orange Oil	1ml Juniper Oil
3ml Palmarosa Oil	

Stir well - if too "stodgy" add more hot water. If too liquid add more ground oats until you have the right consistency. Heat until warm / hot.
Stand or sit in an empty bath, apply the body pack all over feet, legs, buttocks, stomach, chest, back, arms, shoulders and neck. Relax until cool.

shower or run bath and rinse off pack, taking care as the bath or shower may be quite slippery.

It is better if you only do this if you have a shower attachment to your bath otherwise is can be quite difficult trying to run a bath with a body pack on, alternatively your partner could help.

Apply body exfoliating rub, shower again, pat skin dry and apply body lotion.

OATMEAL EXFOLIATING RUB

Grind a cup of whole oats to powder, mix with 50gms ground nuts, and 1 teaspoon maize flour/cornmeal (optional). Rub over body to remove dead skin cells. Do not use on face or delicate skin.

See BODY EXFOLIATING RUB.

SUNTAN OIL 1

This suntan oil has no (or little) sun factor classification - use only when you have conditioned your skin to the sun. Do not use with sensitive, easily burnt skins, for children or for babies.

50ml Hazelnut Oil	20ml Vitamin E oil or Wheatgerm Oil
30ml Sea Buckthorn Oil	15 drops Tincture of Iodine
20 drops Tea Tree Oil	20 drops Carrot Oil

Mix and pour into a labelled and dated dark glass bottle, shake before use. Use within 3 months. Apply often and liberally when sunbathing.

SUNTAN LOTION 2

This suntan oil has no sun factor classification - only use when you have conditioned your skin to the sun. Do not use with sensitive, easily burnt skin, for children or for babies.

50ml Coconut Oil	25ml Wheatgerm Oil
50gms Cocoa Butter	5ml Ylang Ylang Oil
20 drops Tincture of Iodine	1ml Tea Tree Oil
2ml Carrot Oil	

Heat the cocoa butter, coconut and wheatgerm oil in a double saucepan (or microwave) until melted. Whisk until cooled but not set, add the essential oils and tincture, whisk again until cool. Store in a sterilised wide neck jar, label and date, use within 3 months. Apply often liberally when in sun.

FEET

ANTI-BLISTER LOTION

Mix 1 teaspoon of Witch Hazel and 5 drops of Tea Tree Oil. Apply to heels and sides of little toes twice per day to harden the skin and prevent blisters.

ANTI-FUNGAL OINTMENT   ATHLETES FOOT / RINGWORM

25gms Bees Wax	5 drops Moroccan Cedarwood Oil
50ml Olive Oil	50gms Pot Marigold Petals
5ml Tea Tree Oil	*(Calendula Officinalis)*
5ml Kanuka Oil	5ml Manuka Oil
20 drops Clary Sage Oil	20 drops Geranium Oil

Add the marigold petals to the olive oil, heat until nearly boiling, set aside to infuse, preferable overnight*. Heat the wax over a moderate heat, in a double saucepan (or in the microwave with 2 minute blasts on high) until melted. Always keep children and pets away, the wax can reach very high temperatures and should be handled with care. Stir well to cool, when just warm, reheat the marigold infused olive oil, strain through muslin and add oil to the wax, beat well. When just warm, but not set add the essential oils, beating well in. When cool store in a wide necked, sterilised jar. Use as required, apply 3 times per day to infected area, (always cover a ringworm between applications with gauze). Use within 6 months.

NB - Alternatively, buy an over the counter base ointment, melt, add the essential oils, 20ml Olive oil, beat until cool, store and use as above.

* 3ml calendula oil may be added to the olive oil in place of the pot marigold petals.

COLD CUCUMBER AND MINT FOOT SOOTHER

This is ideal for hot sweaty feet and swollen ankles.
Peel 1 cucumber (room temperature), chop and blend until pulped. Put into bowl and add 5 drops of peppermint oil and 5 drops of Tea Tree oil. Mix well. Place bowl of tepid water by the side of the other bowl and have towel ready. Put feet into bowl of cucumber, rub into ankles and top of feet. 'Soak' for 10 minutes, 'wash' feet in bowl of water, pat dry with towel, massage in oil mix of 10ml cold soya oil, 3 drops of peppermint oil and 3 drops of Tea Tree oil. Wrap feet in towel and elevate legs above heart for 20 minutes. This is very soothing when just in from work in the summer!.

Never use any type of mint oil **'neat'** in the bath or on the skin.

CRACKED SKIN TREATMENT

Soak feet in shallow bowl of warm water with 20 drops of Tea Tree oil sprinkled in, pat dry - apply following preparation twice per day.
Mix together 1 tablespoon petroleum jelly, 20 drops of Tea Tree oil and 5 drops of sandalwood - optional - (this is often adulterated, even copied, so make sure that you have the authentic oil).
If symptom persists or feet are painful see a chiropodist.

See NAIL CARE CHAPTER 7
See FOOT CARE CHAPTER 7

DRY SKIN RUB

1 tablespoon Cornmeal (made from Maize) or Salt
1 teaspoon powdered Kelp

Soak feet in shallow bowl of warm water and 10 drops of Tea Tree oil or after a bath. Rub powder into soles and heels to remove dead skin. Do not rub too hard or use on broken or cracked skin as this powder is quite abrasive, rinse and massage in either hand and body lotion or warm foot oil. **Only to be used on the feet.**

SUMMER FOOT COOLER

Mix 7 drops Tea Tree oil, 10 drops peppermint oil, and 10ml soya oil. Massage into the soles of the feet. If you suffer from swollen ankles due to the heat, using upward strokes massage the oil into the ankle/problem area. **Do not use over a large area, this preparation is for feet only.**
Do not use on the face.

FOOT CREAM

See HAND AND BODY LOTION SECTION 4.

WARM FOOT OIL

1 tablespoon olive oil, 1/2 tablespoon wheatgerm oil, 10 drops Tea Tree oil, 5 drops juniper oil and 2 drops ginger oil. Mix olive oil and Wheatgerm oils, warm to blood heat, add essential oils and massage into feet.

Never use ginger oil neat on the skin and never add it to baths.

MISCELLANEOUS

AROMATHERAPY CANDLES

For each candle you will need:
90ml Paraffin Wax
Wax Dye Discs
10ml Stearin
Wick
2 Saucepans
Thermometer
Basin
Cocktail Stick or Skewer
Mould (which can be a cup to a candle mould)

Please keep children out of the kitchen and do not turn heat up too high.

Heat the wax in a saucepan to 180*F - 65*C. In the other saucepan melt the dye and stearin together, heat to the same temperature as the wax and add to the wax. Tie wick in the middle of the cocktail stick or skewer. Balance on edge of mould and let the wick fall into the mould. When slightly cooled add 5ml Tea Tree oil and 5ml citronella or geranium oil. Stir and pour into mould(s) keeping a tablespoon of wax back. Put mould into cold water when set. There will be a dip in the middle. Heat the tablespoon of wax left over and pour into centre of the dip.

Allow to set, trim wick and remove candle from mould. Use as required.

ASHTRAY FRESHENERS

Granulated 'Fullers Earth' can be bought from a chemist, the less expensive alternative is a bag of cat litter. For ashtray fresheners and pomanders it is perfect. It can be dyed, it absorbs oils and does not burn, so it is less of a fire hazard than pot pourri.

Put 2 tablespoons of 'Fullers Earth' into a bowl, pour on a natural food colouring (or halve/quarter the granules and put on 2-4 colours to the separate halves/quarters of the granules). Allow to dry and mix for a rainbow effect. When ready to use, sprinkle on essential oils. Use in ashtrays, pomanders or shoe fresheners etc.

See BLENDS CHAPTER 8

AROMATIC FIRELIGHTERS

Collect all the fir cones that you can, dry them and store in sacks or old pillow cases.

To light a fire, take 6 fir cones and sprinkle on essential oils, 1-2 drops of Tea Tree oil, geranium or citronella oil. Take two pages from a newspaper and roll up quite tightly, so that you have a long thin tube, wrap around your hand until you have a circular 'fire lighter', tuck the end through the middle. Put a fir cone into the centre (or some kindling) and make a base for your fire using several fire lighters, add coal and wood on top, light with a long taper, remember to replace the fire guard.

For a barbecue, take a couple of dried cones and soak in water, then sprinkle with essential oil, throw on dying barbecue (hot ash) after cooking, as an insect repellent whilst eating or if barbecue is still burning put on a high rack to warm and release fragrance.

FRAGRANCE PILLOW

For a quick-no sew- fragrance pillow you will need:
A Quantity of Small Foam Pieces (or cut up enough old clean tights as possible to fill 1/2 a pillow case)
2-3 6"x 4" Plastic Bags
4-6 Tablespoons Fullers Earth (See ASHTRAY FRESHENERS)
An Ordinary Pillow Case
12" x 12" Zipped Cushion Cover

3ml Tea Tree Oil
3ml Lavender Oil   (or see BLENDS-CHAPTER 8).

Equally divide the 'Fullers Earth' between the plastic bags - sprinkle on the oils and knot the bags. (polythene allows the fragrance to escape), pack half the pillow case with foam/tights and place 'fragrance' bags into the middle of the (half) pillow and pack foam/tights around them.
Fold the pillow case over so only half is used, place inside zipped cushion cover. Refresh the 'Fullers Earth as necessary, open polythene bags and sprinkle more essential oils onto the contents (renew the polythene bags to prevent leaking).

FRAGRANCE SACS

To produce pretty fragrance sacs for drawers, car or cupboards you will need 1 metre x 9-10cms wide lace, Ungathered and unhemmed (straight edges), cut into 4 equal pieces with pinking shears. Fold over so the cut edges meet. Sew the right and left sides to form a "sac". Take 8 tablespoons of dyed 'Fullers earth' (See ASHTRAY FRESHENERS) and sprinkle on 1ml Tea Tree oil and 3ml of Lavender oil or any of the blends from CHAPTER 8. Divide into 4 equal parts (2 tablespoons each) and fill 4 polythene bags equally - knot and trim excess polythene. Place one bag in each sac and tie a pretty bright ribbon about 1"- 2" from top. Refresh as necessary.

See WARDROBE FRESHENERS (NO SEW) BEDROOM CHAPTER 5.

POT POURRI

Small Pumice Stone Pieces
Dried Peach Stones
Dried Seeds
Dried Pips
*Fullers Earth Granules
Dried Nuts/Nut Shells
Dried Citrus Fruit Peel
Wood Shavings / Chipped Bark
Small Dried Leaves
Cardamom Pods
Small Dried Flowers
Dried Spices ie. Cloves, Cinnamon Sticks, Vanilla Pods etc.

(Seeds and stones can be painted with natural food colouring for added effect)

*(Cat litter-can be dyed with natural food colouring)

Choose your favourite mixture or use most readily available ingredients.
Put chosen mixture into an airtight container, add Orris Root (from chemist) use 1 tablespoon per cup of mixture.
Patchouli, Sandalwood, Vetiver and/or Myrrh can be used as a fixative. 15ml sprinkled onto 4-5 cups of mixture. Mix well, cover and store for around 4 weeks in airtight box, use as required. Sprinkle on your favourite aromatherapy oils. To top up aroma or use blends for relaxation etc.

See CHAPTER 8

SHOE FRESHENERS

Fill 4 x 6" length ('feet') from two pairs of old clean tights (use doubled so you have just one pair), put a plastic bag inside each 'foot' and fill with pot pourri or 'Fullers Earth' (see ASHTRAY FRESHENERS) and add 10 drops of Tea Tree oil and 10 drops of lavender oil to each 'shoe freshener'. Tie with a ribbon and drop into each shoe. For boots use 12"-15" length of old tights. Perfect for storing shoes and boots, they will keep your cupboards fresh too.

See UTILITY SECTION CHAPTER 5.

TEA TREE OIL PESSARIES

Pessaries are very simple to make, first you need a pessary mould available from specialist shops. Melt 25gms cocoa butter in a glass dish in the microwave or in a double saucepan over moderate heat, stir to cool, add 10 drops lavender oil, 10 drops calendula oil, 5 drops manuka oil and 10 drops Tea Tree oil, pour into mould and allow to set. Store in a sterilised jar in refrigerator for up to 3 months. Use as required, twice per day, for thrush, vaginitis etc. insert with pessary applicator, available from chemists.

WOOD POLISH

For floors and furniture

LIGHT WOOD.

DARK WOOD.

50gms Bees Wax
250ml Linseed Oil (warmed)
50ml White Wine Vinegar (warmed)
5ml Tea Tree Oil   (warmed)
5ml Lavender Oil
20 drops Cedar Wood Oil

50gms Bees Wax
200ml Linseed Oil (warmed)
50ml Walnut Oil (warmed)
50ml Brown Vinegar
5ml Calendula Oil.
5ml Tea Tree Oil

In a large 1 litre Pyrex glass jug melt the bees wax in a microwave (or double saucepan) on high in three minute bursts until melted. (Do keep children out of the kitchen, as hot wax should be handled carefully). Use an oven glove or tea cloth to grip jug handle, the wax reaches a very high temperature to melt.

Dribble in the linseed oil (walnut oil if for dark wood polish), stirring constantly. Add the vinegar drop by drop. Stir well. Stir until blood heat. Add essential oils, stir and pour into lidded wide necked container or Tupperware type container. Cool before replacing lid.

Use as required. This polish has a natural 'insect repellent' fragrance.

Chapter Seven

A–Z
First Aid
Applications

WARNING

100% PURE TEA TREE OIL *MELALEUCA ALTERNIFOLIA,* WITH 1,8 CINEOLE CONTENT 5% OR LESS AND THE TERPINEN-4-OL CONTENT 40% OR HIGHER MUST BE USED. IF THERE IS <u>ANY</u> DOUBT TO THE QUALITY - DO NOT USE IN THIS SECTION.

FOR YOUNG BABIES CONSULT A QUALIFIED AROMATHERAPIST BABIES MUST NOT HAVE MORE THAN 10% SOLUTION: 10ML TO 100ML CHILDREN MUST NOT HAVE MORE THAN 25% SOLUTION: 25ML TO 100ML

PEOPLE WITH A SERIOUS MEDICAL CONDITION SHOULD SEE AN AROMATHERAPIST

Everyone should do a sensitivity test before using ANY essential oil for First Aid applications. Apply a drop of chosen oil to the back of the wrist cover with a plaster. If no reaction after 24 hours it should be safe to use.

PLEASE READ NOTES ON PAGE 8 BEFORE USING THIS SECTION IF SYMPTOMS PERSIST CONSULT DOCTOR

A

ABDOMINAL PAIN

Apply (warmed) 3 drops TEA TREE OIL and 10ml CASTER OIL to abdominal area. Rub gently, cover with cling film (make sure cling film is low in plasticisers), place hot water bottle with medium heat on top and relax.

Alternatively, rub in 2 drops TEA TREE OIL, 2 drops LAVENDER OIL, 2 drops KANUKA OIL and 10ml CASTOR OIL, place a heat pad on abdomen and another to the lower back area, either commercial or home made. See CHAPTER 6 for home made heat pad.

If pain persists or gets worse consult a doctor.

See MENSTRUAL PROBLEMS
See MENOPAUSAL PROBLEMS
See IRRITABLE BOWEL SYNDROME
See ULCERATIVE COLITIS
See COLIC

ABRASIONS

Grazes, scratches, minor cuts, scrapes.

For cuts and scratches, clean well with a solution of 1ml TEA TREE OIL to 50ml of warm water.

For scrapes and grazes soak pad of cotton wool, drag gently across abrasion to remove debris. You may need tepid, running water for stubborn debris. Either hold over a bowl and flood the area with TEA TREE OIL solution or use an eye bath depending on size of wound.

When clean dab with cotton wool & a few drops of TEA TREE OIL and cover. If still bleeding apply pressure for a few minutes.
Bathe and change the dressing twice a day.

Seek medical advice you may need a Tetanus injection.

See CHAPTER 6 for Antiseptic Healing Cream
See SCABS
See SPLINTERS
See WOUNDS

ABSCESS

Large abscesses should been seen by a doctor.

IF ON BODY
Apply neat TEA TREE OIL 3-4 times per day. A warm compress may help, (a warm wet flannel soaked with 10 drops of TEA TREE OIL to surface - place over abscess) It may take a few days until it bursts, drain and treat with neat TEA TREE OIL. Follow instructions for abrasions.

See POULTICE - CHAPTER 6

IF ON FACE
A warm compress made from a piece of cotton wool approx. 2" square, soaked in warm CASTER OIL-1 teaspoon, TEA TREE OIL-5 drops, wrapped in gauze. Apply 2-3 times per day, leave until cool.

ABSCESS IN MOUTH
Consult your dentist Apply 1-2 drops neat TEA TREE OIL to area twice per day until the appointment.

Preventative Keep skin scrupulously clean. Take TEA TREE OIL bath and TEA TREE OIL mouthwash. See CHAPTER 6.

ACHES AND PAINS

Rub in warmed: 5 drops TEA TREE OIL, 5 drops KANUKA OIL & 10 ml OLIVE OIL and apply heat pad as in CHAPTER 6.

See also, RHEUMATISM, ARTHRITIS, TENDINITUS (tender tendons), MUSCLE CRAMPS, ABDOMINAL PAIN.

ACNE

Dab on neat TEA TREE OIL twice a day, if you experience tingling that is uncomfortable or have sensitive skin mix 5ml TEA TREE OIL, 1 ml MANUKA OIL and 1 ml KANUKA OIL with 1ml VITAMIN E OIL OR WHEATGERM OIL and 20ml GRAPESEED OIL. Shake before use. Wet face with warm distilled water and dab on oil twice per day.
Preventative Add 1ml TEA TREE OIL, 10 drops KANUKA OIL and 10 drops MANUKA OIL to 100ml of neutral cleanser and cleanse face twice per day.

See CHAPTER 6 ACNE TREATMENT

AGEING SKIN

See WRINKLES
See CHAPTER 6 for Home-made Preparations.
See SKIN CARE

ALOPECIA

Take 25gms of dried stinging nettles, pour on 50ml hot SOYA OIL blend well in liquidiser and allow to stand overnight, strain through double muslin, until you have a clear (greenish) oil. Add 5 drops ROSEMARY OIL, 20 drops CLARY SAGE OIL, 5 drops TEA TREE OIL, 5 drops KANUKA OIL, 5 drops HORSERADISH OIL, 5 drops BURDOCK OIL and 20ml VITAMIN E OIL Store in a sterilised, dark glass bottle label, date and keep out of the reach of children. Apply to area 2-3 times a day, massage well into the scalp. Always patch test first on a small area initially.
Alternative application - Add 2 teaspoons of the above oil to 2 teaspoons Bay rum, shake well, add 2 teaspoons cider vinegar, shake well, apply to the problem area, following the above guidelines.

Change to a healthier diet, no smoking, limit alcohol, tea, coffee and cola. Follow nutritional guide lines under IMMUNE SYSTEM, adding 1 handful of pumpkin seeds per day and eating oily fish 3-4 times per week. Wheatgerm, lecithin and a tablespoonful of linseeds should be added to breakfast cereals. Eggs, beans, garlic and onions contain the amino acid Cysteine which is beneficial against hair loss, nutritionists usually advise taking a supplement of around 1g to 2gs per day, between meals and with vitamin C, but medical guidance should be sought as Cysteine should not be given to diabetics and other medical conditions may cause a problem.

See HAIR CARE

ANAL FISSURES

Mix 10 drops TEA TREE OIL with 2ml OLIVE OIL and apply to area with cotton wool. Before each bowel movement lubricate area with a teaspoon of petroleum jelly mixed with 2-5 drops TEA TREE OIL. Apply to inside and outside of anus.

Prevention Make sure your diet has enough fibre. Eat at least 3 portions of vegetables and 2 portions of fruit per day. Drinking 6-8 glasses of water daily also helps. If not healed within 2 weeks consult your doctor.

See HAEMORRHOIDS
See CHAPTER 6   HAEMORRHOID TREATMENTS

ANAL ITCHING

Mix 2-3 drops of TEA TREE OIL with 2ml OLIVE OIL and apply to area with cotton wool or gauze. DO NOT SCRATCH AREA YOU COULD SPREAD INFECTION. **If symptoms persist see doctor.**

ANTHRAX

Mainly a disease of sheep and cattle Anthrax is caused by the bacterium Bacillum Anthracis. Anthrax is very contagious and can be transmitted to man through the skin and by inhalation.

Although Anthrax in humans is extremely rare, isolated outbreaks in animals do occur. The first symptoms are painful itching, followed by pimples or boils. These are usually hard with purple/red centres. They appear on the face and neck. **If suspected a doctor/vet should be informed immediately and anyone dealing with sick animals should take strict precautions, ALWAYS follow professional advice.** The nose and mouth should be covered (masks can be sprayed/dipped in a solution of 5ml TEA TREE OIL and 1ml MANUKA OIL to 100ml hot water). Exposed skin can be rubbed with neat TEA TREE OIL. Hands and nails **must** be scrubbed with 100ml of the above solution to which organic washing up liquid has been added.

Clothing, boots and car tyres **must** be sterilised too. The doctor will advise.

AROMATHERAPY

Apart from the medicinal aromatherapy of TEA TREE OIL described under specific headings, TEA TREE OIL can also be mixed with other oils to give relaxing or invigorating blends.

See AROMATHERAPY CHAPTER 8

ARTHRITIS

OSTEOARTHRITIS, in general terms, is an inflammation of a joint, which mainly effects hips, knees, spine and shoulders usually as a result of the natural wear and tear of ageing.

RHEUMATOID ARTHRITIS, is a disease of the connective tissue. This can be genetic and sometimes appears in quite young people.

Stress, lack of exercise, poor diet, allergens, emotional upset contribute to these painful conditions. Gentle exercise, an organic, mainly vegetarian diet containing complex carbohydrates, fresh fruit and vegetables and pure water with lots of relaxation is very effective.

See IMMUNE SYSTEM BOOSTERS

*For relief of inflammation and pain apply hot TEA TREE OIL compresses to affected areas twice a day. Dip a hand towel into a bowl containing 2 pints of hot/warm water, 2 tablespoons CIDER VINEGAR, 10 drops KANUKA OIL and 10 drops TEA TREE OIL.

*Follow application with a gentle massage. Mix together 10ml SOYA OIL, 5ml WHEATGERM OIL, 10 drops TEA TREE OIL, 10 drops ST JOHN'S WORT OIL, 10 drops KANUKA OIL and 4 drops of PEPPER OIL or GINGER OIL.

*Some people find good results with cold compresses. If you did not find the heat particularly helpful repeat using cold water. Substitute GINGER/PEPPER OIL for ROSEMARY OIL.

Skin brushing is very beneficial and helps the body release toxins. You will need a DRY natural bristle body brush (preferably with a long handle). Before and after your bath start at your shoulders. Brush down your arms, back, buttocks, abdomen, thighs, calves to ankles with firm even strokes. Repeat after your bath. A flannel can be used but a natural bristle brush is more effective.

See CHAPTER 6 page 107. For skin brushing to improve circulation.

ASTHMA

Asthma sufferers should be very careful when using essential oils. The falsification of many oils should make people very wary of buying them from just anyone, even if claimed that they supply Aromatherapists!. You should consult a qualified practitioner who will be able to test for an allergic reaction to specific oils. He will advise you of which oils to use, **if any**.

Once you have done this a bowl of boiling water in your room with 5 drops of TEA TREE OIL and 2 drops of ylang ylang. **Do not inhale directly** but let the vapours calm and soothe from a distance.

Ensure pets are not allowed in the bedroom.

Keep dust down to a minimum.

Your diet and environment should be kept as 'organic' as possible.
Avoid tea, coffee, cola and chocolate, smoking and limit alcohol.

See DUSTMITES CHAPTER 5
See CHAPTER 6 - WOOD POLISH

ATHLETES FOOT (TINEA)

TINEA PEDIS is a fungal infection of the foot. The flesh between the toes becomes wet and flaky. It is quite itchy. Toenails can also become infected.

Bathe feet in bowl of warm water containing 2 teaspoons salt and 10 drops of TEA TREE OIL for 15 minutes. Dry thoroughly. Wash towels daily, do not share.

Rub neat TEA TREE OIL between the toes and around the nails 2-3 times a day. (A very good mixture of oils for Athlete's Foot is 2ml TEA TREE OIL and 2ml MANUKA OIL apply as above, store in a dark glass labelled bottle in a cool dark place. - This can be mixed with 4-10ml OLIVE OIL).

Prevent re-infection.
1) Apply neat TEA TREE OIL to feet after going bare foot in public places.
2) Wash socks daily and rinse in solution of TEA TREE OIL (8ml
   to 1 litre). To kill fungal spores.
3) Boil wash towels and add 5ml TEA TREE OIL to rinse water.
4) Always remove dead skin from between toes. This harbours infection -
   you can use the following paste to do this.

ATHLETES FOOT (Cont.)

PASTE I

1 teaspoon Bicarbonate of Soda, 5 drops TEA TREE OIL, mixed to a paste with water, rub between toes.

PASTE II

Mix 25gms ground whole oats, 25gms bicarbonate of soda, 1 teaspoon salt and mix to a paste with distilled water and 5 drops of TEA TREE OIL. Rub between toes and around heels after soaking feet.

See NAIL INFECTIONS
See FOOT CARE
See ANTI-FUNGAL OINTMENT CHAPTER 6
See FEET CHAPTER 6

B

BACK ACHE

This covers a multitude of complaints. You must get a qualified diagnosis from your GP and then try the specific applications for relief.

As a general guide, back pain resulting from prolonged standing, muscle cramps, lifting heavy objects, wearing high heels, over stretching and fatigue may be relieved by the following;

*Relax in a warm bath with 15 drops of TEA TREE OIL and 10 drops LAVENDER OIL.

*Lie on a firm bed, face down or carpeted floor, put a small pillow or pad under tummy for support and have the following mixture of oils massaged into the affected area: 5 drops TEA TREE OIL, 5 drops KANUKA OIL, 5 drops GINGER OIL (never use ginger oil neat on the skin or in the bath). and 30ml GRAPESEED OIL.

*Apply TEA TREE OIL POULTICE. See chapter 6

See CHAPTER 6   DEEP HEAT RUB

*Make sure your mattress does not need renewing.   Your back always needs firm, comfortable support while lying in bed.

*Relax more. Lie on a firm bed, apply a head pad and imagine you are melting into the mattress.

Try AROMATHERAPY blends in CHAPTER 8

*Always 'roll' out of bed carefully, turning onto your side, towards the edge, slowly swing your feet towards the floor, while using your hands on the edge of the mattress to walk yourself into an upright sitting position. Your arms will take the strain not your back.

*For acute pain attacks and inflammation a TEA TREE ice pack and gentle massage of area can help to reduce swelling. Put 5 drops of TEA TREE OIL, 3 drops CALENDULA OIL and 3ml OLIVE OIL (straight from the fridge) onto affected area and apply a bag of crushed ice (wrapped in towel) for about seven minutes. (Ice is not to be used with anyone suffering from heart problems or diabetes). Repeat for two days as necessary.

BACK ACHE (Cont.)
See LUMBAGO
See RHEUMATISM
See ACHES AND PAINS
See MENSTRUAL PROBLEMS
See ARTHRITIS
See STRESS

BACK FRIENDS
See HANGNAILS
See HAND CARE
See NAIL CARE

BAD BREATH

TEA TREE OIL is perfect for refreshing the breath. Not only does it kill the bacteria and fungi responsible for bad breath, it also inhibits plaque build up and whitens teeth. Put a 'pea' sized amount of toothpaste onto your toothbrush, sprinkle on 2 drops of TEA TREE OIL and brush your teeth and tongue - brushing your tongue gently also helps to get rid of the white fur that sticks to your tongue.

*If you need a quick breath freshening rinse, put 2 drops of TEA TREE OIL into 50ml of warm water and swish around mouth.

See TEETH AND GUMS
See THRUSH
See DENTURE SORES
See GUM INFECTIONS
See GINGIVITIS
See TEA TREE OIL TEETHPASTE CHAPTER 6
See ANTISEPTIC MOUTH WASH CHAPTER 6

BALANITIS
See THRUSH

BARBERS RASH
See TEA TREE SALVE CHAPTER 6
See AFTERSHAVE BALM CHAPTER 6
See AFTERSHAVE OIL CHAPTER 6

BED SORES

These can occur anywhere on the body, especially where there is constant pressure. The most common places are buttocks, heels and elbows of bedridden patients.
Apply a few drops of TEA TREE OIL 3-4 times per day. If tingling occurs mix TEA TREE OIL with 1 teaspoon OLIVE OIL.

Prevention Turn patient as often as possible. Change sheets every day. rub massage oil into areas twice daily before sores appear -
(massage oil : 15ml CASTOR OIL 5ml WHEATGERM OIL and 1ml TEA TREE OIL).

See BODY BRUSHING CHAPTER 6, to improve circulation.

BITES AND STINGS
See INSECT BITES
See STINGS

BITES -ANIMALS

In the UK we thankfully do not have the killer disease RABIES, but there is still a risk of infection from bites. You should seek medical advice as soon as possible. You may need a Tetanus injection or booster.

If the skin is broken sprinkle neat TEA TREE OIL immediately and cover - the quicker the better. You must then bathe the area for 5 minutes with a solution of TEA TREE OIL 1ml to 10ml of warm water as soon as you can.

If the wound is still bleeding cover with gauze which has 4 drops of TEA TREE OIL sprinkled onto it and apply, (if there is no bandage handy apply TEA TREE OIL to your hand and press firmly against the wound).

Elevating the wound above heart (if possible) and applying ice pack to bandage can help to stop bleeding.
When bleeding has stopped cover with clean dry bandage. Seek medical advice as soon as possible.

If bitten whilst abroad, flood the wound with TEA TREE OIL and go immediately to hospital. If there is an ice pack to hand, even a pack of frozen peas, it can slow down absorption of infection.

BLACKHEADS

Soak flannel in 100ml hot water and 1ml TEA TREE OIL. Apply to face for 2 minutes and gently rub - repeat twice daily - use TEA TREE OIL face pack and sauna (CHAPTER 6 AND CHAPTER 8) once a week to prevent re-occurrence.
Avoid: the eye area with oils and stretching the delicate skin around eyes.

See TEA TREE OIL FACE PACK CHAPTER 6.
See SKIN CARE
See ACNE TREATMENT CHAPTER 6

BLADDER INFECTIONS
See CYSTITIS

BLISTERS

Blisters are a small sac of serum (a constituent of blood) under the skin's surface. They can be the result of burning, chafing, rubbing, scalding or infection.

Gently rub a mixture of 1 drop TEA TREE OIL, 1 drop CALENDULA OIL and 10 drops OLIVE OIL around area and over blister. You may like to make a felt ring (doughnut shaped) for comfort, especially for blisters on the feet and areas that are pressure points.

If the blister bursts try to keep the 'roof' on, it is natures plaster and will be very sore if removed. Clean area twice per day with cotton wool soaked in a solution of 10 drops TEA TREE OIL to 10ml warm water and allow the air to get to it as much as possible to speed up the healing process. A cushioned 'ring' plaster is ideal.

Prevention
To help prevent friction blisters mix 1 teaspoon of petroleum jelly to 2 drops of TEA TREE OIL and apply daily to blister prone areas before a long walk or exercise.

See BURNS
See CHAFING
See SCABS
See SPECIFIC INFECTIONS
See SCARRING

BODY ODOUR

TEA TREE OIL is a very good deodorant. It neutralises the bacteria that causes the odour and releases it's own unique 'spicy' aroma.

First take a refreshing bath with 10-20 drops TEA TREE OIL or douche with 5 drops TEA TREE OIL to 300ml of water.

Use TEA TREE OIL as a natural underarm deodorant. Apply 2-4 drops to fingertips and rub into underarm area.

For a more 'feminine' aroma use 2 drops TEA TREE OIL to 2 drops of LAVENDER OIL on each side.

See FOOT ODOUR
See HAND CARE

BOILS

Bacteria invades a blocked oil gland or hair follicle, inflammation occurs, and a pus filled abscess forms under the skin. A large red painful bump appears.
At first sign of inflammation, apply neat TEA TREE OIL to the area 3-4 times a day.
If a head begins to form, start applying a warm compress to inflammation, soak a face flannel or lint pad in 1ml of TEA TREE OIL to 20ml of hot water.
Hold on the boil for 10 minutes twice a day then apply neat TEA TREE OIL on and around the 'bump' until the boil bursts, then for 3 days afterwards to ensure all the pus has drained out on tissues.
If you do 'squeeze' the boil, 'disinfect' your hands before and afterwards with neat TEA TREE OIL. (Squeezing is not recommended as scarring can easily occur). See SCARRING.

An equal mixture of OLIVE OIL, MANUKA, KANUKA and TEA TREE OIL can be applied in the same way as above, some people swear by this mixture for boils. Apply a few drops to a gauze pad, cover overnight, secure with surgical tape.

Prevention
Help to prevent boils by adding 2 drops TEA TREE OIL to normal soap or face wash before washing.

See ABSCESS

BREAST FEEDING

Cracked nipples can be very painful. Rub in a little massage oil (10ml VITAMIN E OIL to 1 drop of TEA TREE OIL), dab excess. Apply at least 1 hour before baby's feed. Wipe nipples before feed with sterilised water or a little breast milk.

Preventing problems 2-3 months before the birth gently massage breasts with 1 teaspoon of oil made with 100ml VITAMIN E OIL (available from health food shops) and 5-10 drops of TEA TREE OIL, twice a day. Store oil in a dark glass labelled bottle. Check with midwife before commencing.

After the birth, make sure you ask the midwife to help position the baby on the breast. Keep asking until you get it right.

Nurse with both breasts during each feed and nurse as often as possible.

Keep nipples clean, but do not use harsh soaps, let nipples air dry. Rub your own milk into your nipples, it is high in lubricants.

If you suspect a blocked milk duct, (a small inflammation/hard spot, tender to touch) , anywhere on the breast, consult the midwife, and apply warmth to breast and some of your previous massage oil and massage breast from chest to nipple in circular motions. Allow your baby to suck frequently even if a little painful, nothing clears a blocked milk duct faster than a sucking baby.

If inflammation or pain gets worse or it does not clear after 24 hours, see doctor immediately. You may have Mastitis and need medication. Drink plenty of fluids and do not stop nursing/expelling milk or it could lead to a more serious condition.

Always consult your midwife before commencing.

BREAST INFLAMMATION

If you find a cyst or lump in your breast or experience acute pain/ache you must have an immediate medical check-up.

If you need relief from minor breast infections use a warm CASTOR OIL and TEA TREE OIL compress for 7 days. If breast still inflamed return to your doctor.

To make the compress use 50ml of cold pressed CASTOR OIL to 2ml of TEA TREE OIL, a woollen cloth, a hot flannel, cling film (low or no plasticisers) and a hot water bottle or a heating pad.

Fold the woollen cloth into 4 and saturate with the oil, wring out. Apply hot/warm flannel to breast for 3-4 minutes, discard and put on saturated cloth, cover with cling film and apply heat pad or hot water bottle (it must be comfortable, never too hot). Leave on for 20-30 minutes.

A breast massage with 5 drops TEA TREE OIL, 5 drops JUNIPER OIL and 10ml CASTOR OIL can be beneficial, to ease fluid retention and discomfort.

If pregnant or nursing, consult midwife or doctor, concerning inflammation, before attempting the above.

BREAST TONER
See CHAPTER 6

BROKEN VEINS
See VEINS

BRONCHITIS

As soon as you feel that characteristic 'tightness' gargle with 2-3 drops TEA TREE OIL and 2-3 drops MANUKA OIL (optional) to 50ml warm water. Have a TEA TREE OIL steam inhalation twice a day with 2 pints hot water and 10-15 drops TEA TREE OIL. Place head over bowl and trap the steam with a large towel over head. Close the eyes and breathe through the nose and out through the mouth. If the steam is too hot and uncomfortable, raise head and open towel a little or wait until water is a little cooler.

For a chronic attack a steam inhalation every 2 hours may be beneficial. A chronic attack should always be seen by a doctor.

Rub neat TEA TREE OIL into chest morning and night, not for sensitive skin. (If in doubt, patch test first).

See CHEST VAPOUR RUB CHAPTER 6.

*Contact your doctor if no improvement after a couple of days.

*Contact doctor immediately if you are older, if you have Bronchitis on top of another illness, if you are coughing blood, if you are experiencing chest pains, if you have a fever or if you are short of breath.

BRUISES

Use 2 drops TEA TREE OIL, 4 drops CALENDULA OIL in 10 drops of a carrier oil and an ice pack as quickly as possible on any injury that is likely to bruise. Apply an ice pack at 20 minute intervals and allow area to warm naturally.

Applying neat TEA TREE OIL and CALENDULA OIL will reduce the inflammation and speed up the healing process.

After 24 hours apply 3 drops TEA TREE OIL, 2 drops CYPRESS OIL and a hot compress. These will dilate blood vessels and improve circulation to the area.

*If you have children or a home handyman in the family it may be to your advantage to keep a home-made ice pack in the freezer. Wet a face flannel with water, fold in half. Put it in a freezer bag and freeze. A handy ice pack for bumps.

The ice pack should be applied to the area on top of a piece of gauze or in an emergency a clean tea cloth would do.

See BRUISE BAN I & II   CHAPTER 6

BUMPS
See BRUISES
See ABRASIONS

BUNIONS

This painful and unsightly inflammation of the joint occurs between the big toe and foot. The joint swells up and the skin becomes shiney and red. Apply neat TEA TREE OIL and KANUKA OIL 2 drops of each, 2-3 times a day.

Prevention* After a working day or long walk have a foot bath with 2 pints of warm water and 10 drops of TEA TREE OIL.

Dry feet and rub in massage oil, 2 teaspoons GRAPESEED OIL, 5 drops TEA TREE OIL and 3 drops of CYPRESS OIL to get circulation going. Never wear shoes that are too tight.

BURNS

The most important thing is to cool down the burn as soon as possible. Put burn under cold water, running if possible, for 15-20 minutes.

All but minor burns and scalds should have immediate medical attention. Cover the burn with a gauze compress (a linen tablecloth or sheet for larger areas) soaked in solution of: 1ml TEA TREE OIL to every 500ml water and a teaspoon of salt, go to the doctor or call an ambulance. If clothes are stuck to the burn (or surrounding area) **do not attempt to remove yourself.**

After you have cooled the **minor burn** or scald apply TEA TREE OIL diluted with a little WHEATGERM OIL and 2 drops LAVENDER OIL, cover with lint free, gauze or muslin to allow wound to breathe. (OR SEE BELOW) Keep burn clean. If gauze is stuck to the wound when you come to change the dressing, gently soak it in warm water to remove, DO NOT PULL, this will break the skin. and delay healing.

DO NOT USE ADHESIVE DRESSING OR PLASTERS. Pat dry with a lint free cloth, apply TEA TREE OIL or TEA TREE OIL BURN OINTMENT CHAPTER 6, and cover with a clean, gauze dressing. Do not use cotton wool, fibres may stick to the wound.

See TEA TREE OIL BURN OINTMENT
See BURN CREAM
See SUNBURN
See BLISTERS
See SCARRING

BURSITIS
See RHEUMATISM
See JOINTS
See GOUT

C

CALLUSES
See CORNS

CANDIDA ALBICANS
See THRUSH

CANKER SORES

Wash infected areas with 10 drops of TEA TREE OIL to 50ml of water. Pat dry. Apply neat TEA TREE OIL twice per day.

CARBUNCLES
See BOILS

CARPEL TUNNEL SYNDROME
See REPETITIVE STRAIN INJURY

CATARRH

Congestion can be helped by a steam inhalation of 5-10 drops of TEA TREE OIL to a bowl of steaming water. Put a towel over your head to make a "steam tent", close your eyes and breathe in through your nose, out through your mouth. Repeat for 10 minutes 2-4 times per day as necessary or use 15-20 drops TEA TREE OIL in bath water or in a humidifier.

*Wet a face flannel with hot water and sprinkle on 3 drops of TEA TREE OIL and drape over face - breath through the cloth for 5 minutes.
*If at work put 5 drops in a cup of hot water and inhale.
*In small plastic bag saturate a tissue with TEA TREE OIL and clip, open the bag and breathe deeply the vapours every few minutes. (Do not give plastic bags to children).

See BRONCHITIS
See HAYFEVER
See COLDS AND FLU
See CHEST VAPOUR RUB CHAPTER 6
See SINUSITIS

CELLULITE

The characteristic "orange peel" skin which can effect thighs, buttocks, hips, even stomach and upper arms can be substantially reduced by using the following method over a period of 6-12 weeks.

*In the evening before you bathe or shower do a body brush routine, rubbing in anti-cellulite cream after washing to release toxins from the body as in CHAPTER 6

*Once a week have a mineral bath (warm not hot water) with 4oz sea salt, 1ml TEA TREE OIL. Soak for at least 20 minutes. Rub in anti-cellulite cream or the anti-cellulite oil, as in CHAPTER 6.

*Twice every day rub in a mixture of 20 drops TEA TREE OIL, 10 drops JUNIPER OIL and 20ml SOYA OIL, to affected areas, then kneed and pinch the skin for at least 10 minutes (not for those with varicose veins or thrombosis, if in doubt, consult your doctor).

*Change diet to include at least 3 servings of organic fresh, raw or partly cooked vegetables and at least 2 servings of fresh, organic fruit per day.

Drink 6-8 glasses filtered or pure spring water per day.
Drink Herb teas, fennel and orange blossom etc. replacing coffee, cola and tea. Cut down on red meat and saturated fats, if possible only buy organic produce and eat more sea fish. Eat wholefoods, brown rice, grains, nuts and seeds etc. Olive oil and flax seed oil.
*Take moderate exercise, walking, stretching and gentle movements such as Callenetics are best.
*Relax more. Try to manage stress. Sit down, close your eyes, breathe slow and deep, imagine the stress and tension in your body as a liquid that reaches to the top of your head. Slowly see that liquid draining away from your body through your finger tips until it has all gone.
Repeat as often as necessary.

CERVICITIS
See THRUSH

CHAFING

If you are prone to chafing or you are suffering from it now, rub in 5 drops of TEA TREE OIL to every 1 teaspoon GRAPESEED OIL to afflicted area. Alternatively mix 5 drops of TEA TREE OIL to 1teaspn of petroleum jelly.

CHAPPED HANDS

Remove dead skin cells with oat meal rub and rub in TEA TREE OIL AND OLIVE OIL. Apply TEA TREE OIL hand & body care cream (Chapter 6).

See HAND CARE
See OATMEAL RUB CHAPTER 6

CHAPPED LIPS

Apply a couple of drops of oil mix: 1 drop TEA TREE OIL mixed with 5 drops GRAPESEED OIL, to dry or cracked lips, blot and apply lipstick as normal. Gentlemen can use the TEA TREE OIL lip balm in CHAPTER 6.

If lips become very sore and infected apply a mixture of 5ml glycerine, 5ml petroleum jelly, 1ml TEA TREE OIL. Warm mixture well to incorporate ingredients. Store in a labelled dark glass bottle, apply to lips often.

CHAPPED SKIN
See CHAFING
See SKIN CARE
See CHAPTER 6   MOISTURISING HAND AND BODY CREAM

CHEST INFECTIONS
See BRONCHITIS
See CHEST VAPOUR RUB CHAPTER 6
See TEA TREE OIL POULTICE CHAPTER 6
See COLDS AND FLU
See COUGHS
See EMPHYSEMA

CHICKEN POX SORES

Chicken Pox, a common viral infection in childhood, it is caused by Herpes Zoster, the same virus which is responsible for shingles. The patient is often feverish with itchy spots, blisters then crusts.
A doctor must be consulted at first signs.

TEA TREE OIL with its anti-viral (anecdotal), pain relief and immune-stimulant properties, effectively soothes itching and helps the healing process of the skin. Freedom from itching is invaluable for preventing infection and scarring due to constant scratching. Lavender oil is also highly regarded for bringing relief. **See next page........**

See VIRAL INFECTIONS
See SHINGLES

BABIES
should be bathed in a mild baby 'bubble' bath with 1-2 drops of TEA TREE OIL. Spots/blisters can be dabbed with a mixture of 5-10 drops TEA TREE OIL and 5 drops KANUKA OIL to 25ml VITAMIN E OIL twice a day.

CHILDREN
5 drops in bath. 20 drops (1ml) TEA TREE OIL and 10 drops KANUKA OIL to 25ml VITAMIN E OIL. Dab spots with oil using cotton wool.

ADULTS
15-20 drops in the bath. 2.5ml TEA TREE OIL and 20 drops KANUKA OIL to 15-20ml of VITAMIN E OIL (or use neat TEA TREE OIL). Dab spots with oil, on cotton wool.

In the case of shingles apply along the middle of waist and anywhere you feel pain or tingling, even before spots appear. For severe eruptions soak a clean hand towel in cold water, ring out, sprinkle with 4-5 drops TEA TREE OIL and apply to affected area. (For children or babies a tepid flannel).
*DO NOT APPLY TOO NEAR TO EYES.

See SCARRING
See TEA TREE OIL OATMEAL BATH in CHAPTER 6.

CHILBLAINS

Small painful swellings on feet and hands, which are frequently itchy. Chilblains can be the result of poor circulation and extreme cold.

Apply neat TEA TREE OIL (and KANUKA OIL - optional) to chilblains 2-3 times a day and rub well in.

Give feet and hands a regular, invigorating massage with a mixture of 10 drops TEA TREE OIL, 10 drops ROSEMARY OIL to 10ml WHEATGERM OIL and 3-4 drops GINGER OIL. (NEVER USE NEAT GINGER OIL ON SKIN OR IN THE BATH). When and if you have reason to stand out in the cold, rub massage oil into feet, cover with cling film, (low in plasticisers) not too tight. Put on thick woolly socks or a pair of knee high stocking socks (men included) then a pair of wool socks (thermal). This will help to keep the warmth in your feet. Remember to keep moving to keep the circulation going. You can do the same with hands and wear mittens.

Make sure your diet includes lots of Vitamin C, E and zinc. Eat celery or drink celery juice and green leafy vegetables. Include olive oil and oily fish in diet. Nutritionists usually advise taking Ginkgo Biloba to improve circulation.

CIRCULATORY PROBLEMS

Massage is very good for increasing the circulation of the blood. So is exercise, ie. walking or swimming. A healthy diet is important too, rich in vitamins and minerals. (Citrus fruits, onions, and garlic and wheatgerm are particularly good)

Have a stimulating massage with a mixture of 50ml ALMOND OIL, 10 drops TEA TREE OIL, 5 drops ROSEMARY OIL and 10 drops CYPRESS OIL.

See CHILBLAINS See OEDEMA See CELLULITE See PHLEBITIS, See RESTLESS LEGS See RAYNARDS SYNDROME See BUNIONS
See SKIN BRUSHING CHAPTER 6
See MASSAGE CHAPTER 8

CLAVUS
See CORNS

CLEANSING
See SKIN CARE
See HAIR CARE
See CHAPTER 6

COLDS AND FLU

Spread mainly by coughing and sneezing. The common cold (CORYZA) is a contagious infection of the upper respiratory tract.

Although we have yet to find a cure for The Common Cold, TEA TREE OIL can help to relieve many of the symptoms of colds and influenza by the following methods.

Start at the first signs for best results.

Steam inhalation 2 pints of steaming water 10-15 drops TEA TREE OIL (5 DROPS FOR CHILDREN - **But do not allow young children to do this un-attended or with very hot water).** Place head over bowl and breathe deeply, with eyes closed. Breathe in through the nose and out through the mouth. Place a towel over head (to form a tent) for maximum benefit.

Gargle 2-3 times a day with a solution of 2-4 drops of TEA TREE OIL to 100ml of warm water to relieve sore throats. See next page.
* See SORE THROATS (separate entry)
Young children may find it difficult to gargle.
*Use TEA TREE OIL 'CHEST VAPOUR RUB' See CHAPTER 6

*Humidify home - particularly at night either with a humidifier or bowl of hot water and 10 drops of TEA TREE OIL (be careful of hot water with young children around) or dip cotton wool balls into a solution of: 1ml TEA TREE OIL to 20 ml of hot water, wring but not too much. Tie a length of cotton/string (12" long) around one cotton wool ball on one end and around the other cotton wool ball on the other and hang over radiator, or wet face flannels in solution and drape over radiator.

*Mist-spray the air frequently - put 2ml TEA TREE OIL into 200ml warm water, pour into an atomiser or plant mister, shake well before use and mist air. Especially good for office/shop environment.

*At night sprinkle a few drops of TEA TREE OIL onto 4 corners of your pillow. Or sprinkle a few drops onto hot water in a labelled jug, by the bed.

*Have a warm TEA TREE OIL bath with 15-20 drops of TEA TREE OIL. Make sure you keep warm. Try not to wash hair until the worst is over.

*Saturate 3-4 tissues with a few drops of TEA TREE OIL and put into a small plastic bag. Inhale when needed. (Keep plastic bags out of reach of small children).

*Rub warm TEA TREE OIL into temples - dilute for children and sensitive skin: 2 drops to (20 drops) 1ml grapeseed oil.

*If your nose is red and sore rub in a mixture of 1 teaspoon petroleum jelly (or vitamin E oil for a 'lighter' oil) to 3-5 drops of TEA TREE OIL. (2 DROPS FOR CHILDREN). Coat the nasal area before you blow your nose.

*Massage your aching limbs with a mixture of: 10 drops TEA TREE OIL, 20ml GRAPESEED OIL, 5 drops CYPRESS OIL and 5 drops KANUKA OIL.

Drink a lot of fluids, lemon, blackcurrant, cranberry and citrus juices, or carrot and fresh orange juice mixed. Herb teas especially rosehip and eat fresh organic vegetables and fruit, 'live' yoghurt etc. Doctors sometimes recommend taking a good dose of vitamin C with bioflavonoids every 2 hours, at first signs. Ladies on the pill or HRT should not exceed 1000mg of Vitamin C per day, consult doctor. Home-made chicken soup seems to help.

See TEA TREE OIL POULTICE CHAPTER 6
See IMMUNE SYSTEM
See BRONCHITIS, CATARRH, COUGHS,
See SORE THROATS

COLD SORES   (HERPES SIMPLEX)

These blister-like sores are very contagious. They can be spread to other parts of the body or to other people simply by touch. At the first signs of a cold sore appearing, dab on TEA TREE OIL using a cotton wool bud 3-4 times a day. (Dilute 50% TO 75% with VITAMIN E oil for children).

Make sure that you wear a sunblock when out in the sun, even if no cold sore is present. Once infected, you may still be prone to getting them through cold or heat to the area. Every time you use your toothbrush, rinse in very hot water and rub in a few drops TEA TREE OIL after cleaning teeth.

COLIC

Adults and babies can have uncomfortable bouts of colic. Gently massage the stomach using a mixture of: 1ml (10 drops for babies) TEA TREE OIL, 1ml CHAMOMILE OIL to 100ml CASTOR OIL, and apply a gentle heat pad. If symptoms persist see a doctor.
Sprinkle 2 drops of LAVENDER OIL and 3 drops TEA TREE OIL on to a dampened cotton wool pad. Place over radiator to release soothing vapours.

COLITIS
See ULCERATIVE COLITIS
See COLIC

CONGESTION
See CATARRH

CONJUNCTIVITIS
See EYE INFECTIONS

CONSTIPATION

Constipation can be very uncomfortable and often results in stomach cramps, tiredness and stress. The most common cause is a lack of dietry fibre. Eating 3-4 portions of vegetables, at least 2 portions of fruit; Along with wholegrains, pulses, wheatgerm, dried apricots, (2-3) dried prunes and the drinking of 6-8 glasses of water per day usually cures the problem.
If symptoms persist see a doctor.

Prolonged constipation can lead to general fatigue, unhealthy skin, cellulite, haemorrhoids and some believe even varicose veins.

A TEA TREE OIL massage can also be very beneficial. Mix together 10ml CASTOR OIL, 5 drops ROSEMARY OIL and 10 drops TEA TREE OIL. Lie on a flat, firm surface and rub in the oil, in a circular motion, around the stomach area, for up to 30 minutes. Breathe deeply so that the stomach moves up and down with each breath.

CORNS

A corn is an area of thickened, hard skin on the lower foot area. It can form an inverted pimple whose point presses painfully into the deeper layers of the skin.

It may take several weeks, but TEA TREE OIL is a very effective 'natural' treatment for this painful condition. After bathing abrade the area **gently** with a pumice stone or similar. Saturate a cotton wool bud or the tip of your finger with neat TEA TREE OIL and cover with a plaster. Repeat night and morning.

See FOOT CARE

COUGHS

A cough is a protective response to certain irritants and viral infections that 'disturb' the lining of the lungs. If symptoms persist see a doctor.

Gargle with 2-5 drops of TEA TREE OIL in 100ml of warm water.

Eat foods that boost the immune system, sharon fruit, garlic, kiwi fruit tomatoes, carrots, citrus, wheatgerm, green leafy vegetables, olive oil, garlic and onions. Drink a lot of fluids, Herb teas, fresh organic fruit and vegetable juice.

See IMMUNE SYSTEM
See COLDS AND FLU
See BRONCHITIS
See VIRAL INFECTIONS

CRACKED SKIN

Cracked skin on hands and feet is quite common especially in winter. It can be painful and very unsightly.....

CRACKED SKIN (Cont.)

Mix 5ml TEA TREE OIL, 100ml CASTOR OIL and 100ml WHEATGERM OIL, warm and soak feet and/or hands in oil twice a day. Cover with cotton socks and/or with cotton gloves, before going to bed.

If very painful rub feet with neat TEA TREE OIL into cracks and apply petroleum jelly-cover-repeat twice per day.

See PSORIASIS
See SKIN CARE
See ECZEMA
See CHAPTER 6 FOR DRY SKIN PREPARATIONS

CRADLE CAP

A scalp condition akin to DERMATITIS which affects young babies.
Mix together 25ml warmed EXTRA VIRGIN OLIVE OIL 5ml EVENING PRIMROSE OIL or VITAMIN E OIL and 2-3 drops TEA TREE OIL. Gently massage a few drops into the scalp. leave on as long as possible (overnight) then wash hair with baby shampoo. Repeat as often as necessary.

Prevention
Put 10-20 drops TEA TREE OIL in every 100ml baby shampoo, shake well before each use. Avoid getting into the eye area when rinsing.

CRAMP

Cramp can strike in many areas of muscle - thighs, calf, feet, shoulders, arms, stomach and wrist (writers cramp).

Mix 1ml TEA TREE OIL to every 20ml CASTOR OIL, Rub into the affected part vigorously until the pressure is relieved. Or mix TEA TREE OIL and SOYA OIL as above, with 5 drops GERANIUM OIL, apply heat. For stomach cramps rub in either of these TEA TREE OIL blends and place heat pad on top of stomach area.

See RESTLESS LEGS
See CIRCULATORY PROBLEMS
See MUSCLES
See ACHES AND PAINS
See MENSTRUAL PROBLEMS
See DEEP HEAT RUB CHAPTER 6

CROUP

A barking cough often caused by laryngitis. It is quite common in children up to 4 years of age. Do not confuse with wheezing, CROUP is a honking seal-like noise caused by inflammation of the larynx. It usually occurs at night **Any difficulty breathing or noisy breathing lasting more than a couple of minutes should be reported to the doctor immediately or take directly to hospital.** First aid for CROUP, **or until doctor arrives**, is to take the child to a warm room and fill with steam - put 10 drops TEA TREE OIL AND 10 drops LAVENDER OIL into steaming bowl/bath of water. Do not put child into the water, but let him breathe the vapours. Boil kettle or anything to add a lot of moisture to a warm (small) room. Never leave the child alone. Hold child gently but firmly and away from hot water to avoid accidents. Rub chest with a mixture of: 3 drops TEA TREE OIL, 3 drops LAVENDER OIL, 3 drops PALMAROSA OIL and 20ml VITAMIN E OIL.

CUTICLES
See HANDCARE

CUTS
See ABRASIONS

CYSTITIS

This painful infection of the bladder affects women much more than men. It causes lower back pain, a burning sensation as if passing very hot water, frequent painful urination

Medical advice should be sought. Drinking large amounts of water or cranberry juice/powder often relieves symptoms. Eat plenty of onions, garlic and plain 'live' yoghurt. If symptoms persist see a doctor again.

TEA TREE OIL should not be taken internally without medical supervision.

*Make a solution of 10 drops TEA TREE OIL to 250ml warm water, using cotton wool - swab the area of vagina, always front to back (with a clean piece of cotton wool each time), <u>every time</u> urine is passed.

*Use 15 drops of TEA TREE OIL and 10 drops MANUKA OIL in a 'sitz bath' (just enough warm water in bath to cover vaginal area, lie back with knees apart).

*Massage lower back and lower abdomen (twice daily) with 5ml CASTOR OIL to 3-5 drops of TEA TREE OIL. Apply heat pad to areas.

D

DANDRUFF

Hairdressers and dermatologists agree that dandruff is the single most common scalp complaint their clients have. TEA TREE OIL is very effective at clearing up this problem, depending on the severity of the condition, you can use it in a variety of ways.

For dry/normal hair rub scalp with a mixture of 1 Tablespoon EXTRA VIRGIN OLIVE OIL and 1-2ml of TEA TREE OIL leave on for 10 minutes and wash twice with your normal shampoo (to which you add 3-5ml of TEA TREE OIL per 100ml of shampoo). Use every week.

For greasy hair rub scalp with a mixture of: 5ml lemon juice, 5ml Witch Hazel, 10ml glycerine and 1-2ml TEA TREE OIL, leave on for 5-10 minutes and shampoo twice with your normal shampoo (with 3-5ml of TEA TREE OIL added to 100ml of shampoo), leave on hair for at least 5 minutes.

*For a stronger dandruff shampoo, use up to 10ml TEA TREE OIL to 100ml shampoo. Use twice per week initially then once per week.

See HAIR CARE
See HAIR CHAPTER 6

DENTAL PROBLEMS
See TEETH & GUMS
See CHAPTER 6

DENTURE SORES

Rub infected area of gum with a couple of drops of neat TEA TREE OIL twice per day. Clean dentures well, put a few drops of TEA TREE OIL in cleaning paste or make your own SEE CHAPTER 6 and clean dentures thoroughly, not just the 'teeth', then rub neat TEA TREE OIL into every part of denture. You can make your own denture soak with 1 tablespoon salt and 20 drops of TEA TREE OIL to 75 ml hot water, it is better to clean with paste first, then soak for 30 mins or overnight, rinse well and wear.

See ANTISEPTIC MOUTHWASH CHAPTER 6
See TEETHPASTE AND DENTURE PASTE CHAPTER 6

DEODORANT

TEA TREE OIL is a very effective deodorant, it kills the bacteria that is responsible for body odour. Apply neat TEA TREE OIL to area under arms. For a more feminine aroma mix 50/50 with LAVENDER OIL. For sensitive skin, mix with a little SOYA OIL or water soluble gel.

See BODY ODOUR
See DEODORANT CHAPTER 6

DEPRESSION

Clinical depression must have medical attention. A case of mild depression or 'feeling down' can be alleviated by a refreshing spa bath with 5 drops of TEA TREE OIL, 5 drops YLANG YLANG and 5 drops BENZOIN. To simply 'feel good' have a gentle massage with the uplifting massage oil in CHAPTER 8.

See AROMATHERAPY CHAPTER 8

DERMATITIS
See ECZEMA
See SKINCARE
See DANDRUFF

DHOBI ITCH
See THRUSH

DIABETIC SORES

Diabetics should take particular care of feet and lower legs. Cracked infected skin and sores, even ulcers, are quite common. TEA TREE OIL does have some very good results with these conditions.

Bathe the sores in warm, boiled, water and add 10 drops TEA TREE OIL. Gently apply a mixture of: 3ml TEA TREE OIL to 5ml OLIVE OIL and 5ml VITAMIN E OIL, twice per day. Cover area with gauze, elevate legs every 3 hours if possible for 30 minutes. See Circulatory Problems.

Prevention
Apply TEA TREE OIL SUPER ANTISEPTIC HEALING CREAM. CHAPTER 6 morning and night to feet and lower leg. Massage in an upwards direction, towards heart.

DIAPER RASH
See NAPPY RASH

DIARRHOEA

If symptoms are severe or persist you must see your doctor. To alleviate mild diarrhoea switch to a plain diet of rice and rice water for 24 hours. Boil organic rice for 30 minutes, in pure filtered water, strain and drink the water with a pinch of salt, sweeten with honey if necessary. Eat the rice at 2 hourly intervals with plain 'live' yoghurt, 'Total' sheep's/ewes yoghurt is the best.

Drink at LEAST 6 glasses of pure, filtered water per day.

Cleanliness is essential. If you do not want to re-infect your system or others. 'Douche' after every bout with 5-10 drops TEA TREE OIL to 100ml warm water wiping front to back or add a few drops to bidet. Put a few drops of TEA TREE OIL on a tissue and wipe the toilet seat and finally, after washing your hands put 2 drops on your hands with soap, rub and rinse.

See ABDOMINAL PAIN
See COLIC
See IRRITABLE BOWEL SYNDROME
See ULCERATIVE COLITIS

DRY HAIR
See HAIR CARE
See DANDRUFF
See CHAPTER 6

DRY SKIN
See SKIN CARE
See CRACKED SKIN
See ECZEMA
See PSORIASIS
See CHAPTER 6

DYSMENORRHOEA
See MENSTRUAL PROBLEMS
See ABDOMINAL PAIN

E

EAR INFECTIONS

An ear infection should be seen by a doctor as soon as possible. If a minor infection and the eardrum is undamaged, the following TEA TREE OIL applications can be beneficial: mix together 3ml warmed ALMOND OIL or OLIVE OIL, 2-4 drops (1 drop for babies) TEA TREE OIL and 2 drops CALENDULA OIL. Use an ear dropper and drop a little into each ear. Tilt head for 3-5 minutes to keep the ear 'full' and then drain. Massage a few drops of the oil around ear and along the bone behind the ear. Repeat on the other side. Apply gentle heat to the ears (a hot water bottle with cover or wrapped in a towel).

If the earache is thought to be from a throat infection gargle with 2-4 drops TEA TREE OIL in a glass of warm water. (Not for young children).

See SWIMMERS EAR
See THROAT INFECTIONS
See TINNITUS
See TEA TREE OIL EAR PLUGS CHAPTER 6

ECZEMA

Red, inflamed, irritated skin, rashes, flaky skin, itching and even small blisters are mostly associated with DERMATITIS/ECZEMA. It can be hereditary, the result of an infection or an allergic reaction. Test a small patch of infected skin first for 24 hours before you apply any remedy to a large area. Choose whichever method is effective for the particular problem.

DRY, FLAKY ECZEMA AND ALSO CRACKED SKIN try 2ml TEA TREE OIL mixed with 20ml CASTOR OIL, 20ml WHEATGERM OIL and 30ml ALMOND OIL, shake well and apply gently to dry skin twice a day.
WEEPING ECZEMA Mix 2ml TEA TREE OIL and 2ml CALENDULA OIL with 15ml warm (boiled) milk, shake well, apply direct to sores. You could also try TEA TREE SALVE and OATMEAL MILK SOOTHER.
To ease ITCHING the following may be helpful: Take 20g nettle tea, pour on 50ml boiling water, steep for at least 10 minutes, strain until clear and allow to cool. Add 20ml distilled witch hazel (omit if skin broken), 5 drops ROSEMARY OIL, 5 drops TEA TREE OIL and 5 drops ST JOHN'S WORT OIL. Shake well before use, apply with cotton wool. Always patch test first.

ECZEMA (Cont.)

Add 10-15 drops of TEA TREE OIL to bath water, or have a TEA TREE OIL 'OATMILK' BATH. See CHAPTER 6.

Try to eat a plain varied diet, fresh, organic, mainly vegetarian including at least 2 servings of fruit, 3 servings of vegetables and 1 serving of whole-grains. Drink a good amount of pure water, and fresh vegetable juices, herb teas are very beneficial for clearing the system, try nettle and rosehip, with a little honey. Eczema is sometimes thought to be an allergic reaction to pollutants, foods, chemicals, pets, stress etc.

See STRESS
See IMMUNE SYSTEM BOOSTERS
See CHAPTER 6

EMPHYSEMA

From the first diagnosis of this disease - take control - do not smoke, do not passive smoke, do not go outside when the air quality is bad. Avoid things you may be allergic to. Go for gentle walks in fresh air. With your doctors advice tone up those chest muscles, shoulders and upper arms, try swimming, it is a good form of exercise, but do be careful of chemicals in the water.

Maintain your ideal body weight. Eat little and often, fresh organic vegetables and fruit, plenty of wholegrains. ask your doctor to prescribe good antioxidants and take them. Relax, cut out stress.

Try not to use sprays around the house. TEA TREE OIL polish and TEA TREE OIL as a deodorant will cut down on a couple of sprays.

Add 5-10 drops TEA TREE OIL to hot water in bowl or sink. Place head over bowl, put a towel over your head to trap the steam and breathe. Inhale through the nose, exhale through the mouth for 10 minutes.

Add 5-8 drops TEA TREE OIL to a hot wet face flannel and apply to chest area for 5 minutes.

See DEODORANT
See STRESS
See CHEST VAPOUR RUB CHAPTER 6
See IMMUNE SYSTEM BOOSTERS

ENDOMETRIOSIS
See PERIOD PAIN

EYE INFECTIONS

DO NOT USE ESSENTIAL OILS IN AN EYE BATH, DO NOT BATHE EYES WITH ESSENTIAL OILS. IF THEY HAVE CONTACT WITH THE EYE, WASH COPIOUSLY WITH COLD WATER, IF STINGING PERSISTS SEEK MEDICAL ADVICE.

Eye infections should be reported to a doctor. Sometimes eye problems can be a symptom of a more serious disease that needs urgent medical attention. After professional diagnosis minor eye irritations can be treated at home.

Foreign body in eye: If it is imbedded seek urgent medical advice. For specks that are visible, use the corner of a soft, dry, clean, cloth/tissue and gently try to move speck to the corner of eye, where it can be removed. Sometimes tears, an eye bath with cool, boiled water, or pulling the top lash gently over the bottom lash can help. If persistent seek medical advice.

Sore and itchy eyes can be treated with a chamomile infusion (teabag or 1 heaped teaspoon chamomile steeped in 300ml boiling water and strain), adding a pinch of salt. (If using chamomile tea bags for the infusion, save to go cold and use as eye pads). Bathe eyes with a cotton wool pad for each eye. Place a cold chamomile tea bag on each eye for 10 minutes.

Inflamed eyes and conjunctivitis can be soothed with warm fennel water 200ml and 2 pinches of salt. (Boil 1 tablespoon crushed fennel seeds in 500ml boiling water for 10 minutes. Allow to cool, drain and use in eye bath). Either use an eye bath or a piece of cotton wool, and bathe. Use a new piece of cotton wool each time, DO NOT dip a used piece of cotton wool into the water.

For tired eyes weak Jasmine tea in an eye bath is also beneficial, a little cool organic cucumber juice and cucumber slices work wonders too.

For styes and infection of the eyelids bathe with warm marigold water: place 1 teaspoon pot marigold petals *(Calendula Officinalis)* into a heat proof jug, pour on 300ml boiling water and 2 pinches of salt, steep for 15 minutes and strain. Allow to cool slightly, until just warm and using a new piece of cotton wool each time, bathe each eye. Repeat twice per day.

For a vapour bath (Styes/Infections) put 5-10 drops of TEA TREE OIL in a bowl of steaming hot water and place head over the bowl for 10 minutes. With eyes closed let the vapours reach the eyelids, keep at a comfortable distance or allow water to cool slightly. Repeat twice per day.

Never store any of the above mixes, always use the same day or discard.
See CUCUMBER EYE POULTICE CHAPTER 6

F

FEMININE HYGIENE

TEA TREE OIL is very effective as a 'natural' cleanser as it does not interrupt the natural flora of the vagina, but can guard against infection, odour and itching. Douche with 5 drops TEA TREE OIL to 250ml warm water (shake/stir well) and cotton wool (new piece each time) front to back.

See BODY ODOUR
See TOXIC SHOCK SYNDROME
See THRUSH

FEVER

A fever is an abnormally high body temperature over 37 degrees Centigrade. It can be due to over exhaustion, hot weather, as well as a bacterial or viral infection. In most cases a fever is a good thing as it means that the body is fighting the infection. If more than **one** degree higher than the norm, or persistently high, seek medical advice as soon as possible.

TEA TREE OIL is an anti-bacterial substance, it can help stimulate the immune system, and it has DIAPHORETIC properties (induces sweating) when the body is unwell. Drink lots of fluids, fruit juices, cool Herb teas to avoid dehydration. It may also have anti-viral properties too.

To bring a high temperature down, while you are waiting for a Doctor to arrive, lie in a tepid bath containing 5 drops of TEA TREE OIL and 7 drops PALMAROSA OIL and 7 drops CHAMOMILE OIL (3 drops of each for children, 1 drop of each for babies). **Alternatively**, (it may be better FOR BABIES AND YOUNG CHILDREN) sponge the body with a pre-soaked flannel of: 500ml tepid water and 1-2 drops of TEA TREE OIL and 2 drops PALMAROSA OIL and 2 drops CHAMOMILE OIL (**always avoid the eye area).** A cool air fan is also beneficial. A cooling body oil can be made using: 40ml SOYA OIL, 3 drops TEA TREE OIL, 5 drops PALMAROSA OIL, 2-3 drops CHAMOMILE OIL and 1 drop PEPPERMINT OIL. (Halve essential oils for babies). Massage a little oil gently into back and chest, EXCLUDING the face, and place a plain tepid (flannel) compress on forehead. (Never use mint oils neat or in the bath).

Use TEA TREE OIL humidifiers.   See COLDS AND FLU

FLAKY SKIN
See ECZEMA
See SKIN CARE
See PSORIASIS
See CHAPTER 6

FLEAS
See INSECT BITES
See VETERINARY SECTION 17 CHAPTER 5
See ALL AROUND THE HOUSE SECTION 1 CHAPTER 5

FLU
See COLDS AND FLU
See BRONCHITIS
See SINUSITIS

FOLLICULITIS

Similar to impetigo, but an infection of the scalp. Use a few drops of TEA TREE OIL mixed with a few drops olive oil, massaged into infected area twice per day, wash as normal. An alternative mix is: 10 drops TEA TREE OIL, 10 drops MANUKA OIL and 20-40 drops OLIVE or ALMOND OIL. Apply as above.

See HAIR CARE
See DANDRUFF
See HAIR CHAPTER 6

FOOD POISONING

ALWAYS SEEK MEDICAL ADVICE AT FIRST SIGNS OF FOOD POISONING.

To avoid food poisoning: when preparing raw meat or eggs for cooking and salad or lightly cooked vegetables, there is a very high risk of contamination from hands. It is possible to transfer harmful bacteria from hands onto salad vegetables and/or preparation areas.

After handling meat, eggs or egg shells, wash and scrub hands with soap, water and 2-5 drops of TEA TREE OIL. Wash kitchen surfaces and utensils that were in contact with them separately. Use 1 litre of very hot water, organic washing up liquid and 2ml TEA TREE OIL. Boil wash the dishcloths, or wipe areas with disposable kitchen towel.

See DIARRHOEA

FOOT BATH

For a refreshing foot spa, add 5-10 drops of TEA TREE OIL to a bowl of warm water and soak feet for 10-15 minutes, or rub in a mixture of 5 drops TEA TREE OIL and 1 tablespoon OLIVE OIL.

See FOOT ODOUR
See FEET CHAPTER 6

FOOT CARE

We generally take our feet for granted, we never appreciate how hard they work for us until they start to ache. Following a few simple guidelines should help to alleviate discomfort.

Never wear tight or ill fitting shoes, keep heels to a minimum. After a few hours on your feet, elevate feet to a 45 degree angle to your body and relax for 20 minutes. Massage feet and toes often to get circulation going, Massage oil: 1 teaspoon OLIVE OIL, 5 drops TEA TREE OIL and 3-4 drops WINTERGREEN OIL. Let the air get to your feet, kick off those shoes whenever possible. Soak your feet in a TEA TREE OIL 'footbath', and massage with TEA TREE OIL HAND AND BODY CREAM. Treat yourself to a pedicure.

Many swear by *hot and cold treatments - with shower attachment spray feet with hot water then with cold, alternating between both for 5 minutes. Massage feet with TEA TREE OIL and OLIVE OIL. (*Do not do this if suffering from Diabetes or heart condition until checking with doctor).

See FEET CHAPTER 6

FOOT INFECTION

To prevent picking up foot infections from swimming baths etc., rub in TEA TREE OIL before and after the activity. Avoid slippery surfaces.

CRACKED HEELS see CRACKED SKIN

See ABRASIONS
See NAIL INFECTIONS
See NAIL CARE
See ATHLETES FOOT
See CORNS
See VERRUCAE AND WARTS

FOOT ODOUR

Massage 5 drops TEA TREE OIL and 1 teaspoon OLIVE OIL (mixed) into feet, use a TEA TREE OIL 'footbath' as often as possible. Put 2 drops of TEA TREE OIL into your shoes at night or use TEA TREE OIL SHOE FRESHENER - CHAPTER 6.

For chronic foot odour, before you go to bed wash your feet, dry and massage in neat TEA TREE OIL - 5-10 drops per foot. Apply loose cling film to each foot and put on pair of socks. In the morning unwrap and put on more TEA TREE OIL, put a clean pair of socks on, cotton ones are better. You should be odour free all day. (When washing socks, put a few drops of TEA TREE OIL in the final rinse water.)

See BODY ODOUR

FOREIGN BODY
See SPLINTER
IN EYE - SEE EYE INFECTIONS

FOREIGN BODY IN EAR

Flood with 10ml CASTOR OIL with 2-5 drops TEA TREE OIL and leave for a few minutes. Drain and wipe entrance of ear with cotton wool. If symptoms persist see a doctor.

See EAR INFECTION
See SWIMMERS EAR
See TEA TREE OIL EAR PLUGS CHAPTER 6

FROSTBITE

If frostbite is suspected do seek medical advice - do not warm up affected parts, (go from freezing to cold conditions), gently apply 1-2 teaspoons VITAMIN E OIL, 5 drops TEA TREE OIL and 5 drops LAVENDER OIL to affected skin, by dabbing lightly with soaked cotton wool. This will help with the pain. Apply oil mixture three times per day until healed.

Prevention If out in cold weather for a long time, rub in a mixture of 5 drops TEA TREE OIL, 3 drops WINTERGREEN OIL, 2-3 drops GINGER or PEPPER OIL, and 2 teaspoons Petroleum Jelly (warming the mixture helps to mix ingredients), cover feet loosely with cling film and put on 3 pairs of socks - or 2 pairs of stocking 'feet' and a pair of ordinary socks. The more 'loose' layers the better - (not too tight because of circulation). Keep moving do not stand still for long periods. **Do not use mix on broken skin. (Never use ginger or pepper oil neat on the skin or in the bath).**

FUNGAL INFECTIONS

TEA TREE OIL is a very effective fungicide. Rub in neat to infected area. For delicate skins, TEA TREE OIL should be diluted 1-3ml per 10ml OLIVE OIL. Please see specific infections, before treating area.

See THRUSH
See FEMININE HYGIENE
See EAR INFECTIONS
See GUMS
See NAIL INFECTIONS
See RINGWORM
See SORE THROATS
See ANTI-FUNGAL OINTMENT CHAPTER 6

FURRY TONGUE
See BAD BREATH
See MOUTHWASH CHAPTER 6
See TEETH PASTE CHAPTER 6

FURUNCLE
See BOIL
See ABSCESS

G

GASTRITIS
See ABDOMINAL PAIN
See DIARRHOEA

GENITAL HERPES
See HERPES

GERMS

TEA TREE OIL has a strong germicidal action. It is effective against most household germs.

With a 1.5% dilution of TEA TREE OIL (1.5ml TEA TREE OIL diluted in 1 teaspoon of vodka or alcohol from chemists and 100ml hot water - stir well) wipe down surfaces, telephones, etc. anywhere germs may be lurking.

Pour above solution into a spray mister, shake before use and mist air to kill germs in sick room etc. Or put a 1.5% solution of TEA TREE OIL into a humidifier.

When washing clothes, handkerchiefs, towels nappies etc., put 5-8ml of TEA TREE OIL in final rinse water, if possible leave to soak for at least 30 minutes. Unlike most germicides for clothes, TEA TREE OIL is gentle on delicate fabrics.

GINGIVITIS

Massage 2-3 drops TEA TREE OIL into gums twice per day. Use a mouthwash of 100ml warm water and 2-3 drops TEA TREE OIL, wash all around mouth 1-2 times per day.

Add 2 drops of TEA TREE OIL to toothbrush when cleaning teeth. Make sure toothbrush is kept clean, wash well at least once per week (once per day if you have a mouth infection). Wash toothbrush in a cup of boiling water and 5 drops of TEA TREE OIL. Swish around and let stand for at least 30 minutes.

See TEETH AND GUMS
See DENTURE SORES
See BAD BREATH
See TEETHPASTE CHAPTER 6

GOUT

A painful swelling, usually of the big toe joint. Gout is akin to arthritis and can attack any joint, turning the skin red and hot, and the affected joint is swollen and tender.

Where possible keep the joint elevated, apply TEA TREE OIL neat and put on an ice pack. You may find a charcoal poultice beneficial. Mix 30-50gms of powdered activated charcoal with 1-2ml TEA TREE OIL and enough FLAXSEED OIL to prepare a thick paste. Apply to the joint and leave on for 4 hours, or overnight. (Charcoal does stain, so use large old socks, preferably cotton, to cover joint). An effective rub for gout sufferers is: 10 drops KANUKA OIL, 2 drops ROSEMARY OIL, 3 drops TEA TREE OIL, 3 drops WINTERGREEN OIL mixed with 10ml SOYA OIL.

Eat a 1/4lb to 1/2lb cherries per day, or 1 tablespoon of organic cherry concentrate. Some people swear by this to avert a bad attack. Also celery and celery juice, the seeds can be used instead of salt for flavouring.

AVOID alcohol, anchovies, brains, bouillon, gravy, stock cubes, heart, herrings, liver, meat extracts, muscles, sardines, and sweetbreads.

GO EASY on asparagus, dried beans, cauliflower, lentils, mushrooms, oatmeal, dried peas, shellfish seafood, spinach, wholegrains, wholemeal breads and yeast.

Do drink 6-8 glasses of pure filtered water per day. Rosehip tea, peppermint tea, celery, dandelion and yarrow tea is also very good.

See ARTHRITIS SEE JOINTS

GRAZES
See ABRASIONS

GREASY HAIR
See HAIR CARE

GREASY SKIN
See SKIN CARE

GUM INFECTIONS

Massage in a few drops of TEA TREE OIL. Grip gums between your thumb and first finger and gently rub.

See MOUTH ULCERS See TEETH AND GUMS
See DENTURE SORES See GINGIVITIS

H

HAEMORRHOIDS

Have a TEA TREE OIL 'sitz' bath - knees raised in 10 centimetres of warm water and 10 drops of TEA TREE OIL in bath.

Dab haemorrhoids with 1 teaspoon cold Witch Hazel to 2 drops cold TEA TREE OIL. Repeat twice per day and this will help with pain and swelling.

See ANAL FISSURES
See ANAL ITCHING
See HAEMORRHOID CREAM 1&2 CHAPTER 6
See CIRCULATORY PROBLEMS

HAIR CARE

TEA TREE OIL is one of the best hair care products I have found. The gentle, yet powerful, antiseptic action is good for all hair types, greasy, dry, normal and for scalp conditions such as dandruff, dermatitis, eczema. It even helps to control nits and head lice. It assists in the regulation of the sebaceous glands, helps to get rid of dead skin cells, and fights fungal and bacterial infections, while amazingly your hair looks healthier and is more manageable!!

For general hair care, put 1ml TEA TREE OIL into a mild or pH neutral shampoo. I use baby shampoo and/or conditioner. Wash hair as normal, always shake bottle well before use.

For a final rinse, rub into scalp 5 drops TEA TREE OIL and 20ml Cider vinegar, leave on for 1 minute and rinse with clear, warm water.

For excessively dry or heat damaged hair, apply the following warmed oil: 20ml WHEATGERM OIL, 3 drops TEA TREE OIL and 5 drops ROSEMARY OIL, warm the oil and apply to hair, pay particular attention to the ends, wrap hair in plastic and a warmed towel, leave on for at least 30 minutes or overnight. Wash as normal, always use a 20 minute conditioner.

See HAIR CARE - CHAPTER 6
See CRADLE CAP
See DANDRUFF
See HEADLICE
See FOLLICULITIS

HAIR REMOVAL

After waxing, sugaring, shaving or cream, rinse and rub in cold TEA TREE OIL and LAVENDER OIL mixed with 15ml SOYA OIL. Especially good for underarms when a deodorant would sting, OR use the TEA TREE OIL SALVE and/or the AFTER SHAVE OIL or BALM / CHAPTER 6.

TEA TREE OIL can be used after plucking eyebrows with tweezers. Either add 3 drops TEA TREE OIL mixed with a teaspoon of GRAPESEED OIL, or use TEA TREE OIL SALVE / CHAPTER 6, apply any of these with cotton wool to area. Be careful, if TEA TREE OIL does come into contact with the eyes, rinse with a copious amount of pure water.

See DEODORANT
See BODY ODOUR
See TEA TREE OIL SALVE

HALITOSIS
See BAD BREATH
See TEETH AND GUMS

HAND CARE

Your hands do have a lot of work to do in 24 hours, so they need pampering at every opportunity, to keep them looking and feeling good. TEA TREE OIL, with its gentle moisturising, anti-bacterial, anti-fungal action is invaluable.

Before you put your hands into water or go outside to do the gardening etc., rub in TEA TREE OIL barrier cream as in Chapter 6.

Alternatively, add 2-5 ml TEA TREE OIL to every 100ml of your normal handcream.

For chapped, dry and rough hands, treat them to an oatmeal rub (See Chapter 6) rinse (never use hot water) and massage in a mixture of 100ml olive oil, 10ml WHEATGERM OIL and 1ml TEA TREE OIL - a few drops of LAVENDER OIL added also gives a lovely aroma and adds to the beneficial effect. Repeat twice a day initially until hands improve.

See NAIL CARE
See CRACKED SKIN
See HANGNAILS
See HANDS CHAPTER 6

HANGNAILS

Hangnails are characterised by little triangles of split skin, they form around the fingernails and even toenails. Hangnails or backfriends can be very uncomfortable - they catch on everything. They are particularly common among clerical staff who handle a lot of paper, the paper absorbs the natural oil from fingertips and the skin splits. Soak fingers in 20ml OLIVE OIL & 10 drops TEA TREE OIL for 15 minutes. With small, sharp scissors clip the loose skin as short as you can, without cutting the healthy skin.

Prevention* - rub in a 2-3 drops of TEA TREE OIL in 10ml OLIVE OIL into area around fingers every day.

See HANDCARE
See NAILCARE

HAYFEVER

An allergic form of rhinitis, hayfever attacks in the late Spring and Summer months, it causes inflammation in the lining of the nose, along with watery eyes and sneezing. The suggestions below will not cure, but they may help.

Gargle with cooled boiled water 100ml to 2-3 drops TEA TREE OIL. Rub the chest, around the nose and the sinus area with oil made from 10ml SOYA OIL and 3-5 drops TEA TREE OIL. Put a few drops of TEA TREE OIL onto your handkerchief/tissue and carry it with you. Spray the house with 200ml water and 2ml TEA TREE OIL (emulsified in alcohol from chemists) in an atomiser. Or use a humidifier.

See COLDS AND FLU
See EYE INFECTIONS

HEADACHES

Put 2 drops TEA TREE OIL and 2 drops LAVENDER OIL in 1 tablespoon GRAPESEED OIL and massage into temples, around neck and earlobes.

A TEA TREE OIL inhalation can relieve a congestive headache. A cold compress against forehead works wonders especially with curtains closed.

Feverfew tablets, available from chemists is said to be beneficial, also a relaxing bath with a few drops of Melissa oil (pure Melissa oil is expensive).

See COLDS AND FLU
See COLD COMPRESS CHAPTER 6

HEADLICE

Everyone, no matter who, can get infected with headlice; they cause intense itchiness of scalp and surrounding areas. The lice lay little grey/white eggs that attach to the hair shaft (nits), they are often prevalent in schools. TEA TREE OIL will kill the lice but not until they have hatched, so repeat treatment every 2-3 days, for 3 applications. (Always avoid eye area).

Wash hair in shampoo (neutral) adding 5-10ml TEA TREE OIL to every 100ml shampoo and leave on for 10 minutes before rinsing.

Wash all combs, brushes, hair slides, etc., in hot water and 10 drops of TEA TREE OIL. See DANDRUFF See HAIR CARE.

A SCALP RUB TO ERADICATE INFESTATION

Dissolve 10ml TEA TREE OIL in 1 tablespoon Vodka, mix with 50ml warm water and rub into the scalp of every member of the family, (for sensitive or broken skin - use 5-10ml TEA TREE OIL with 50ml OLIVE OIL instead). Leave on for either 1 hour or cover with a showercap and leave on overnight. (Repeat every 2-3 days for 3 applications). Wash out with 5-10% TEA TREE OIL shampoo as above. In the final rinse water add 1 tablespoon cider vinegar and 2-5 drops TEA TREE OIL.

Prevention
add 3ml TEA TREE OIL to every 100ml of normal shampoo, leave on hair for 5 minutes before rinsing, wash hair every day during outbreak.

HEAT EXHAUSTION

Heat exhaustion is caused by excessive loss of body fluid, which results in a rise in body temperature. Find some shade or a cool, darkened room, drink water a little at a time. Freshly squeezed orange juice with a pinch of salt is also very good.
Sponge down with 500ml tepid water and 3 drops TEA TREE OIL 2 drops PALMAROSA OIL, stir/shake well. Splash pure water on face and neck.

HEELS AND ROUGH DRY SKIN

Heels with excess dry skin are uncomfortable. After soaking or bathing, liberally apply equal amounts of TEA TREE OIL and OLIVE OIL, cover with cling film (low in plasticisers), put a clean sock on and leave overnight. Rub away as much rough skin as you can with an abrader or coarse towel. Repeat this often to keep under control.

See FOOT CARE
See CRACKED SKIN

HERPES

Cold sores, shingles and genital herpes are all problems caused by the infection (virus) HERPES SIMPLEX I & II. They are characterised by itching and very painful blisters. At the first sign of tingling, apply neat TEA TREE OIL to the sore spot and repeat 2-3 times per day. Initially mix TEA TREE OIL with Vodka (alcohol) 1ml to 5ml respectively, do not use alcohol if skin is sore, broken or weeping, always patch test first.

GENITAL HERPES

This is very contagious. At first signs of discomfort, douche with 2-3ml TEA TREE OIL to 100ml warm boiled water (stir/shake before use). Wash 4-5 times per day, this may help to prevent the attack.

Dab blisters as soon as evident with neat TEA TREE OIL.

An anti-viral douche oil mix which may alleviate symptoms is: 3 drops TEA TREE OIL, 3 drops LAVENDER OIL, 3 drops NIAOULI OIL and 5 drops HOUTTUYNIA CORDATA OIL, mix well and dilute as necessary, with 1-2 dessertspoons of VITAMIN E OIL, depending on skin sensitivity. It is also possible to add 5 drops of each of the above essential oils to 500ml warm water and mist the air, always shake the atomiser well, before use.

Have a bath with 20 drops of TEA TREE OIL to 12 cms water, splash area with knees apart. See IMMUNE SYSTEM BOOSTERS

HIGH BLOOD PRESSURE

Diagnosis and treatment by your own GP is important. Caution should be taken when using essential oils. ROSEMARY OIL SHOULD BE AVOIDED, always check on the bottle in case of contra-indications.

Your optimum weight should be maintained and a low fat (hard fats) low salt diet should be followed. See IMMUNE SYSTEM BOOSTERS.

Certain essential oils, diluted, can be beneficial, mix 50ml SOYA OIL with 5 drops LEMON OIL, 3 drops TEA TREE OIL and 10 drops YLANG YLANG. Massage 1 teaspoon of oil mix gently into solar Plexus, soles of feet and temples. Never have bath water too hot, sprinkle 5 drops LEMON OIL, 5 drops YLANG YLANG and 3 drops TEA TREE OIL onto water, for a morning bath. Omit the lemon oil for an evening bath, before bedtime.

See STRESS
See CHAPTER 8 But remember do not use Rosemary Oil.

HIVES

Hives can be very uncomfortable, burning and itching with red blisters, small boils and spots similar to being stung by nettles. It can be caused by allergens - the sun, dust, stress, etc.

Apply neat TEA TREE OIL to affected area twice per day. Or apply TEA TREE OIL SALVE - CHAPTER 6 twice per day. When bathing put 10 drops TEA TREE OIL into bath. Try applying TEA TREE OIL cold compress to area, rinse flannel or small hand towel in cold/tepid water with 5-10 drops TEA TREE OIL added and apply to area 3 times a day.

See NETTLE RASH
See ECZEMA

HOT FLUSHES
See HIGH BLOOD PRESSURE
See MENOPAUSAL SYMPTOMS
See FEVER

HOUSEMAIDS KNEE

Treat as for HEELS AND ROUGH DRY SKIN

See RHEUMATISM
See CRACKED SKIN
See SKIN CARE
See JOINTS

HYPERVENTILATION

If you suddenly start to hyperventilate for no apparent reason, you should seek medical advice, as soon as possible.

For First Aid purposes:
Sit down, try to be calm and relax. Place 1 drop of TEA TREE OIL and 2 drops CHAMOMILE OIL in a paper bag and breathe into the bag. (If you have spasmodic attacks, carry a strong paper bag around with you, it will give you reassurance when travelling - if oils are included store in a small plastic bag until ready to use).

See STRESS
See ASTHMA

I

IMMUNE SYSTEM BOOSTERS

"CASTOR OIL HEAT PACKS CAN FORTIFY IMMUNE SYSTEM"

This is based on what Dr Shealy PhD Head of Shealy PhD & Healthcare in Missouri thinks. Taken from the writings of psychic healer Edgar Cayce.

For an efficient immune system start with 25ml warmed CASTOR OIL and add 1ml TEA TREE OIL. Thoroughly soak a flannel and place on top of stomach. Cover with cling film and place on a hot water bottle, as hot as you can stand it. Leave this on for 30-45 minutes. Do this every day for a month. Then 3 times a week.

TEA TREE OIL has proved very good for immune response. Try taking a TEA TREE OIL bath twice a week (10 drops in bath). Rub oil (50 drops TEA TREE OIL to 50ml VITAMIN E OIL to 50ml CASTOR OIL - and 20 drops FLOUVE OIL - optional) warm and rub into body, hands and soles of feet twice a week.

The more conventional way is to eat a varied, balanced diet with plenty of **fresh**, **organic** fruit and vegetables including citrus, garlic and onions, tomatoes, sharon fruit, kiwi, carrots, green leafy vegetables and 'live' ewe's yogurt. Wholegrains, nuts, seeds and wheatgerm. Use cold pressed oils such as flaxseed oil and olive oil in salad dressings. Take plenty of fresh air and gentle sustained exercise. No smoking or passive smoking.
Cut out tea, coffee, cola, chocolate, sugar, junk food, fried foods, smoked, processed or canned foods, excess salt and hard fats from your diet.
Do drink plenty of pure filtered or spring water, herb teas and/or fresh organic vegetable juices.

A, C, rich foods, - tomatoes, sharon fruit, carrots, parsley, guava, mango, etc
E, - wheatgerm oil, sunflower oil, wholewheat, sunflower seeds, nuts etc
Selenium , - Brazil nuts, wholewheat, shrimps, green lentils, mushrooms etc
Zinc, - sardines, shrimps, wholemeal bread, chicken, pumpkin seeds, eggs etc

See AROMATHERAPY SECTION CHAPTER 8
See TEA TREE OIL BODY BRUSHING CHAPTER 6
See HEALING CHAPTER 6

IMPETIGO

A very infectious skin disease usually caused by either Streptococcus or Staphylococcus bacteria. This uncomfortable infection mainly affects children and can be seen on the face, scalp, neck, hands, knees, legs and nappy area, in large inflamed patches or spots which blister and crust over. This infection should not be left and if affecting a large area of the body should be seen by a doctor, as it could lead to other, more serious, complications.

Mix together 5ml WHEATGERM OIL, 10ml GRAPESEED OIL and 1-2ml TEA TREE OIL. Apply oil 2-3 times a day with cotton wool to area.

Make sure the infected person eats a diet for healthy skin including carrots, carrot juice, sharon fruit, oranges, wheatgerm and plain 'live' yoghurt.
A favourite recipe drink is 50ml fresh pressed orange juice, 50ml fresh pressed carrot juice and 1 tablespoon cider vinegar, honey may be added if desired. Drink once a day.

See IMMUNE SYSTEM BOOSTERS

INFLAMMATION
See ARTHRITIS
See GOUT

INFLUENZA
See COLDS AND FLU

INGROWING TOENAILS
See NAIL CARE.

INSECT BITES

A small red inflamed spot with a speck of blood in the centre is most likely caused by an insect bite. They can become red and itchy after a few hours. Flies, fleas, ants, gnats, mosquitoes, (even spiders) etc can all give a nasty bite. Apply 1 drop TEA TREE OIL direct to bite as soon as possible. Apply twice per day until disappeared, usually 2-4 days. This will help with the healing process and avoid infection. If persistent seek medical advice.

If abroad, splash on TEA TREE OIL and seek urgent medical advice.

See STINGS
See HOUSEHOLD SECTION (to rid home of parasites) CHAPTER 5
See FLEAS CHAPTER 5

INSECT REPELLENT

Use 2 drops TEA TREE OIL on exposed skin and rub in well. It will repel most biting insects, mixed with GERANIUM OIL can also be very effective. Mix with 1 teaspoon SWEET ALMOND OIL for sensitive skins.

For alfresco parties mix TEA TREE OIL with CITRONELLA OIL and sprinkle on barbecue candles or sprinkle on pan of hot water - keep out of reach of children to avoid accidents.

See IN THE GARDEN CHAPTER 5 See MISCELLANEOUS CHAPTER 6

INSOMNIA

For a relaxing night's sleep put 2 drops of LAVENDER OIL and 2 drops of TEA TREE OIL on pillow, then relax. Close your eyes and imagine you are sinking deep into the mattress, feel your limbs, body and head sinking deeper and deeper. It may help to curl up in the foetal position and imagine that you are back in the womb, floating in the dark, warm, comfortable and contented.

IRRITABLE BOWEL SYNDROME

Avoid trigger foods, citrus, coffee, tea, alcohol, wheat, cheese, artificial sweeteners, excess fats etc. Eat 'live' ewes yoghurt, on empty stomach, available in most supermarkets. Replace cows milk with goats or rice milk available from health shops. Do not get stressed as there is a strong connection between the two. See STRESS

Eat little and often, drink plenty of fluids (but not actually with food), herb teas such as peppermint and fennel are particularly beneficial, they should be taken 30 minutes before food and/or 30 minutes after food.

During an attack try a TEA TREE OIL massage and heat pad. At the onset of pain, massage oil gently (10 drops TEA TREE OIL, 10 drops CHAMOMILE OIL to 50ml CASTOR OIL and 5 drops of JUNIPER OIL) into tummy and apply a heated pad/hot water bottle. Lie down and relax for 30 minutes. Wild yam may help being an anti-spasmodic. See THRUSH.

ITCHING

Itching can be a sign of infection, allergic reaction, sting, bite, skin condition or parasite. You will need to find the cause and treat accordingly. **If itching occurs from using TEA TREE OIL dilute or discontinue use.**

See ECZEMA See THRUSH & See SKIN CARE
See HIVES   See IMPETIGO & See PLANT STINGS
See HEAD LICE See FLEAS   See INSECT BITES & See STINGS

J

JET LAG

TEA TREE OIL mixed with GERANIUM OIL is an effective alleviator of Jet lag. Mix together a few drops with 20ml GRAPESEED OIL, and store in a small, dark glass bottle. Keep with you when travelling and rub onto skin when necessary. They are also an effective insect repellent. Or apply a few drops of neat oil to a cup of steaming water and breathe in the aroma.

JOINTS

When a joint has been stressed from over work, rub in a mixture of: 1ml cold TEA TREE OIL, 1ml cold KANUKA OIL, 1ml cold JUNIPER OIL and 30ml cold SOYA OIL. Wrap in cling film (low or no plasticisers) and apply ice pack for 20 minutes and elevate joint. (Not to be used for people with heart disease or diabetes). After 24 hours switch to heat pad.

For inflammation, mix a deep heat, oil rub with: 50ml CASTOR OIL, 1ml TEA TREE OIL, 1ml of JUNIPER OIL, 1ml KANUKA OIL, 10 drops GINGER OIL and 1ml WINTERGREEN OIL. Rub into stiff joint, wrap in cling film (low or no plasticisers) then wrap in a hot towel. Relax and elevate the afflicted joint, (greatly dilute for children or for sensitive skin).

Do a boost massage for the joint. Whichever joint is affected: for wrist firmly compress tendons in forearm and firmly massage in 2 drops of TEA TREE OIL, 1 teaspoon CASTOR OIL, 2 drops of KANUKA OIL and 2 drops GINGER OIL. For ankle, massage the calf, for knee massage the thigh, for elbows massage the upper arms.

ST JOHN'S WORT OIL is very effective for painful joints and swelling, gently massage in 5 drops mixed with 1 teaspoon CASTOR OIL, 3 drops KANUKA OIL and 3 drops TEA TREE OIL.

Do not use neat ginger oil undiluted on the skin or in the bath.

See ARTHRITIS
See ACHES & PAINS
See GOUT
See VIRAL INFECTIONS
See COLDS AND FLU

K

KNEE PAIN

If pain and swelling are evident, do not apply a heat pad, check with doctor as to cause of swelling. You may need to wear an elastic bandage.

If swollen after exercise apply ice pack. (Unless you have heart problems or diabetes).

If swelling or pain persists see doctor.

See JOINTS
See ARTHRITIS
See GOUT
See ACHES AND PAINS
See RHEUMATISM

L

LARYNGITIS

Do not talk, do not even whisper, write everything down. Gargle with a TEA TREE OIL solution and have a steam inhalation 3-4 times a day. (Listed under 'Colds and Flu').

Avoid cold drinks. Warm Herb teas are soothing especially Slippery Elm Bark with honey. Stockists include: Herbalists, Homeopaths or try your local Health food shop.

See SORE THROATS
See COLDS AND FLU
See VIRAL INFECTIONS

LEECHES

The best thing to do if you pick one of these is to dab on neat TEA TREE OIL to loosen the grip. Dab wound with neat TEA TREE OIL. As a repellent rub in a few drops TEA TREE OIL to lower limbs and especially socks, if you are going to be walking through swampy areas.

LEUCRRHOEA

See THRUSH

LICE

These can be picked up from mattresses and close contact with humans and animals who have lice.

BODY LICE

Rub the whole body down with 2ml TEA TREE oil emulsified in a teaspoon of Vodka, and mix with 100ml warmed, boiled water, until infestation clears. Massage in a solution 1ml TEA TREE OIL and 50ml GRAPESEED OIL (shake well before use), 3 times per week.

PUBIC LICE

Cut pubic hair as short as possible and rub in a mixture of 2ml TEA TREE OIL and 10-20ml GRAPESEED OIL every day for 2 weeks or until clear.

*Add (2ml) 40 drops TEA TREE OIL to the bath water, bathe every day for at least 5 days, repeat after 1 week. Apply oil as above after bath.

*Check hair for head lice. See separate entry listed under head lice.

*Sponge mattress with 5ml TEA TREE OIL in 100ml alcohol (available from chemists), work in a ventilated room and wear rubber gloves. Keep out of the reach of children. Any of this mixture stored should be labelled and locked away in a high cupboard.

*Wash clothing and bedding, any that cannot be boiled, soak in a solution 5-8ml TEA TREE OIL to 1 litre of water for 1 hour, before washing.

*Boil wash towels every day. Add 5-8ml TEA TREE OIL to final rinse.

See HEAD LICE
See INSECT BITES
See ALL AROUND THE HOME CHAPTER 5

LUMBAGO

Severe pain in the Lumbar area of the back. Qualified diagnosis is essential. Bed rest - as long as the mattress is firm - heat and massage works wonders, so too does a hot bath before retiring. Sprinkle in 5 drops TEA TREE OIL, 2 drops ROSEMARY OIL and 2 drops JUNIPER OIL. A hot poultice is very soothing and then a massage.

For a massage oil mix 5 drops of TEA TREE OIL, 2 drops of JUNIPER OIL, 5 drops KANUKA OIL, 7 drops ST JOHN'S WORT OIL, 1 drop of GINGER OIL, 1 teaspoon of WHEATGERM OIL and 1-2 tablespoons of SWEET ALMOND OIL. Rub into lower back, cover with cling film (low in plasticisers) and apply heat pad or hot water bottle - keep it warm.

For sciatica, use the above massage oil 2-3 times per day, on the affected areas and down the spinal column, for sensitive skin, dilute essential oils with another 1 tablespoon of GRAPESEED OIL, or more depending on sensitivity of the individual.

See BACK PAIN
See ACHES AND PAINS
See ARTHRITIS
See RHEUMATISM
See DEEP HEAT RUB
See TEA TREE OIL HOT POULTICE CHAPTER 6

M

MASSAGE
See CHAPTER 8

MASTITIS
See BREASTFEEDING

MEASLES

If you have a sore throat, a barking cough, eyes that are sensitive to the light and a rash on your face, neck to trunk and on limbs it is probable that you have Measles. **You must go to the doctor for diagnosis at first signs.**

A feverish bout can be helped by sponging down the body with a flannel dipped in tepid water to which 1 drop of TEA TREE OIL and 3 drops PALMAROSA OIL and 2-3 drops CHAMOMILE OIL has been added.
See FEVER.

For a sore throat gargle with 2 drops of TEA TREE OIL in 50ml warm (boiled) water. Mix well. (Children invariably find it difficult to gargle) Have steam inhalations (not unattended) and mouth washes instead.
If **spots** become very itchy, bathe in warm bath with 10-20 drops of TEA TREE OIL added. See ECZEMA (itching)   See TEA TREE OIL SALVE.

Make sure you have a humidifier in the room or put a bowl of hot water with 10 drops TEA TREE OIL to 1 litre water. Keep out of reach of children.

Have regular steam inhalations. In a bowl put hot water, 5-10 drops of TEA TREE OIL and cover head with towel to make 'STEAM TENT'. Inhale through the nose and exhale through the mouth. Do not leave unattended.

See EAR INFECTIONS and See VIRAL INFECTIONS
See SORE THROATS and See ACHES AND PAINS

MENOPAUSAL PROBLEMS

HOT FLUSHES
Sponge the body and/or face (halve the amount of oils for the face) with mix of: 2 drops TEA TREE OIL, 2 drops PALMAROSA OIL, 1 drop PEPPERMINT OIL and 2 drops CLARY SAGE OIL in 150ml tepid water. Avoid the eye area. Label and date bottle, shake well. Use within 2 weeks.

CHAMOMILE OIL is said to be very good for hot flushes, and has a nice calming effect, mix 5 drops with 5 drops LAVENDER OIL and 5ml SOYA OIL, store in small bottle in handbag and dab onto pulse points as necessary.

Therapeutic spas are beneficial. Oatmeal baths (CHAPTER 6) with sea salt, 10 drops ROSEMARY OIL, 10 drops LAVENDER OIL and 10 drops TEA TREE OIL. (**AVOID ROSEMARY OIL if you have high blood pressure**)

Drink Herbal Sage and Nettle tea with honey, especially good for hot flushes. Soya products added to the diet are beneficial during menopause.

Calcium and Magnesium rich foods may also help. Seaweed's (kelp, nori and arame etc.) is a good source. See IMMUNE SYSTEM BOOSTERS.

Do not drink tea and coffee or soft drinks but do eat lots of salads and drink fruit juices and vegetable juices. They do say that a juice made from beetroot tops, beetroot, and carrots taken twice a day has quite a beneficial effect. Try 3 parts carrot juice to 1 part whole beetroot (and tops) juice.

Massage the abdomen and lower back with a massage oil containing 30-50 ml EVENING PRIMROSE OIL, 5 drops ST JOHN'S WORT OIL, 10 drops CYPRESS OIL and 10 drops of TEA TREE OIL.

There are numerous Herbs that women are turning to in place of conventional HRT. See your doctor and ask him about the following, they are available from Health shops, also practising Homeopaths and Herbalists:

SAGE improves mental clarity and calms night sweats.
MOTHERWORT sedative and eases hot flushes.
GINSENG balances body helps stress management.
GINKGO BILOBA assists concentration and circulation.
PURPLE CONE FLOWER stimulates the immune system and calms inflammation.
CHASTE-TREE eliminates hot flushes. Can guard against osteoporosis.
DONG QUAI calms flushes. Stops menopausal anxiety.
WILD YAM contains Saponins. Used widely in medicines. Eases headaches. Is used to make natural progesterone cream.
DANG SHEN a natural energy tonic wine. Helps combat fatigue.
NU ZHEN ZI a liver and kidney tonic wine.
BLACK COHOSH balances hormones.
NATURAL AGNUS CASTUS is an all round helper of women's problems.

*A natural HRT - progesterone cream is available on doctors prescription, For information: see USEFUL ADDRESSES at the back of book.

MENSTRUAL PROBLEMS

CRAMPS

Take a warm mineral bath with a handful of sea salt and 10 drops of TEA TREE OIL, 10 drops CHAMOMILE OIL and 5-10 drops of NEROLI OIL. (Neroli oil is expensive, 10 drops LAVENDER OIL can be substituted).

Massage oil made with 10 drops of TEA TREE OIL, 50ml SOYA OIL, 5 drops CYPRESS OIL and 5 drops of NEROLI OIL. Massage into abdomen, lower back and back of neck and shoulders. Apply heat pad to abdomen and lower back. Rest in a darkened room.

Eat little and often, a well balanced, varied diet is essential. Instead of binging on carbohydrates at certain times of the month, eat foods rich in magnesium. Nuts (not salted or roasted), dried fruit, wholegrains, dark green leafy vegetables, wheatgerm, seafood, seaweeds.

Drink vegetable juices - 10ml beetroot juice (beetroot and tops used), 30ml carrot juice, 30ml fresh pressed orange juice is very good - drink twice a day, it is also very good for PMT.

Do not take salt or eat a lot of processed foods, try to eat plenty of fresh fruit and vegetables and drink plenty of fluids such as raspberry leaf tea, vegetable juices and pure filtered or spring water.

Agnus Castus is a safe natural herb that can alleviate PMT problems, ask your doctor about its benefits and also Starflower oil or Evening Primrose oil capsules. Herbs that may help are: (see a Herbalist for further details), Milk Thistle, Wild Yam Extract, ChasteBerry, Pasque flower, Black Cohosh, Vervain, Dandelion Leaf/Root, Dang Gui (Chinese Angelica) etc. If prone to headaches, feverfew may help. Professional advice should be sort, before using any of these herbs, especially if on medication of any kind.

See OEDEMA See THRUSH

MIGRAINES
See NEURALGIA
See HEADACHES

MONILIASIS
See THRUSH

MOTION SICKNESS
See NAUSEA

MOUTH ULCERS

Dab 1 drop TEA TREE OIL on to the ulcer with the tip of your clean finger or cotton wool bud. Repeat 2-3 times per day.
Mix a TEA TREE OIL mouth wash by adding 2 drops to 50ml of warm water and rinse mouth twice per day

PREVENTION When brushing your teeth in a morning add two drops of TEA TREE OIL to your toothbrush on top of the toothpaste, and clean your teeth as normal, this will lift plaque, freshen the breath and guard against mouth infections. After 7 days, use once per week.
*It is thought that an unhealthy diet can also cause mouth ulcers.

See IMMUNE SYSTEM BOOSTERS
See TEETH AND GUMS
See GINGIVITIS
See TEETH PREPARATIONS CHAPTER 6

MUSCLES

Muscles that are overworked can give pain. At first signs apply a mixture of: 10 drops cold TEA TREE OIL, 30ml CASTOR OIL, and 10 drops KANUKA OIL, massage in and apply an ice cold flannel or towel. After 24 hours apply TEA TREE OIL MIXTURE and a heat pad to ease soreness.

CRAMPS

Massage vigorously with a deep heat rub. (1ml TEA TREE OIL to 50ml ALMOND OIL and 10 drops JUNIPER OIL, 10 drops KANUKA OIL and 3 drops PEPPER OIL). Stretch fingers and toes as you rub. Wrap area in cling film (low in plasticisers) and apply heat pad or hot water bottle. Drink plenty of fluids. If cramp is a result of vigorous exercise, try a glass of fresh pressed orange juice and a pinch of salt. If symptoms persist seek medical advice.

SPASMS

Massage in the following oil: 30ml SOYA OIL, 5 drops TEA TREE OIL, 5 drops MANDARIN OIL and 5 drops CLARY SAGE OIL.

See ACHES AND PAINS
See JOINTS
See DEEP HEAT RUB CHAPTER 6
See SPRAINS

N

NAIL CARE

Finger and toe nails are made of keratin, a protein which is found in skin cells. Like skin, nails can become dry, flaky and susceptible to infection and fungal disease.

You can add TEA TREE OIL direct to your normal hand cream 1ml per 100ml. It would be beneficial for your nails to use the TEA TREE OIL BARRIER CREAM (Chapter 6) before your hands are immersed in water or before you do jobs like the gardening etc.

See HAND AND BODY CARE CREAM CHAPTER 6

To keep your nails healthy, bathe once a week in warm water with a few drops of TEA TREE OIL added, pat dry and manicure them. Rub in TEA TREE NAIL OIL which is made by adding 1ml of TEA TREE OIL to 10ml LINSEED OIL, 5ml WHEATGERM OIL and 5 drops of OIL OF MYRRH. This should help to keep finger and toe nails strong and healthy.

See NAIL CONDITIONING OIL CHAPTER 6

CUTICLES

TEA TREE OIL does make a good cuticle remover, after a bath or after you have soaked your nails for at least 10 minutes, in quite warm water and 1 tablespoon OLIVE OIL. Apply a drop of TEA TREE OIL to each cuticle, rub in and leave for 5 minutes. Take an orange stick dipped in TEA TREE OIL and gently ease back each cuticle. You must be very gentle, so that you do not damage the soft tissue. You can also use your fingernail or towel to gently push back cuticles.

INGROWING TOE NAILS

Soak the feet daily in warm water with 2 teaspoons of salt, and 10 drops of TEA TREE OIL, pat dry and rub in 1ml TEA TREE OIL and 1ml OLIVE OIL. This will soften the nail and help to prevent infection. When nail is soft it is easier to cut with a small, sharp pair of nail scissors. If pain persists consult a qualified chiropodist.

Prevention Cut nails straight across, never below the top of the toe.

CUTTING NAILS

Always soak in warm water and OLIVE OIL, massage in TEA TREE OIL before cutting, this will ensure that they do not split or break.

NAIL INFECTIONS

TEA TREE OIL is very effective against fungal nail infections. Mix together 1 ml of TEA TREE OIL and 1ml OLIVE OIL and 10 drops of WHEATGERM OIL. Soak infected nail twice per day until infection cured. For a stronger antidote try rubbing in neat TEA TREE OIL twice a day, making sure all of the nail is covered by dipping a cotton wool covered orange stick in TEA TREE OIL and 'cleaning' underneath each nail.

Prevention Clean underneath nails every day with an orange stick dipped in TEA TREE NAIL OIL as above and see CHAPTER 6.

See HAND CARE

NAPPY RASH

This can be a very painful and distressing condition, which affects most babies at some time during their time in nappies.

For younger babies less than a 5% solution of TEA TREE OIL is recommended, for older babies not more than 10% solution. 3-10ml of TEA TREE OIL to 100ml of SUNFLOWER OIL, shake well before use. Do a skin test first - apply to small area 5-6 times in 24 hours, if no reaction apply to the nappy rash everytime the nappy is changed (every 2 hours). Give the baby's bottom some air. Let him kick happily without his nappy for as long as you can watch him. It is not advisable to leave him alone without a nappy on. If symptoms persist longer than 48 hours, without improvement, consult midwife. *Do not use Tea Tree Oil solution for longer than 10 days at a time.

NAUSEA

Some people become nauseous with petrol/diesel fumes or fishy smells - try massaging TEA TREE OIL into acupressure points - the webbing that joins the thumb and index finger with 'deep' pressure and rapid massage movements. You can do both at once using both hands.

The other point to try is reached by putting the palms together with fingers in each wrist and massaging firmly with the fingertips for several minutes with TEA TREE OIL. (A good substitute is LAVENDER OIL).

If nausea persists for a few days you must consult your doctor.

NECK PAIN

On the first sign of inflammation and stiffness apply 10-15 drops cold TEA TREE OIL mixed with 10-20ml SOYA OIL, cover with gauze or a clean tea towel and apply an ice pack. This will also reduce swelling after ice has reduced inflammation. **Only apply ice pack if you do not suffer from heart problems or diabetes.** Leave for 1 hour to warm naturally and then soothe with warmed TEA TREE OIL MIX as above and apply heat pad.

A warmed large towel loosely wound (like a neck collar) around neck can be beneficial.

After applying the above oil roll up a towel and place it against small of back when sitting. It will better align the spine and give more support.

Whiplash injuries and/or persistent or chronic neck pain must have medical attention.

See DEEP HEAT RUB CHAPTER 6
See MUSCLE CRAMPS
See ARTHRITIS
See JOINTS

NERVES
See STRESS
See NEURALGIA

NETTLE STINGS
See PLANT STINGS

NEURALGIA

A trapped, compressed or irritated nerve is the most common cause of neuralgia. The most effective answer is heat, either a warming massage oil, poultice or heat pad. This will greatly help discomfort.

Apply warm 'TEA TREE OIL MASSAGE RUB' made from 10 drops TEA TREE OIL, 20ml GRAPESEED OIL, 10ml WHEATGERM OIL, 10 drops KANUKA OIL, 2 drops PEPPER OIL and 10 drops of ST JOHN'S WORT OIL. Massage gently into the affected area (not to be used on the face - see below). Apply heat pad for 20 minutes. When going outside always cover up and keep warm the affected area. For a hot poultice see Chapter 6.
(Never use neat pepper oil on the skin or in the bath).

FACIAL NEURALGIA

Mix together 3 drops of TEA TREE OIL, 10ml GRAPESEED OIL, 5ml VITAMIN E OIL, 2 drops of JUNIPER OIL and 2 drops OREGANO OIL. Massage in gently to the affected area. **Remember to patch test first.**
A similar oil can be made with 10ml GRAPESEED OIL, 5ml VITAMIN E OIL, 3 drops TEA TREE OIL, 3 drops CHAMOMILE OIL, 3 drops ST JOHN'S WORT OIL.

Always avoid eye area.

A steam inhalation can also be beneficial. Into a bowl of steaming water add 5 drops of TEA TREE OIL and 5 drops LAVENDER OIL. Position face as comfortably as possible over the rising steam and let the vapours soothe away the pain, close eyes..

NIPPLES
(Cracked and sore).
See BREAST FEEDING
See SCABIES

NITS
See HEAD LICE
See LICE

NOSE BLEEDS

Give your nose one last blow with a soft tissue, to remove any clots. Pack your nose with wet cotton wool soaked in 1ml TEA TREE OIL to 100ml of water and 10 drops LEMON OIL, shake/stir well. Apply pressure to fleshy part of nose for 5-7 minutes. If bleeding doesn't stop repeat process, leaving cotton wool for further 20 minutes before taking out

An ice pack may also help. If persistent or heavy consult medical advice.

Apply TEA TREE OIL at 1.5% (1.5ml TEA TREE OIL to 100ml OLIVE OIL) to inside of nose, on a small piece of cotton wool or rolled up tissue, 2-3 times a day for 7 days. It will help keep down STAPH BACTERIA, stop itching and prevent crusting.

Breathe in humidified air with a few drops of TEA TREE OIL as often as possible. Dry air can sometimes bring on nose bleeds in the susceptible.

See COLDS AND FLU
See SINUSITIS

O

ODOUR
See BODY ODOUR
See FOOT ODOUR
See DEODORANT
See BAD BREATH
See DEODORANT CHAPTER 6

OEDEMA

This is a condition caused by the body holding on to excess water. It may be because of a more serious condition, so it is advisable to see your doctor initially. (***Do not use Rosemary oil in case of high blood pressure, hypertension or epilepsy).**

Morning and night vigorously massage a little of the following oil into the hands, the soles of the feet, the abdomen and the solar plexus (in clockwise direction). 20 drops TEA TREE OIL, 5ml WHEATGERM OIL, 100ml SOYA OIL, 20-30 drops CYPRESS OIL, 20 drops ROSEMARY OIL and 10 drops KANUKA OIL.

Warm baths or warm showers (never hot) with a few drops of TEA TREE OIL, GERANIUM OIL and CYPRESS OIL can be very beneficial.

Dry body brushing before a bath or shower can help too. Take a natural bristle brush and gently brush body in long even strokes, from the neck, down to the ankles and toes.

A diet high in fresh, organic vegetables, fruit and wholegrains, low in salt, sugar and refined (white) carbohydrates, can help with oedema, drink plenty of pure filtered water, (6-8 glasses of water per day). Rosehip tea, dandelion tea, dandelion juice, celery juice and parsley juice are all natural diuretics. Avoid alcohol and smoking.

See IMMUNE SYSTEM BOOSTERS
See BODY BRUSHING CHAPTER 6
See MASSAGE CHAPTER 8 ***See note above**
See MENOPAUSAL PROBLEMS
See CIRCULATORY PROBLEMS

P

PAIN
See ACHES AND PAINS
See RHEUMATISM

PANIC ATTACKS

Mix a few drops each of YLANG YLANG, LAVENDER AND GERANIUM OILS apply to a tissue, inside a small plastic bag, ideal for handbags, or for use with an aromatherapy lamp. Use when required. Dilute 2 drops of each in 1-2 teaspoons SWEET ALMOND OIL and massage into shoulders.

PARASITES
See INSECT BITES
See LICE and HEAD LICE
See TICKS
See SCABIES
See VETERINARY CHAPTER 5

PARONYCHIA
See ITCHING
See NAIL INFECTIONS

PEDICULOSIS
See HEAD LICE
See IMPETIGO

PERIOD PAIN
See MENSTRUAL PROBLEMS

PHLEBITIS

This is only for people diagnosed with superficial phlebitis and with the knowledge of their doctor. It is to help reduce pain.
Rest the leg when pain starts, elevate 15-30 cms above the heart and apply a few drops of TEA TREE OIL and KANUKA OIL diluted in SOYA OIL, very gently massage in, then apply warm moist heat, (a damp towel with a hot water bottle). Try not to stand still for long periods as it is best to walk gently, to keep circulation flowing. On long journeys stop frequently to allow gentle exercise. Elevate leg as best as you can in the car. Take a hot water bottle with you. Carefully apply 3 drops each TEA TREE OIL and KANUKA OIL in 1-2 teaspoons SOYA OIL, and then introduce gentle heat.
See CIRCULATORY PROBLEMS

PIERCED EARS

When you have your ears pierced, you must take care not to get an infection. Swab area with a few drops of TEA TREE OIL on some cotton wool, two to three times per day, until healed. If you have sensitive skin, dilute with OLIVE OIL. (10 drops TEA TREE OIL mixed with 2ml OLIVE OIL)
Every time you use your earrings wipe them with TEA TREE OIL or the TEA TREE OIL MIX before you wear them.

PIMPLES
See SPOTS
See BOILS
See BLACKHEADS

PLANT STINGS AND RASHES

Cover immediately with cold TEA TREE OIL as this should stop pain and itching. Dilute with OLIVE OIL in the case of sensitive skin. Apply as necessary, let a fan blow over it to cool area and to stop itching.

See POISON IVY

PLAQUE
See TARTAR AND PLAQUE
See TEETH AND GUMS

PMT

Relax and sink into a warm refreshing spa of a TEA TREE OIL bath - add 10-15 drops and 10 drops GERANIUM OIL, pamper yourself - breath deeply. Stress always adds to symptoms.

See MENSTRUAL PROBLEMS

PNEUMONIA
See COLDS AND FLU
See BRONCHITIS

POISON IVY

Apply neat TEA TREE OIL (or dilute with GRAPESEED OIL for sensitive skin) as soon as possible, then apply as necessary up to 3 to 4 times per day. If very itchy a cold compress or a cool air fan applied to the area does help alleviate the condition.

See HIVES
See ECZEMA (ITCHING)

PRICKLY HEAT
See HIVES
See ECZEMA (ITCHING)

PSORIASIS

Psoriasis is different for everybody, so are the remedies. What works for one person does not always work for another. Here is the list of 'FIRST AIDS' for sufferers. Find the one that suits you best.

TEA TREE RUB OIL

> 100ml ALMOND OIL, 10ml WHEATGERM OIL, 10ml TEA TREE OIL, 10ml CALENDULA OIL. Mix and apply as necessary.

WATER BASED TEA TREE OIL LUBRICANT

> Mix 7ml TEA TREE OIL with 75ml tube water based lubricant or KY JELLY. Smooth on as necessary. (SYLK can also be used)

TEA TREE OIL SUPER ANTISEPTIC HEALING CREAM
See RECIPE in CHAPTER 6

TEA TREE JELLY

> Mix 10ml TEA TREE OIL with 100ml petroleum jelly (warmed), Mix together drop by drop until incorporated. Apply as necessary.

* If skin is very dry apply cling film (low or no plasticisers) over top of treatment for maximum absorption.

Never have bath water hot.

* Cold TEA TREE OIL mixed with equal quantities of SOYA OIL and an ice pack is good for itching skin.

Gargle with a 2 drops of TEA TREE OIL in water as often as necessary.

See ECZEMA (ITCHING)
See SKIN CARE
See HAIR CARE

PYORRHOEA
See GINGIVITIS
See TEETH AND GUMS

R

RAYNARDS SYNDROME

Characterised by very cold hands and feet Raynards syndrome, is due to a circulatory problem. Vigorously massage into the hands, lower legs, arms and feet, a mixture of the following oils: 30ml ALMOND OIL, 5 drops TEA TREE OIL, 10 drops CYPRESS OIL, 5 drops JUNIPER OIL and 5 drops GINGER OIL. Repeat massage as often as necessary. (Never use neat ginger oil on the skin or in the bath).

When going outside in the cold, massage a little of the above oil mixture into the hands and/or feet, cover with cling film (low in plasticisers) and put on a pair of mittens/socks. Twirl your arms up and over (like a cricket bowler) 10 to 60 times to get the circulation going, and so warm up the hands. Stamp feet to warm those too.

See CIRCULATORY PROBLEMS
See FROST BITE

REPELLENT
See INSECT REPELLENT

REPETITIVE STRAIN INJURY (R.S.I.)

RSI, writers cramp or typists wrist is not something that happens overnight, it is an accumulative trauma disorder, that develops over a period of time; due mainly to repeated stressful movements of the hands and wrist.

If you are 35 to 60 years old and are doing a repetitive job using your hands it is best to take preventative measures, take a break every 2 hours if only for two minutes, stretch your arms above your head, bring them down and move your wrists round and round in circular motions. Bend your neck forward then back, do a circular motion with your chin, try to make the letter O with your chin try to make it bigger and bigger. Then lastly apply your normal handcream with 1ml of TEA TREE OIL added and rub your palms together and your hands vigorously.

In the evening **or** at the first sign of numbness, cramping or tingling, massage in a little of the following cold oil: 5ml TEA TREE OIL, 50ml

SOYA OIL, 1ml CYPRESS OIL, rub well in with circular firm movements from elbow to fingertips, pull and push fingers as you massage each one in turn. Apply an ice pack for at least 10 minutes to each wrist and hand.

RESPIRATORY INFECTIONS
See BRONCHITIS
See ASTHMA

RESTLESS LEGS

Whenever you find your legs twitching involuntary, get up and walk. It is particularly annoying at bedtime when you and/or your partner are trying to get to sleep.

Before going to bed, have a warm bath, sprinkle in 10 drops of TEA TREE OIL and 10 drops of LAVENDER OIL. Massage your legs, paying special attention to lower legs and calves. The best massage oil to use for restless legs is a mixture of 50ml ALMOND OIL, 5ml VITAMIN E OIL, 10 drops TEA TREE OIL, and 1ml CYPRESS OIL. Some people also swear by warming up exercises (gentle stretches) before getting into bed.

See CIRCULATORY PROBLEMS

RHEUMATISM

Rheumatism is basically muscle pain, TEA TREE OIL is very good at soothing away pain.
Massage the area with a massage oil made with 50ml ALMOND oil, 1ml TEA TREE OIL, 1ml ELEMI OIL, 1ml JUNIPER OIL and 1ml KANUKA OIL, twice per day. Apply heat pad if necessary.

Have a refreshing spa bath with 10 drops TEA TREE OIL and 5 drops CYPRESS OIL.

Body brushing is very therapeutic for rheumatism as it helps to release toxins from the system. Brush the body with a natural bristle body brush at least once per day, starting at the shoulders brush the skin in long firm, even strokes right down to the toes. Massage in the massage oil as above.

See BODY BRUSHING TO IMPROVE CIRCULATION CHAPTER 6
See ACHES AND PAINS
See ARTHRITIS
See MUSCLES
See DEEP HEAT RUB CHAPTER 6

RHEUMATOID ARTHRITIS
See ARTHRITIS

RHINITIS
See COLDS AND FLU
See HAYFEVER
See SINUSITIS

RINGWORM

Characterised by a patch of scaly red itching skin that forms a raised ring with a pink centre Ringworm is a fungal skin complaint.

TEA TREE OIL is very good at eradicating ringworm. You can use TEA TREE OIL at the first signs, unlike most ringworm creams, it does not matter if the scaly patch of skin turns out to be impetigo or eczema, TEA TREE OIL treats all three.

Mix 5ml of TEA TREE OIL with either 20ml of water based lubricating gel or 10-20ml of OLIVE OIL (store in a dark glass, labelled bottle) and apply to ringworm 4 times per day, Until 1 week after it disappears. Impetigo and ringworm are highly contagious, you must cover with a gauze pad until they disappear. (Adults may use neat TEA TREE OIL).

A mixture of 3ml TEA TREE OIL, 3ml MANUKA OIL, 3ml KANUKA OIL and 10-20ml OLIVE OIL can be used instead, apply as above.

If on the scalp dab 4 times per day with 5ml TEA TREE OIL diluted with 20-30ml OLIVE OIL and wash hair daily with a normal shampoo containing 10ml TEA TREE OIL & 5ml ROSEMARY OIL to 100ml Shampoo

It is very important to wash clothes, bedding, towels, brushes, combs, hair slides and hands in a solution of 10ml to 1 litre of water and soap.

See IMPETIGO See ATHLETES FOOT
See ANTI-FUNGAL OINTMENT CHAPTER 6

ROPE BURNS
Treat as for BURNS

ROSACEA - ACNE
See VEINS

ROUGH SKIN REMOVER
See SKINCARE
See HAND CARE
See OATMEAL RUB Chapter 6

S

SANITARY APPLICATIONS
See TOXIC SHOCK SYNDROME
See THRUSH
see SKIN CARE

SCABIES

Quite common in sheep farming areas scabies is transmitted by the mite Sarcoptes Scabies, it can be picked up from anything from clothing to coins. Small red pimples appear as the hatched mites burrow their way out of the skin. The areas usually affected are the groin, genitals, nipples and hands.

To treat, wash the infected part with a solution of 3-5ml TEA TREE OIL to 100ml of warm water. Apply, three times per day, a water based lubricating gel that has been mixed 5ml TEA TREE OIL to 25 ml water based gel, or 25ml GRAPESEED OIL

Add 20-40 drops of TEA TREE OIL to a bath. Add 5ml TEA TREE OIL to every 100ml of your normal shampoo and conditioner.

Boil wash bedding, towels and flannels. Wash clothes well and add 8ml TEA TREE OIL to 1 litre of rinsing water soak for 1 hour. Wash brushes, combs, and slides in the same solution.

Sponge down mattress and pillows with 5ml TEA TREE OIL in 100ml solution of alcohol (available from chemist). Keep out of the reach of children, if stored it should be labelled, and locked away in a high cupboard.

See ALL AROUND THE HOME / DUSTMITES / CHAPTER 5

SCABS

It is best to let scabs heal and disappear by themselves, but if they are unsightly or infected, then they may benefit from the following treatment.

Apply TEA TREE OIL direct to scab. If stuck to a bandage, soak the area in warm water with 5 drops of TEA TREE OIL added. Bathe with water, pat dry and apply 1 drop of TEA TREE OIL and 1 drop CALENDULA OIL, cover with gauze so that wound can breathe while healing.

SCALDS
See BURNS

SCALP
See HAIR CARE
See DANDRUFF
See CHAPTER 6

SCARRING

To help to prevent unsightly scarring, gently apply the following to the healing wound. Mix together 10 drops TEA TREE OIL, 10 drops CALENDULA OIL, 10ml VITAMIN E OIL (or WHEATGERM OIL), 1 Teaspoon warmed honey, keep stirring until cool, gently apply a little to the area twice per day. Store in a sterilised pot, in a cool dark place, use within 3 months.

SCIATICA
See LUMBAGO
See BACK PAIN
See RHEUMATISM

SCRATCHES
See ABRASIONS
See SPLINTERS

SEPTIC FINGER

Cuts and wounds must be kept clean and free from infection. If your cut becomes itchy, red and swollen or develops a green pus underneath the skin, then it is turning septic.

At the very first signs soak the wound in hot water with 1 dessertspoon salt and 10 drops of TEA TREE OIL. Pat dry and rub on a few drops of neat TEA TREE OIL, cover and repeat three times per day until infection subsides. If persists longer than 48 hours without improvement, area gets bigger, or pain gets worse consult your doctor.

See TTO SUPER ANTISEPTIC HEALING CREAM CHAPTER 6

SHAVING
See HAIR REMOVAL
See DEODORANT
See AFTERSHAVE OIL CHAPTER 6

SHINGLES

Apply 1ml TEA TREE OIL, 10 drops OREGANO OIL, 10 drops ST JOHN'S WORT OIL, 10ml VITAMIN E and 10-20ml SOYA OIL to area that is tingling, before spots arrive, twice per day.
Add 10 drops of TEA TREE OIL to calamine lotion and apply to spots, three to four times per day, shake well.
Have an oatmeal and TEA TREE OIL bath, (in a muslin bag put a handful of ground whole oats. Hang bag around cold tap and allow bath water to run in through bag), add 20 drops of TEA TREE OIL to water.
For pain relief apply a cold TEA TREE OIL compress to painful area.

See SCARRING
See SUPER ANTISEPTIC HEALING CREAM CHAPTER 6

SIDE STITCH

If you are prone to a sharp temporary pain in your side (waist area), after exertion, it is probably 'The Stitch'. It is possible to guard against and alleviate this uncomfortable problem. If pain persists consult doctor.

When pain hits - STOP - press the points of your fingers, into the part where the pain is, gently but firmly massage in TEA TREE OIL & SOYA OIL. Breathe deeply and slowly. Breathe in the vapours of the TEA TREE OIL then breathe out long and slow. Continue for 5 minutes, this should then have alleviated the pain. If pain becomes worse when pressure is applied, see your doctor as soon as possible, for a check up.
Prevention Before you start any form of exercise, massage your diaphragm, lie on your back and massage 3-4 drops of TEA TREE OIL with 20ml OLIVE OIL into the area of the diaphragm. A warmed diaphragm is unlikely to have stitch spasm.

SINUSITIS

When you begin to feel the first signs of sinusitis, make a TEA TREE OIL steam tent and repeat twice per day. Put 5-10 drops of TEA TREE OIL into a large bowl of hot, steaming water, or as hot as is comfortable. **Keep out of the reach of children**. Lean over the bowl and drape a large bath towel over your head to form a tent. Inhale the vapours through your nose and exhale through your mouth.

If you have an attack at work. Fill a cup full of hot water and 5 drops of TEA TREE OIL breathe in the vapours as often as necessary.
If symptoms persist see a doctor

SINUSITIS (Cont.)

If you have a lot of dry heat at home, hang humidifiers containing water and TEA TREE OIL over the radiators. SWEET ORANGE OIL can be added too.

Some doctors extol the virtues of a nostril bath. Mix together, 2-4 drops of TEA TREE OIL and 30ml warm water, pour into a small glass. Tilt head back, close the right nostril with thumb and sniff/draw half the solution up the left nasal passage, then gently blow your nose - repeat with the other side. Or you could dampen a small wad of cotton wool with the above mix, small enough to fit inside the nasal passage, and gently dab the inside of the nose. Use a new piece of cotton wool for each nostril repeat twice a day.

See CATARRH
See COLDS AND FLU

SKIN BRUSHING

Skin brushing is an ideal way to keep skin in tip top condition and to rid your body of accumulated toxins, that cause problems like cellulite, arthritis, rheumatism to name but a few.

Use only a DRY, NATURAL bristle, body brush preferably with a long handle, making firm even strokes, brush the body all over from shoulders, back, chest, buttocks, abdomen, front and back of legs right down to the ankles and toes. Soak in a refreshing TEA TREE OIL spa bath made from a handful of sea salt, 10 drops TEA TREE OIL, 5 drops of CYPRESS OIL and 5 drops of LEMON OIL Rub/dry skin with a course towel to remove dead skin cells, and massage with 20ml SOYA OIL, 10 drops TEA TREE OIL and 5 drops LEMON OIL.

See SKIN BRUSHING TO IMPROVE CIRCULATION CHAPTER 6

SKIN CARE

Skin care must really begin from within. A healthy balanced diet including natural, organic fruit, vegetables, wholegrains, seeds, nuts, with 6-8 glasses of filtered water, herb teas and vegetables juices will help to keep skin healthy, toned and fresh. Used in conjunction with basic cleansing and moisturising, with natural unadulterated products, could ensure your skin remains clear, glowing and youthful all through your life.

TEA TREE OIL has been proven to penetrate the skin layers, oxygenating, repairing and cleansing cells below the surface. As it cleanses it will also moisturise, keeping the skin supple and help to retain the natural elasticity.

Your skin will always reflect what you put into your body, what you put on to it and your state of mind (stress etc). If you bombard your system and skin with chemicals it could eventually lose its natural bloom.

BODY

FOR GENERAL SKIN CARE

* Add 10-20 drops of TEA TREE OIL to your bath water. This is very beneficial as it will achieve 3 actions in one.
1) The waters and oil will cleanse and moisturise the skin,
2) The steam will open pores in facial skin, ready for cleansing.
3) The vapours will be inhaled to work internally, and will generally make you feel 'better'.

For a morning invigorating spa bath mix: 10 drops TEA TREE OIL, 5-10 drops GERANIUM OIL added to water.

For an evening relaxing soother bath mix: 5 drops TEA TREE OIL, 5 drops BENZOIN (optional), 10 drops LAVENDER OIL added to water. Use a face flannel, body brush or loofa to rub away dead skin cells from body.

For an invigorating male body oil mix: 50ml SWEET ALMOND OIL, 5 drops TEA TREE OIL, 10 drops FRANKINCENSE, 10 drops ROSEMARY OIL and 5 DROPS CEDARWOOD OIL.

For an enlivening woman's body oil mix: 50 ml SWEET ALMOND OIL, 5 drops TEA TREE OIL, 10 drops YLANG YLANG OIL, 10 drops LEMON OIL and 5 drops GERANIUM OIL.

For a more mature lady's body toning oil mix: 50ml SWEET ALMOND OIL, 5 drops TEA TREE OIL, 10 drops SANDALWOOD OIL, 10 drops LAVENDER OIL and 10 drops ROSEWOOD OIL.

Or use TEA TREE OIL HAND & BODY CREAM CHAPTER 6 **or** add 2-3ml of TEA TREE OIL to your own toiletries, shake well before each use.

See SKIN BRUSHING See BODY EXFOLIATING RUB CHAPTER 6
See CELLULITE See ANTI-CELLULITE CREAM AND OIL CHAPTER 6

FACE

Start by removing dead skin cells. For this you can use an ordinary face flannel. Stir water vigorously and moisten flannel (warm water to which 2 drops of TEA TREE OIL has been added), rub over face, from outside in, taking care not to drag the skin directly under and around the eyes.

FACE (Cont.)

If face has greasy skin add 1 drop LEMON OIL to the water for the flannel. **Do not get into eyes, if stinging occurs wash copiously with cool water.**

You may like to use the TEA TREE OIL facial exfoliating cream (chapter 6). Avoid eye area completely. Tone and moisturise facial skin afterwards. See FACE CHAPTER 6

DRY SKIN

Never use hot water when cleansing.

Body - moisturise everyday by massaging in a little dry skin moisturising oil - 1ml TEA TREE OIL 1ml LAVENDER OIL, 10ml WHEATGERM OIL, 150ml OLIVE OIL or GRAPESEED OIL. Put all ingredients in large, labelled, dark glass bottle with airtight stopper, shake well before each application. See BODY CHAPTER 6 See BODY OIL (previous page).

Heels, elbows and knees - after bath rub in 5 drops TEA TREE OIL mixed with 1 teaspoon petroleum jelly. After every 3 days exfoliate. (See page 177).

Face - mist face with water, mix face oil 1ml TEA TREE OIL, 50ml VITAMIN E OIL, 10ml AVOCADO OIL. Shake well. Store in a labelled dark glass bottle. Apply 1/2 teaspoon twice per day, avoiding eye area.

Facial dry skin - See also Chapter 6 for face packs, cleansers, toners and moisturisers.

See OATMEAL MILK BATH / CHAPTER 6

GREASY SKIN

Body - Take a warm to hot bath with 2 tablespoons lemon juice (or 5 drops LEMON OIL) and 5 drops TEA TREE OIL and 10 drops of JUNIPER OIL.

Face - Tone the skin with the following strawberry skin freshener. As often as necessary:- 30gms fresh garden mint, 30gms Cleavers, 150gms fresh strawberries, 1 pint cider vinegar, 1ml TEA TREE OIL. Wash and dry fruit and herbs, place all ingredients, except TEA TREE OIL, into a liquidiser, turn to highest setting, liquidise until smooth. Strain through a fine mesh sieve and then strain again through muslin, until liquid is clear. Pour into a large dark glass bottle. Add TEA TREE OIL. Shake well before use, dilute as required, with distilled water, to suit skin. Always patch test before use, initially. See Facials in Chapter 8.
See TEA TREE OIL and Lemon clay face pack (Chapter 6).

NORMAL SKIN
See FACE See BODY CHAPTER 6

CHAPPED SKIN

Chapped skin usually affects the hands
When your skin becomes very red and sore and even cracked, avoid washing the area as much as possible. If your hands are affected, rub with anti-bacterial glycerine, mix 3-5ml TEA TREE OIL to 50ml glycerine and apply everytime you should have washed your hands. Shake well before use.

At night rub in a mixture of 1ml TEA TREE OIL, 10ml WHEATGERM OIL and 10ml SUNFLOWER OIL. Cover with cotton gloves if possible.

To remove dry skin use Oatmeal rub for hands (chapter 6). Apply hand cream liberally and repeat once a week.
Prevention Whenever you go outside in winter rub TEA TREE OIL SUPER ANTISEPTIC HEALING CREAM into hands and cover with gloves. Use a barrier cream before washing up and/or wear rubber gloves.

See CRACKED SKIN
See CHAPPED LIPS
See CHAPTER 6
See TRANSDERMAL ABSORPTION   CHAPTER 4
See SUNBURN

SKIN INFECTIONS
See ECZEMA
See PSIORSIS
See IMPETIGO
See RINGWORM
See ATHLETES FOOT
See BOILS
See ABSCESS
See SCABIES

SNAKE BITES

Whether TEA TREE OIL is beneficial to snake bites is purely anecdotal, there is no evidence. Seek medical attention, if at all possible try to remember the type of snake that bit you. Gently clear poison from the surface of bite. Bind area, if on arm or leg, very tightly above bite towards heart, (release for 1 minute every half hour). Immobilise the limb with a splint. Apply ice, if handy, apply neat TEA TREE OIL, if handy. - Do not delay, carry the person and seek medical attention immediately.

SORE THROATS

Fill an all purpose atomiser spray bottle with a mixture of 50ml warm water, 2 drops TEA TREE OIL and 2 drops MANUKA OIL shake well before use and lightly mist-spray throat, 2-3 times a day. Do not attempt if under 12 years of age or are suffering from asthma or a serious medical condition. If symptoms persist more than 48hrs, without improvement, see doctor.

See COLDS AND FLU

SPIDER BITES

It has recently been reported that we now have venomous spiders in the South of England. If bitten apply neat, cold TEA TREE OIL to area every few hours. If an allergic reaction to the bite appears consult doctor immediately. (Dilute with SOYA OIL for children and sensitive skin).

If abroad, soak area in TEA TREE OIL, if you have it near, apply cold to area and seek medical attention immediately. See SNAKE BITES.

See INSECT BITES
See STINGS

SPLINTERS

Surface splinters, thorns, metal filings etc., remove as soon as possible with tweezers or needle (soaked in neat TEA TREE OIL). Soak area if possible in salt water with 10 drops TEA TREE OIL to clean perforation. Apply neat tea Tree oil and cover.

If splinters are in the eyes or buried deep beneath the skin seek professional advice immediately.

See ABRASIONS
See SEPTIC FINGER
See SPLINTER THORN STEAM EXTRACTOR CHAPTER 6
See POULTICE CHAPTER 6

SPOTS
See BLACK HEADS
See ACNE
See BOILS
See VIRAL INFECTIONS
See SKIN CARE - GREASY SKIN
See BODY See FACE CHAPTER 6

SPRAINS

Apply 10 drops TEA TREE OIL and 10 drops ELEMI OIL to sprain, cover with towel and apply ice pack. Elevate leg to help to stop the swelling. **Seek professional advice.** Usually an elastic bandage is applied but this should never be too tight. After a few hours heat may help with the pain. Apply the above oils and a heat pad.

See ACHES AND PAINS
See MUSCLE PAINS
See BRUISE BAN CHAPTER 6

STAINED TEETH
See TEETH AND GUMS
See CHAPTER 6

STIFFNESS

Have a nice warming bath with 5 drops TEA TREE OIL and 5 drops ROSEMARY OIL. Massage area with 1/2 teaspoon oil made with 50ml SOYA OIL, 1ml TEA TREE OIL, 5 drops CYPRESS OIL, 5 drops ROSEMARY OIL and 1ml WHEATGERM OIL - cover with heat pad.

See ACHES AND PAINS
See MUSCLE PAINS
See MASSAGE CHAPTER 8

STINGS

* BEE STINGS - Honey bees actually leave their sting in the skin. Scrape it out carefully, do not squeeze, it may release more poison. Apply 1 drop TEA TREE OIL, 1 drop LEMON OIL and ice cube.

* WASP STINGS - Apply TEA TREE OIL and Bicarbonate of soda paste by mixing 1 teaspoon bicarbonate of soda with a few drops of TEA TREE OIL and water. Leave on for 15 minutes. In an emergency apply neat TTO.

* ANTS - Apply neat TEA TREE OIL to stop the painful itching. Children should be given a 25-50% solution (diluted with GRAPESEED OIL).

* **Watch carefully for signs of an allergic reaction, it can be anything from: fainting, dizziness, vomiting, swelling anywhere on body (tongue, hands feet, ankles, etc.), hoarseness, sore throat, chest tightness, shortness of breath, wheezing, headache, coughing, fever, muscle cramps, spots, skin rashes, skin discoloration or anything unusual.**

If any of these do occur take to the nearest medical centre, urgently.

STINGS (Cont.)

If abroad, or the person has a known allergy to the type of sting, apply TEA TREE OIL, if handy, and seek **urgent** medical attention.

For an effective insect repellent mix 50ml SOYA OIL, 3-5ml TEA TREE OIL and 3-5ml GERANIUM OIL. Store in a dark glass bottle and apply as necessary.

NETTLE stings apply TEA TREE OIL to affected area and cold compress if itching is severe.

See PLANT STINGS
See INSECT BITES
See SPIDER BITES

STOMACH CRAMPS

Gently massage abdominal (and lower back if possible) area with the following massage oil: 10ml SOYA OIL, 5 drops YLANG YLANG OIL, 2 drops TEA TREE OIL and 7 drops CHAMOMILE OIL, apply heat pad.

See MENSTRUAL PROBLEMS
See IRRITABLE BOWL SYNDROME
See MUSCLES

STRESS

Muscles knot and tense when we are under stress. Massage in a little of the following oil: 1 tablespoon SOYA OIL, 3 drops TEA TREE OIL and 5 drops LAVENDER OIL (see massage chapter 8) into the back of the neck, along shoulders. See PANIC ATTACKS.

Apply gentle pressure to temples with finger tips and massage in a little of the above oil, massage ear lobes too. Take a relaxing bath with 5 drops of TEA TREE OIL and 10 drops of LAVENDER OIL

Lie on your bed or sit in a comfortable chair, place a cup or bowl of hot water near, add the following oils: 3 drops YLANG YLANG OIL, 1 drop TEA TREE OIL, 5 drops BENZOIN and SANDALWOOD OIL, breathe deeply, breathe in the relaxing aroma, imagine it entering your body and slowly draining away the stress and tension. Feel the stress draining down through your fingers, through your toes, down into the floor and finally disappearing.

STYES
See EYE INFECTIONS

SUNBURN

Avoid burning your skin at all costs. Use a sensible factor 15, or above, on the first day, wear a hat. Do not spend a long time outside, unless shaded. (Children should use a sun block). Gradually come down the factor scale as necessary, re-apply during time in the sun, especially after swimming. Try to keep out of the sun between 11.00am to 2.30pm, when it is at its hottest.

If you do suspect burning, immediately find shade, apply cooling compress. A flannel moistened a mixture of 1 pint of cool water or milk with 10 drops TEA TREE OIL and 1ml LAVENDER OIL. Apply cool air fan.

In an emergency spread a pot of cold, 'live', plain yoghurt liberally over area. If very painful or you suspect severe burning seek medical attention.

You **must** seek urgent medical advice if burns are very severe, they cover a large area, blister, are very red and sore, or the skin is cracked and weeping. Do not risk going out in the sun until skin has completely healed.

Apply an after-sun soother (Chapter 6). Do not use soap, but bathe in oatmeal 'milk' soother. Put 1 cup oats in large heat proof jug, pour on cool water allow to stand for 10 minutes, strain through large fine mesh sieve into bath. Run tepid bath water through sieve, add 1 pint milk or 3 table-spoons milk powder, add 10 drops TEA TREE OIL, 20 drops LAVENDER OIL and soak in bath for 10-15 minutes. Do not rub skin, gently pat dry.

After bath - before bedtime apply a little of the oil mixed as follows; 50ml WHEATGERM OIL, 30ml SEA BUCKTHORN OIL, 5ml TEA TREE OIL, 5ml LAVENDER OIL, 5ml CALENDULA OIL. Apply and wrap in cotton sheet.

A cold/tepid TEA TREE OIL COMPRESS can be soothing. See CHAPTER 6

See BURNS
See SKIN CARE
See BODY   CHAPTER 6

SWIMMERS EAR

Infection after swimming is quite common. If you are susceptible to infections apply 'waterproofing' to each ear, before you enter the water. Mix together 1 teaspoon warmed OLIVE OIL and 2 drops TEA TREE OIL. Tilt your head to one side and apply mixture in dropper to ear, wiggle your ear, massage outside and drain off excess. Repeat with other ear. This can help to guard against infection. If persistent seek medical advice.

See TTO EARPLUGS CHAPTER 6

T

TARTAR AND PLAQUE
See TEETH AND GUMS
See CHAPTER 6

TATTOO

To avoid infection after having a tattoo, wash area with a few drops of TEA TREE OIL in 50ml warm water. At first sign of infection, rub in a mixture of 5 drops TEA TREE OIL and 20 drops of OLIVE OIL.
If infection persists consult doctor.

TEETH AND GUMS

For healthy teeth and gums 'think small' when purchasing your toothbrush. It will be easier to reach into those corners. Soft rounded bristles are always preferable, consult your dentist if in doubt.

When brushing your teeth put a 'pea' sized amount, of your normal toothpaste, onto your toothbrush. Add 2 drops of TEA TREE OIL and clean your teeth as normal. You will be pleasantly surprised at how clean and fresh your mouth feels, your teeth will become whiter too. After 7 days, use TEA TREE OIL once a week to maintain whiteness.

To floss your teeth, smooth TEA TREE OIL along flossing tape or flossing string and floss as normal.

To make your own plaque spotter, coat lips with lip balm or petroleum jelly. Put one capful of natural food colouring into mouth. Swish around and spit out, the plaque will be coloured, and so easier to remove. Clean teeth with TEA TREE OIL paste, see below.

Stained teeth - or helping to prevent plaque and tartar, make your own TEA TREE OIL TEETHPASTE. Mix 1/2 a teaspoon bicarbonate of soda with 1 drop of TEA TREE OIL, and a pinch of salt, add water drop by drop until a stiff paste - brush teeth well and rinse very well.

TEA TREE OIL mouth wash to kill bacteria and freshen breath mix 2 drops of TEA TREE OIL in 1/2 a cup of warm water and swish around mouth for 1 minute.......

TEETH AND GUMS (CONT.)

See GINGIVITIS
See DENTURE SORES
See CHAPTER 6

TEETHING

Before you apply to baby's gums do a sensitivity test with a 10% solution of TEA TREE OIL, 1 drop TEA TREE OIL and 1 drop CHAMOMILE OIL to 10 drops ALMOND OIL. Try a patch test over 48 hours, APPLY OFTEN **to wrist**. If no reaction mix 1 drop TEA TREE OIL and 1 small drop CHAMOMILE OIL with 1 teaspoon ALMOND OIL and put a drop of mixture on finger or gauze pad, massage baby's gums. (Mix 1 tablespoon ALMOND OIL to 4 drops TEA TREE OIL and 4 drops CHAMOMILE OIL. Store in sterilised dark glass bottle in cool place. use when required). Use within 7 days or discard.

Apply a few drops of mixture to teethers to help prevent infections.

A persistent high temperature may not be due to teething always consult a doctor.

TEMPERATURE
See FEVER

TENDINITIS (TENDER TENDONS)

Like the pain of overused muscles Tendinitis - an inflammation in and around the tendons can be quite sharp. It is not wise to exercise through pain - if persistent seek medical advice.

Immediately after exercise apply 10 drops TEA TREE OIL with 2ml SOYA OIL and a covered ice pack, to reduce swelling and to soothe pain. (do not apply ice pack if suffering from heart disease or diabetes).

Allow area to warm up naturally to room temperature, then give the affected part a warm TEA TREE OIL bath, this will raise temperature and increase blood flow. Massage in warmed mix of 2ml TEA TREE OIL, 50ml SOYA OIL and 1 ml CYPRESS OIL, 10 drops WINTERGREEN OIL. Apply heat pad and raise afflicted part above heart if possible.

See MUSCLES
See DEEP HEAT RUB CHAPTER 6
See RHEUMATISM

THORNS
See SPLINTERS
See SEPTIC FINGER

THROAT INFECTIONS
See SORE THROATS
See COLDS AND FLU

THRUSH

Candida Albicans is a yeast fungus that grows naturally in warm moist places on the body and in the intestines. It is a natural flora, and in the normal context is quite harmless. But if the balance is upset by antibiotics, medical conditions, stress, the pill, HRT, chemical douches, strong soap and deodorants etc., infection can spread and the skin can become red, itchy and sore, with a white discharge from the vaginal area. TEA TREE OIL is very effective, killing off the harmful bacteria - whilst still being kind to the skin tissue.

You should always have a qualified doctors diagnosis and advice, at the first signs of a discharge, or if persistent.

Have a sitz bath, put 2ml TEA TREE OIL and 10 drops LAVENDER OIL into bath. Run in a few inches of warm water, sit in water, legs apart for 5-10 minutes or use a bidet.

Avoid scratching infected areas. It is possible to transfer infection to other parts of the body.

On waking in the morning wash hands. Add 10 drops TEA TREE OIL to a small amount of water in washbasin, scrub under nails with soap and water (even rubbing your eyes can spread infection to eyelids, so be careful).

Use natural, water soluble lubricant during intercourse. Mix 2-3 drops of TEA TREE OIL to a teaspoon of lubricating jelly. This helps to guard against infection. Using a condom will protect your partner.

Douche area with 5-10 drops TEA TREE OIL to 100ml of warm water on cotton wool. Always douche vagina front to back, do not use the same piece of cotton wool twice. Make sure partner has treatment too, this will prevent re-infection.

Apply to tampon and insert the following: mix 3-5 drops TEA TREE OIL to 1 teaspoon of water soluble jelly (ie KY or SYLK). Leave in overnight. If irritation occurs or excessive stinging discontinue use.

THRUSH (CONT.)

Avoid foods containing yeast or that have been fermented, until infection clears. Cheese, wine, beer, alcohol, bread, doughnuts, soy sauce, miso, quorn, mushrooms, vinegar, pickles, etc. and cut sugar intake.

Eat fresh organic fruit and vegetables to boost immune system. Garlic, onions, sharon fruit, tomatoes, kiwi fruit, carrots, papaya etc. and eat 'live' ewe's yoghurt before each meal, and before going to bed, on an empty stomach. Cranberry powder/tablets from Health food shops can be beneficial, also a *tea made from pot marigold petals (*calendula Officinalis*).

At home, wipe toilet seat with neat TEA TREE OIL after use.

When travelling, wipe toilet seat before and after use with TEA TREE OIL on paper tissue.

Keep underwear clean. It is possible to become re-infected with Thrush from washed and laundered underwear. As an extra precaution rub in a few drops of TEA TREE OIL into part of clothes that touch infected area and launder as normal or put 5ml of TEA TREE OIL into final rinse water.
Cotton underwear is preferable to nylon if you are susceptible to thrush

For oral Candida (white spots on roof of mouth), rinse thoroughly with 5-10 drops TEA TREE OIL in a glass of warm water, swish around for 5 minutes, and spit out. *Marigold tea, is also beneficial as a drink and a rinse.

See IMMUNE SYSTEM BOOSTERS
See TEA TREE OIL PESSARIES CHAPTER 6

TICKS

Ticks are nasty, greyish white, round creatures related to the spider. If one becomes embedded into the skin do not try to pull it out, it may break off at the head and cause infection.
Dab tick with neat TEA TREE OIL at regular intervals. After 3-4 applications, if it has not let go, grip with tweezers dipped in TEA TREE OIL and rock gently back and forth until it losses its grip. Dab area with neat TEA TREE OIL twice a day, until healed.
Prevention Cover up well when walking through grassy farmland - apply insect repellent to exposed skin: 1 tablespoon SOYA OIL, 7-10 drops TEA TREE OIL and 7 drops GERANIUM OIL.

TINEA
See ANTI-FUNGAL OINTMENT CHAPTER 6
See ATHLETES FOOT   See RINGWORM   See SHAVING RASH

TINNITUS

A constant noise 'inside' the ear, (not related to outside sources). Many people suffer with this distressing condition, it can range from a ringing sound to a constant banging noise. The cause is difficult to pin down, it can be from poor posture, shock, rotting teeth, infection, constant loud noise (ie machinery), damage to ear drum, allergy, certain drugs, poor circulation and blocked sinuses, hayfever, colds, even lack of sleep, etc.
Diagnosis by a qualified practitioner is essential.

Sometimes acupressure can help, or taking a supplement of ginkgo biloba.

A warm compress made from: 1 flannel moistened with 250ml warm water, 3 drops TEA TREE OIL, 7 drops SANDALWOOD OIL and 7 drops of LAVENDER OIL, wring out and place against each ear for 10 minutes.

Or an oil made from 1ml SOYA OIL, 1 drop TEA TREE OIL, 1 drop SANDALWOOD OIL and 2 drops LAVENDER OIL, mix and massage into temples and along the bone behind the ear.

See SINUSITIS
See CIRCULATORY PROBLEMS

TIRED FEET
See FOOTCARE
See COOL MINT FOOT SOOTHER CHAPTER 6

TIREDNESS

An aromatherapy lamp or a cup of hot water, sprinkled with a few drops of TEA TREE OIL and a few drops GERANIUM OIL or SWEET ORANGE OIL can work wonders, or any of the methods in chapter 8.

TONSILLITIS
See SORE THROAT
See COLDS AND FLU
See LARYNGITIS

TOOTHACHE

Book appointment to see dentist. In the meantime apply 1-2 drops TEA TREE OIL to tooth with dropper or dab with gauze pad. Rinse mouth with 2 drops of TEA TREE OIL and a large pinch of salt in 25ml warm water. Do not swallow liquid.

Avoid applying heat to cheek, as it may make the infection worse, even if it does help the pain.

TOXIC SHOCK SYNDROME

TSS is a quite rare but very serious, even fatal, illness caused by a type of bacteria. The bacteria can live happily on our bodies, until in certain circumstances a few strains can manufacture and release a toxin that causes TSS in susceptible people.

Around 40 cases occur per year out of the U.K. population. The use of tampons seems to give an increased risk of TSS. Cases in men, children and non-menstruating women can also occur. Menstruation in itself can give an increased risk of TSS.

To reduce the risk of TSS it is important during menstruation to practice good hygiene, changing sanitary towels at least every 4 hours, during the day. Never leave tampons in for longer than 10 hours. Always wash and scrub hands with a few drops of TEA TREE OIL, in soap and water, before and after, you change sanitary protection. Douche vaginal area night and morning or have sitz bath, see Thrush.

Boil wash bath towel every day while menstruating.

See THRUSH
See FEMININE HYGIENE

TRAPPED NERVE

Take warm to hot bath with 10 drops of TEA TREE OIL. Rub in warmed massage oil to area and apply heat pad.

To mix oil take 50ml GRAPESEED OIL, 1ml WHEATGERM OIL, 1ml TEA TREE OIL, 1ml ST JOHN'S WORT OIL and 10 drops PEPPER OIL (never use PEPPER OIL neat or in the bath). Store in a labelled dark glass bottle and shake before use.

If pain persists seek medical advice.

See SCIATICA
See MUSCLES
See TENDINITIS
See NEURALGIA
See DEEP HEAT RUB   CHAPTER 6

TRAVEL SICKNESS
See NAUSEA

TYPISTS WRIST
See REPETITIVE STRAIN INJURY
See SPRAINS

U

ULCERATIVE COLITIS

Recurrent diarrhoea, depression, pain, ulcerative colitis is often caused by stress and poor eating habits. A well balanced, varied diet is essential. Herb teas such as chamomile & agrimony, slippery elm capsules or golden seal is sometimes prescribed by Herbalists. When all else fails a diet low in salicylates can bring about a marked improvement. Omit aspirin, all carbonated and 'coloured' drinks, all colourings and preservatives, spicy foods etc. For a list of low salicylate foods, contact a dietician/nutritionist.

Twice a day or when pain strikes you could try massaging stomach, solar plexus, lower back and soles of feet with a massage oil made with: 20ml CASTOR OIL, 10-15 drops CHAMOMILE OIL, 5 drops TEA TREE OIL, 10 drops YLANG YLANG.

See DIARRHOEA
See DEPRESSION
See STRESS
See ABDOMINAL PAIN
See IMMUNE SYSTEM BOOSTERS

ULCERS
See MOUTH ULCERS
See DIABETIC SORES
See VEINS

URETHRITIS
See CYSTITIS

URTICARIA
See HIVES

V

VAGINAL HYGIENE
See FEMININE HYGIENE
See THRUSH
See TOXIC SHOCK SYNDROME (TSS)

VAGINITIS
See THRUSH
See TEA TREE OIL PESSARIES CHAPTER 6

VARICOSE ULCERS

Apply oil as below (VEINS) as a preventative measure.

FOR TREATMENT See DIABETIC SORES (LEG)
See BED SORES
See IMMUNE SYSTEM BOOSTERS

VEINS

For varicose veins, always wear support stockings or support tights. Keep legs moving even when standing still, (walk on the spot at regular intervals). Your doctor may be able to prescribe 'paroven', a natural plant extract.

For alleviating pain from varicose veins try to elevate legs as often as possible, or for at least 2 hours during the day.

Lightly apply the following oil: mix 25ml SOYA OIL, 10-20ml VITAMIN E OIL, 10 drops TEA TREE OIL, 1ml CYPRESS OIL, 1ml LEMON OIL and 10 drops JUNIPER OIL and apply from ankle up in long gently firm strokes. Then elevate as suggested. Apply oil 1-2 times per day if possible. Do not use on broken or sore skin. (This may increase sensitivity to sunlight, in susceptible people). See DIABETIC SORES

Elevate end of bed by 2" with telephone directories or out of date mail order catalogues. Apply the above oil before going to bed.

Prevention Never: keep legs crossed for long periods, wear too high a heel, or wear tight filling jeans or underclothes. Always eat a well balanced, varied diet. Constipation may contribute to this condition. Always try to keep to your optimum weight. Herbs rich in silica and bioflavoniods are said

THE TEA TREE OIL ENCYCLOPEDIA

VEINS (CONT.)

to strengthen the walls of a vein, grapeseed pycnoginals (PCO'S), stinging nettle (dried) tea, melilot etc. Foods rich in rutin and lecithin may improve elasticity of veins, buckwheat, apricots etc.

Broken veins/capillaries (spider veins) apply the same mixture of oil and treat as for varicose veins. See a qualified practitioner for easy removal.

BROKEN VEINS ON FACE (Rosacea).

Broken veins and flushing to the face (cheeks) can be helped by massaging in the following oil: 20ml VITAMIN E OIL, 1 drop TEA TREE OIL, 2 drops LEMON OIL, 2 drops CHAMOMILE OIL, 2 drops MYRRH, 2 drops PALMAROSA OIL, mix well. Do not have contact with the eye area. Always use sunblock when out in the sun, and a good moisturiser when outside. **Tone the skin** with 1 tablespoon rosewater and 1 drop myrrh, 1 drop tea tree oil, 1 drop calendula oil and 1 drop palmarosa oil on cotton wool.

The diet, sun damage, steroid creams, or hormonal changes may play a part in this condition. The food, as above, (varicose veins) can be helpful, also a good wholefood diet, no caffeine, no alcohol and no smoking. Avoid 'yeasty' foods, Candida Albicans could be a likely cause, especially if you also have a vaginal discharge. See THRUSH

See CIRCULATORY PROBLEMS

VERRUCAES

Small black dots at the centre of a wart like infection, often on soles of feet. Verrucae oil can be made by mixing 10ml TEA TREE OIL with 10ml MYRRH RESIN. Store in dark brown glass bottle. Shake before use. Apply to verrucae 3-4 times per day. Apply clean plaster each time. After about 5-6 days inspect site, if area discoloured and soft the black dots in centre should be carefully removed using needle (dipped in neat TEA TREE OIL). Continue applying verrucae oil and covering with a plaster 3 times a day for 6 weeks or until healed.
Remember to keep area covered, at home and in public places, verrucaes are very infectious.
Neat TEA TREE OIL can also be applied as above, in place of the 'verrucae oil'. ***Prevention*** To help prevent the risk of verrucaes forming, apply neat TEA TREE OIL to soles of feet, before and after, going barefoot in public places - beware of slippery surfaces.

VIRAL INFECTIONS

When one person in the household is infected with a virus, the chances are that other members of the family will become infected too. An anti-viral household spray should help to combat a virus spreading through the air. The solution can also be used to wipe telephone mouthpieces, toilet seats, door handles etc. In a 1 pint atomiser spray (plant mister) put 500ml of warm water, 3ml TEA TREE OIL, 3ml NIAOULI OIL, 3ml HOUTTUYNIA CORDATA, 3ml LEMON OIL and 3ml LAVENDER OIL. Always shake well before use.

An anti-viral oil to use is: 30ml SOYA OIL, 20 ml VITAMIN E OIL, 2ml TEA TREE OIL, 2ml NIAOULI OIL, 2ml HOUTTUYNIA CORDATA OIL and 2ml LAVENDER OIL. Apply to viral sores, use as a massage oil to back. Add 2-3 drops of the above essential oils to an aromatherapy lamp, the bath or to a humidifier.

Echinacea (purple coneflower) is often taken for viral infections, tablets, tincture and a refreshing tea (dried root) is available from Herbalists.

See IMMUNE SYSTEM BOOSTERS
See SHINGLES
See CHICKEN POX
See COLD SORES
See HERPES
See COLDS AND FLU
See MEASLES

W X Y Z

WARTS

Small hard growths (some with a cauliflower head appearance) affecting hands, fingers, face, elbows or knees. They are thought to be contagious.
Dab wart at first signs with neat TEA TREE OIL 3-4 times a day. May take over 6 weeks to clear, depending on size, and how long you have had it etc.

WATER RETENTION
See OEDEMA

WAXING
See HAIR REMOVAL

WHEEZING

A wheezing child must have medical attention as soon as possible.

See ASTHMA
See BRONCHITIS
See COLDS AND FLU

WHITEHEADS

See ACNE
See BLACKHEADS
See BOILS

WOUNDS

Deep wounds should have medical attention as soon as possible. Sprinkle with TEA TREE OIL, cover and apply pressure to stop bleeding. If severe, ring for an ambulance.

See CUTS AND ABRASIONS
See BITES
See SPLINTERS

WRINKLES

To soften wrinkles, apply to face and neck, 1 tablespoon oil made from: 25ml BORAGE OIL, 25ml VITAMIN E OIL, 10-20 drops ROSE OIL (Pure rose oil is very expensive so optional substitute: 5 drops SWEET ORANGE OIL, 5 drops MYRRH and 10 drops PALMAROSA OIL) and 2 drops TEA TREE OIL.

Patch test a small area on face for 48hrs. Massage in warmed oil twice a day (avoid contact with eyes, if stinging occurs wash well in cool water). Cover with a warm towel to help absorption.

ROSE TONER To keep skin firm, tone skin with rose toner daily.

To make toner: take 100gms pink or red, fragrance rose petals, 100ml white wine vinegar, 500ml distilled water, 2ml ROSEWOOD OIL and 5 drops TEA TREE OIL. Place rose petals, vinegar and 100-200ml of the water into a liquidiser and blend on high speed until smooth, leave overnight. Strain through a fine mesh sieve and through double muslin, squeeze out all the liquid. Add to the rest of the distilled water, add TEA TREE and ROSE-WOOD OIL. Shake well and use a little on cotton wool, after cleansing and before moisturising. Bottle, label, date and use within 8 weeks.

ANTI-WRINKLE CREAM To keep skin moisturised, apply twice per day.

1. You could buy a base, natural, pH neutral cream and add 10 drops ROSE-WOOD OIL, 10 drops CALENDULA OIL, 10 drops PALMAROSA OIL and 5 drops TEA TREE OIL - per 50gms of cream, warm the cream gently, stir in the warmed oils, stir until cold and return to jar. OR....

2. Take 15gms Beeswax, 15gms Anhydrous lanolin (you can use 30gms beeswax, or emulsifying wax, if allergic to lanolin) and melt over heat in a double saucepan, or in a glass (pyrex) jug in the microwave, on 3 minute bursts on high, do not leave unattended. (The wax mix reaches a very high temperature, children and pets must not be allowed in the kitchen). Remove from heat with oven gloves, even in the microwave the jug gets very hot. Stand on a heatproof, non-slip mat and stir until just warm, dribble (stir) in 25ml (warmed) rose water, 25ml (warmed) VITAMIN E OIL, 25ml (warmed) BORAGE OIL while stirring to cool, (if curdling occurs, warm oil again, until liquefied and stir vigorously until just warm), then add the above essential oils, plus 10 drops SWEET ORANGE OIL, stir until cool. Store in sterilised glass jar, label, date, use within 6 months. To apply warm 1 teaspoon in palms, by rubbing vigorously, spread onto face and neck, massage in.
See SKIN CARE   See CHAPTER 6

YEAST INFECTIONS
See THRUSH

ZOSTER
See SHINGLES
See VIRAL INFECTIONS
See HERPES

Chapter Eight

The Essence Of Aromatherapy & Massage

Aromatherapy

The ancient Egyptian, Hebrew, Indian and Chinese cultures are known to have practised an early form of aromatherapy for both ritual and medicinal purposes, harnessing the power of natural plant resins and perfumes to balance the body and heighten spiritual awareness.

Aromatherapy is becoming popular once again, as people look to the more holistic form of therapies, to help in combating the unbalancing effects of modern day life. The holistic approach is to treat the body as a whole, spiritually, physically and emotionally rather than to treat the individual symptoms of a particular illness.

Organic plants and their oils, like ourselves, have a potent energy; synthetics and chemicals may be able to mimic the healing properties of plants, to some degree, but they will never possess the actual life-force that works in harmony with our systems and so balances our whole being.

One of the most eminent writers on the subject is Dr Deepak Chopra, and to explain the concept of aromatherapy there is no better way than to quote from his best selling book "PERFECT HEALTH", a must for every bookshelf.

"The odours that can be detected by the nose must first
dissolve in the moisture of the nasal tissue and are then
passed on by specialised olfactory cells straight to the
Hypothalamus in the brain.......... "

".......The fact that smells go straight to the Hypothalamus
is very significant, for this tiny organ is responsible for
regulating dozens of bodily functions, including
temperature, thirst, hunger, blood sugars level, growth,
sleeping, waking, sexual arousal and emotions such as
anger and happiness. To smell anything is to send an
immediate message to 'the brain's brain' and from it to
the whole body..... "

".......At the same time the message of an odour goes to
the brain's limbic system which processes emotions and
to an area called the hippocampus, the part of the brain
responsible for memory, which is why smells bring back
past memories so vividly. Kitchen smells, flowers and
perfumes can all trigger a sense of "deja-vu"

How to obtain the best quality oils

It is prudent to consult a qualified Aromatherapist when dealing with essential oils. Some of the oils can be as dangerous as drugs in inexperienced hands. An Aromatherapist can supply the oils for home use and give advice on how to use them to their best effect.

When purchasing oils be aware that some labels marked 'Aromatherapy Quality' are not always pure essential oils. Try to find a reputable supplier who relays as much information about the oil as possible, either on the label, or in a separate fact sheet. Make sure that your Aromatherapist knows the supplier, the suppliers background and the way the oils were distilled. It is vital that all these queries are satisfied, if you are to be assured that the oils are pure and unadulterated.

'Cutting' by chemicals and or cheaper alternatives is quite common, and very difficult to detect. The suppliers who care about the art of aromatherapy will have done all the research work necessary. They will have traced the oil they purchase right back to the distillation process and, usually, even to the plantations themselves. They will be proud to supply as much information as possible to the end user, and you will know that you have the best quality oil, with the best therapeutic properties, available.

Remember the essentials

No organic oil could ever truly have a synthetic counterpart. Not only would the synthetic not carry a living plants life-force, it would never be able to copy the many and varied molecules that work synergistically together, to create the unique therapeutic properties of a pure oil. That is why the term 'nature identical' has never worked in reality.

The synergy of molecules and constituents not only give organic oils their unique aroma, it also gives them their therapeutic value and indeed their toxicity. Only a qualified diagnostic Aromatherapist, who understands this synergy, should ever attempt to mix and use the more toxic, aromatherapy medicinal blends. Essential oils must never be taken orally as a medicine, unless under a qualified practitioners supervision.

The elderly, pregnant women and children do have to be very careful when using essential oils. In the case of pregnancy some quite innocent sounding oils should be avoided altogether. Oils such as Sage, Clary Sage, Parsley Basil, Rosemary and Cedarwood to name but a few. My advice would be to stop aromatherapy, as soon as you decide to start a family, unless otherwise directed by your doctor.

The elderly, children and babies should only use very diluted forms of essential oils diluted in approximately 90% to 25% of carrier oil.

Essential oils should not be stored for long periods as some of the constituents may change into different forms; especially citrus oils such as Neroli, Lemon, Mandarin etc. They should only be bought fresh and not stored for too long. This also applies to oils that have been left open without a top. Essential oils should really have a 'use by' date on the bottle for safety reasons. Oils, mixes and preparations should be stored in labelled, airtight, dark glass bottles, away from direct sunlight and preferably in a cool place.

Never use an aromatherapy oil without first doing a skin sensitivity test, whether it is for an inhalation or a massage. Put a drop of the oil onto your wrist and cover for at least 24 hours. If no reaction it should be safe to use. Do not use oils you are sensitive to, even for inhalations. It is advised not to use neat oils everyday and only use when needed for a specific condition.

Apart from first aid applications, essential oils can be enjoyed in a variety of ways:

IN THE BATH

A few drops of essential oil works wonders when relaxing in the warm waters of a bath. Be aware that not all essential oils can be used in the bath, ie mint, ginger, pepper, horseradish, etc. always check the label before using.

AS AN INHALATION

*Add 5-10 drops to a bowl of steaming water - gently inhale vapours.

*5+ drops added to water in an aromatherapy lamp (follow instructions).

Add a few drops to a handkerchief (or tissues in a small plastic bag). (Be very careful of young children with hot water, plastic bags and candles).

AS A MASSAGE OIL (Mixed with a carrier oil)

Massage into skin using firm even strokes.

See MASSAGE BLENDS - Do not use neat essential oils for massage.

AS A 'PERFUME' (For home made Pot Pourri etc.)

Sprinkle onto matured Pot Pourri, or dyed Fullers Earth in ashtray.

AS A HUMIDIFIER (Home made)

Sprinkle dampened cotton wool balls with oil and tie one cotton wool ball to each end of an 12" piece of string and drape over radiators. Or purchase one of the many commercial humidifiers that are readily available.

Each oil has its own characteristics, here is a simple guide to the more popular oils. Use one choice from whichever section you feel fits your particular mood. Either use a few drops in the bath (unless otherwise stated), or in an aromatherapy lamp. **Oils should not be used neat (on the skin) in this section**

THERAPEUTIC OILS - WHEN FEELING UNDER PAR

Tea Tree	Lavender
Niaouli	Rosemary
Eucalyptus	Juniper (often adulterated with turpenine oil)

UPLIFTING OILS - WHEN GLOOMY - WITH HEADACHE

Clary-sage	Ylang Ylang
Melissa (very expensive oil often adulterated and sold cheaper)	Tea Tree
	Lavender
Ginger (never use neat Ginger oil on skin or in the bath.)	Geranium

EXHILARATING - NEEDING MOTIVATION - GET UP AND GO

Neroli* (Expensive often adulterated)	Peppermint (Mint oils must never be used neat or in the bath)
Grapefruit*	Lemon*
Lime*	Mandarin*

ENTERTAINING GUESTS - SETTING THE RIGHT ATMOSPHERE

Bergamot	Rosewood
Lemon	Sandalwood
Geranium	Neroli* (See above)

* All citrus oils should be stored in dark bottles in a cool place - only buy fresh oils. **Never** use bergamot, lemon, grapefruit oils on skin that is exposed to sunlight.

SOOTHING - WHEN FEELING NERVY AND STRESSED

Benzoin
(Benzoin is a known allergen. Caution
if prone to allergies, otherwise do not
forget to do a sensitivity test)

Geranium

Cedarwood

Petitgrain* (often adulterated with
cedar oils)

Mandarin*

Neroli* (expensive-often adulterated.)

Lavender

RELAXING - NEEDING TO TAKE THE PRESSURE OFF

Benzoin (See above)

Chamomile

Sandalwood

Ylang Ylang

SLEEP INDUCING - FOR INSOMNIACS

Lavender

Ylang Ylang

Chamomile

Palmarosa

APHRODISIAC - SETTING THE MOOD

Benzoin (See above)

Sandalwood

Patchouli (is often adulterated with cedar oils)

Ylang Ylang   Savoury

MEDITATION - DEEP THINKING

Frankincense   Myrrh   Cardamom

Benzoin (See above)   Caraway   Juniper (See above)

Sandalwood   Cedarwood

*All citrus oils should be stored in dark bottles in a cool place - only buy fresh oils.

OVER BURDENED - HAVING TOO MANY RESPONSIBILITIES

* Rosemary   Rosewood

Palmarosa

* Rosemary oil should be used with caution or avoided if
suffering from high blood pressure.

PRONE TO TANTRUMS - ESPECIALLY CHILDREN

*Chamomile   *Lavender

* Please remember that children and babies should only come
into contact with essential oil that has been greatly diluted.

FEARFUL - PRONE TO PHOBIAS

Chamomile   Frankincense

Sandalwood   Lavender

Ylang Ylang   *Marjoram

* Marjoram should not be used on the young, without the
assistance of a qualified Aromatherapist. Use with care.

GRIEF - SUFFERING LOSS

Marjoram   Tangerine (Citrus oils must be fresh
(See above)   they do not keep very well)

* Ginger   Ylang Ylang

Frankincense   Sweet Orange

* Do not use neat ginger oils on the skin or in the bath.

Massage

Massage with natural oils is the perfect way to assist the body's healing process. It can soothe away nervous tension, headaches and stress. The gentle rubbing action activates the skin's nerve endings, stimulates the circulation and helps the rejuvenation of the cells.

Singularly or with a partner, massage is very therapeutic as well as calming, especially for fractious children - (use less than half of the amount of essential oils for children).

See following pages for massage blends and carrier oils. Do not use neat essential oil for massage. Before you start have a warm bath or shower, this will help the absorption of the oils and nutrients into your skin.

Place a large towel on the floor or bed, sit on the towel, pour 1/2 teaspoon of your chosen massage oil into the palm of your left hand, gently massage your right shoulder, rising up into the neck area, with a circular anti-clockwise motion. (Use your right hand clockwise and your left hand anti-clockwise, for areas behind your back).

Using both hands (both in an anti-clockwise motion this time) massage a little oil into your temples, between your eyebrows (1 hand), behind your ears and your ear lobes (both hands). Using your right hand, massage from the dip at the back of the neck, up to the base of your skull with light, warming circular movements.

Massage your chest, arms, legs and feet with light, but firm, long circular motions, always work towards the heart (from feet upwards, scalp downwards and clockwise, circular motions in the middle - Solar plexus).

Massage is not recommended for people with varicose veins or deep vein thrombosis. If you have a medical problem, or are unsure of your health, you must always consult a qualified practitioner before beginning any massage techniques.

To improve circulation

Add 2 drops Juniper oil, 3 drops Wintergreen oil and 2 drops of Tea Tree oil to your carrier oil, ie. 10ml soya oil, mix well. Apply massage oil to the back of the ankle, using your thumb and forefinger rub and pinch gently, for a few minutes, repeat on the other side. Apply oil to your knuckles, massage the base of your feet from arch to heel, and then repeat on the other foot. Still sitting, and again apply oil to your knuckles, firmly stroke from back of knee, upwards to top of thighs (buttocks). Wrap yourself in a towel and lie back with legs raised by (covered) cushions for 10 minutes.

Solar plexus and stomach   (not to be attempted in pregnancy)

Comfortably, but firmly, press your oiled palm into the solar plexus (between your ribs and your stomach) and massage in a clockwise direction only. Use the same method lower down, for the stomach. This is essentially beneficial for women's problems. Massage in 1 teaspoon of soya oil mixed with 3 drops of Clary sage oil - **never substitute with sage oil.** For a man, 3 drops of Moroccan Cedarwood oil in 1 teaspoon of soya oil should be used.

Scalp

Massaging your scalp is particularly good for tiredness and loss of hair. Using your fingertips (lightly moistened with: 1 teaspoon grapeseed oil and 3 drops of Tea Tree oil), firmly massage scalp as if washing your hair.

Back

Ask your partner to massage your back: lie on your stomach with your bare back uppermost. They should apply a massage oil to your neck and smooth down the centre of your back. Massage neck in light circles using thumb and fingers. Resting both hands on your shoulders (either side of neck/spine) and keeping hands still, gently but firmly, massage fleshy part of back (below neck) with thumbs in a circular motion, using shoulders as a pivot for both sets of fingers. Then with the same thumb movement, move palms up and down either side of the spine, in a slight circular motion, out across the shoulder blades to the arms. Back across the tops of the shoulders to the nape of the neck with a scissor like pinching motion, gently squeezing as you go. Take the thumbs down either side of the spine keeping them about 1-2cms out from the spine, down to the coccyx and continue out to the sides of the back, slowly return (along the sides) up to below the arms, and across the shoulder blades. Finish by letting your palms flow across the oiled back, up and down in slow circular movements, for a couple of minutes. You must never press too firmly and you must never cause the recipient any pain.

Feet and hands

Massaging feet and hands can be very therapeutic. Vigorously follow the contours with firm, flowing strokes. Pay particular attention to the soles of the feet, rub in a circular motion with knuckles to invigorate circulation.

Many reflexology points can be stimulated by using this simple technique, boosting the immune system and generally giving the recipient a feeling of well-being. This coupled with the discerning use of essential oils can boost physical and mental alertness and well-being.

The following blends are personal favourites, everyone has their own likes and dislikes, you can experiment or consult an Aromatherapist, who will advise you on blending your own oils. To make a massage oil: first select a carrier oil and add *25-30 drops of your chosen oil or blends of oils.

DELUXE MASSAGE CARRIER BLEND

        10ml Borage oil
        10ml Avocado oil
        10ml Wheatgerm oil
        10ml Sea Buckthorn oil
        50ml Grapeseed oil
        *25-30 drops selected essential oils

STANDARD MASSAGE BLEND

        75ml Sweet Almond oil
        10ml Wheatgerm oil
        *25-30 drops selected essential oils.

Pour oils into a 100ml, dark glass bottle, label, date and use within 3 months. Always store in a cool, dark place. Shake well before each use.
For a serious or persistent medical condition you must be diagnosed and treated by a qualified Aromatherapist in conjunction with your doctor.
People with high blood pressure or epilepsy use Rosemary oil sparingly or omit altogether.

For relaxing to exhilarating blends and a list of oils and their qualities please see the following pages:

THERAPEUTIC BLEND

Symptom: feeling under par - colds and flu.

        5 drops Tea Tree oil
        10 drops Oregano oil
        7 drops Niaouli oil
        7 drops Lemon oil

Add to one of the above carrier oils and apply a little of the warmed oil to the skin on back and chest, cover for 10 minutes, then massage in.

*UPLIFTING BLEND

Symptom: mildly depressed/headache/chilled.

> 7 drops Ginger oil
> 15 drops Ylang Ylang oil
> 8 drops Sandalwood oil

*EXHILARATING BLEND

Symptom: lacking motivation/energy.

> 10 drops Mandarin oil
> 10 drops Thyme oil
> 15 drops Rosewood oil

OR

> 10 drops Tea Tree oil
> *10 drops Rosemary oil
> 10 drops Sweet Orange oil

*(CAUTION - HIGH BLOOD PRESSURE SUFFERERS)

*RELAXING BLEND

Symptom: feeling pressured, cannot take anymore.

> 6 drops Geranium oil
> 10 drops Ylang Ylang oil
> 7 drops Benzoin
> 7 drops Sandalwood oil

*SOOTHING

Symptom: feeling nervy and stressed.

> 10 drops Clary Sage oil
> 10 drops Benzoin
> 10 drops Ylang Ylang oil

SLEEP INDUCING

Symptom: insomnia.

> 10 drops Ylang Ylang oil
> 20 drops Chamomile oil

OR

> 20 drops Lavender oil
> 10 drops Benzoin

APHRODISIAC

Symptom: low sex drive.

> 10 drops Benzoin
> 5 drops Savoury oil
> 5 drops Sandalwood oil

OR

> 5 drops Ginger oil
> 7 drops Savoury oil
> 10 drops Ylang Ylang oil
> 5 drops Cedarwood oil

MEDITATION

Promotes deep thinking.

> 5 drops Juniper oil
> 5 drops Patchouli oil
> 5 drops Benzoin
> 5 drops Sandalwood oil
> 5 drops Cardamom oil
> 5 drops Frankincense oil

*Mix with selected carrier oils, and apply a little of the warmed oil to the skin (back and chest), cover for 10 minutes, then massage in.
Remember: For children, you must halve (or less) the essential oils.

Facials

Facials are very therapeutic and relaxing, as well as helping to keep the skin toned and young looking.

See CHAPTER 6 / SECTION 3 for cleansers, moisturisers, toners and skin fresheners to use under the following headings.

1) **Tie back hair**, if applicable.

2) **Wash face** (remove make-up if applicable) with a flannel soaked in warm water and a very mild soap. Baby oil makes a very good eye make-up remover, rinse. Pat dry, with a soft towel.

3) **Cleanse** the face and neck using a cleansing milk/cream. Massage in using firm even strokes, wait 5 minutes and remove with cotton wool. Always work from the outside in, taking care not to stretch the delicate skin around the eyes. Avoid the eye area, baby lotion may be used instead.

4) **Freshen** the face and neck with a skin freshener to tone the skin and remove traces of cleanser. Avoid the eye area.

5) **A facial sauna** deep cleanses the pores, improves the circulation and helps to eliminate toxins. Avoid in cases of broken veins/capillaries (rosacea), or medical conditions, such as asthma, etc.

Facial sauna blends

Add the following essential oils to a bowl of steaming water, place towel over head and bowl, close eyes and inhale through the nose, exhaling through the mouth for 10 minutes. Pat face dry with cotton wool.

DEEP CLEANSING

5 drops Tea Tree oil
3 drops Rosemary oil
2 drops Lime oil

GREASY SKINS

3 drops Tea Tree oil
3 drops Juniper oil
3 drops Lemon oil

NORMAL SKINS

3 drops Tea Tree oil
5 drops Pettigrain oil
1 drop   Benzoin

DRY/SENSITIVE SKINS

2 drops Tea Tree oil
3 drops Galbanum
7 drops Palmarosa oil

REMOVING DEAD SKIN CELLS

5 drops Tea Tree oil.
5 drops Geranium oil
5 drops Lemon oil.

MATURE SKINS

2 drops Tea Tree oil
5 drops Patchouli oil.
5 drops Rose oil
(Rose oil is very expensive, often
adulterated & sold much cheaper)

6) **Apply a nourishing face pack** and relax for 20 minutes. I like to apply to the face and neck. This will feed the skin, draw more toxins out from the pores and give a much clearer, healthier complexion. Remove with soft tissues and wash off the excess, splash the face and neck with cold water, this will help to keep your muscles toned. Pat face and neck dry.

7) **Tone the skin** with a toner from chapter 6.

8) **Apply a moisturiser** and lightly massage in with finger tips - always work from outside in to avoid stretching the skin unnecessarily.

9) **Gently tap** along the jaw line with fingertips to tone and improve the circulation. Tap the hollow from each side of the nose to the corners of the mouth. Tap cheek bones lightly around the sides of the nose. From the outside edge of the eyebrows, tap along to the centre, gently massage and tap the temples either side of the face. Raise eye brows and stroke up from the tear duct to outside edge of eye brow.

10) **Massage** face including neck and ears following the contours of the skin. Do not stretch the skin.

MY OWN FAVOURITE BLENDS ARE: (Fill in as necessary)

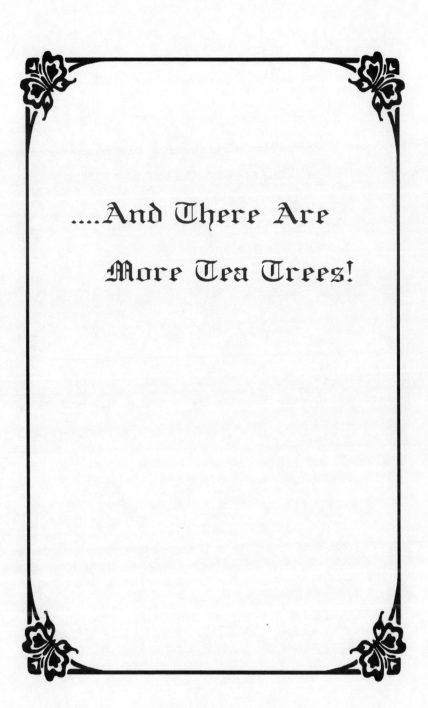

.....And There Are
More Tea Trees!

Before the Australian botanical names were classified, Captain James Cook, on landing first in Australia and then in New Zealand, named the many aromatic trees he found there as 'Tea Trees'. Although the 'Tea Trees' do not all come from the same genera, they are of the same botanical family (*Myrtaceae*) and they do share similar therapeutic properties.

Listed below are a few of the many 'Tea Trees' that we now are able to obtain essential oils from:

NIAOULI OIL

The Broad Leaf Paperbark Tree, *Melaleuca Quinquenervia* and *Melaleuca viridiflora*. These trees are grown in New Caledonia, Tasmania and parts of Europe. They are used as a strong antiseptic especially of the urinary system. The high Cineole content (40%-60%) suggests that some people may find it a skin irritant if used in high concentrations. As with the Cajuput oil (below) it is effective in Rheumatic preparations and as an inhalant for the respiratory system. Scientific research in France suggests that it has anti-viral properties. Niaouli is also used in Veterinary products.

CAJUPUT OIL

White (pale) Tea Tree, *Melaleuca Cajuputi,* and *Melaleuca Leucadendron*. These trees found in Asia and Australia are used extensively in medicine and as an insecticide. The Cineole content being much higher (50%-75%) than that of *M. Alternifolia* it is not used on the skin in high concentrations. But is useful as an ingredient in Rheumatic preparations and as an inhalant. It is a useful sudorific (induces sweating).

Other Tea Trees from the *Melaleuc*a genus are: *M. Bracteata, M. Hypericifolia, M. decussata, M. Thymifola, M. Erucifolia, M. Linarifolia, M. Minor*, etc. Some of these oils are mixed with *M. Alternifolia* by less scrupulous companies. Care should be taken not to buy a *Melaleuca* oil without its type name displayed and only from a reputable supplier.

EUCALYPTUS OIL

Another probable 'Tea Tree' named by Captain Cook, *(Eucalyptus Globulus, E. Polybractea, E. Smithii, E. Radiata, E. Dives, E. Citriodora. etc.)* also known as Gum trees, It is the leaves of the Eucalyptus that contain the essential oil. There are over 250 constituents incl. Cineole (75%-90%), so it should not to be used on the skin in a high concentrations. It is included in Rheumatic embrocations, Cough medicines, Colds, Flu, (respiratory) Nasal decongestants, Medicinal skin ointments and Insecticidal preparations.

THE NEW ZEALAND TEA TREES

The 'Tea Trees' from New Zealand are from the same family *Myrtaceae*, but are from the genus *Leptospermum*. They have been used medicinally for centuries by the Maori people.

MANUKA OIL (Tairawhiti Manuka)

Leptospermum Scoparium, still grows wild and is harvested from the East Cape area. Although it grows in other areas, the trees from the East Cape seem to give a more anti-microbial activity. Manuka oil has a pleasant, heavier medicinal, more earthy, balsamic aroma than Tea Tree oil, and has a much thicker (more complex) consistency. It is steam-distilled from the combined, leaves, flowers and small terminal branches. In tests Manuka oil seems to be about 20 times stronger than the *M. Alternifolia* against Gram positive bacteria, but not quite as good against Gram negative bacterium. It shows exciting results against Tinea, (Athletes foot and Ringworm). It has passed conformity and toxicity tests in France (1992) and has been used internally (under medical supervision), so a low toxicity is suggested. Obviously more tests need to be carried out, but Manuka oil seems to have a very promising future in the Cosmetic, Pharmaceutical, and Veterinary Industries. Like the Melaleuca Alternifolia, the future of the oil of Manuka is in our hands....

Principle constituents are: Leptospermone 15>%, Isoleptospermone 5% Flavesone 5>%, Calamanene 16>%.

KANUKA OIL

Leptospermum Ericoides is distilled as Manuka oil above, and has a pleasant spicy, medicinal aroma, not as heavy as Manuka, but not as light as Tea Tree; the consistency also mirrors this analogy. It is similar (but not quite as active) to Tea Tree in anti-microbial activity. Kanuka oil has very good analgesic (pain killing) and skin penetration properties. Especially beneficial to arthritic and rheumatic conditions. ......And a very promising future in the Industries, as for Manuka.

* Essential Oils can also be distilled from this family: *Leptospermum Pertersonii, L. Citratum, L. Liversidgei,* etc.

* A honey made by bees feeding on the flowers of the *Leptospermum Scoparium* has caused quite a stir in New Zealand. Scientific tests are very promising, the honey seems to have high anti-microbial activity and has applications for Surgical Procedures (to reduce scarring), Stomach Ulcers, Irritable Bowel Syndrome, Ulcerative Colitis etc. and Urinary Tract Infections.

.... And Into The
21st Century

The 1990's are an exciting time for the oil of the *Melaleuca Alternifolia*.......

Commonwealth Industrial Gases in Australia have perfected the use of Tea Tree oil in industrial air ⁀nditioning systems. This has proven to inhibit the growth of mould, bacteria and fungi. Less germs, less respiratory infections, less food contamination, less unsightly mildew on walls, more peace of mind. An effective prevention of Legionnaires disease in our hospitals perhaps ??? And maybe opening the way for an anti-viral gas ???

Chlorinated phenols, such as topical disinfectants (Dettol) are a relatively inexpensive alternative to Tea Tree oil. Many leading medical and surgical researchers have concluded that they are limited in their continual use because of the build up of resistance to them by pathological organisms.

Botanists are exploring the possibilities of fungal treatments for trees.
New research is underway for the effectiveness of Tea Tree oil as a natural fungicide and pesticide for our fruit... Not before time. Let us hope that it can replace harmful pesticides and fungicides that poison our systems and land.

It is being tested in agriculture. Scandinavian farmers are using Tea Tree oil for cattle diseases. Denmark has reported success with Tea Tree oil for Mastitis in cows. In Australia it has possible uses for delousing sheep, tick treatments, fungal foot diseases and pest control.

The Cosmetic, Toiletry and Pharmaceutical Industries are becoming interested in Tea Tree oil for its 'active' anti-bacterial and anti-fungal characteristics.

It is used to inhibit fungal growth in carpets & soft furnishings.

Perhaps new research will somehow find an application for helping to alleviate the spread of Aids. I for one welcome the extended use of Tea Tree oil from the *Melaleuca Alternifolia* - I hope that research goes from strength to strength as world-wide demand grows. Perhaps the answer would be to just use Tea Tree oil *M.A.* with the low Cineole and the high Terpinen-4-ol content for topical medicinal and cosmetic applications, and encourage the research into cultivation in similar climates around Australia, Asia, Zimbabwe, California etc. The oil would probably be slightly different but it still may have viable world wide agricultural and botanical applications without putting a strain on the valuable supplies in New South Wales.

Or maybe mixing the *'Melaleuca Alternifolia'* with another broad spectrum 'Tea Tree oil' ie. Manuka oil (*Leptospermum Scoparium*), would be the answer .... Time and demand will tell.......

.......AND FINALLY

The computer will never match the brain's ability of independent free will - there is a vital energy missing - just as synthetic compounds will never have the same broad spectrum capabilities that natures own blends have.

An excerpt below from Nina Turpin's book *"The Healing Wonder From Down Under"* raises the issue of looking to nature to provide the 'solution' to the 20th Century and maybe even the 21st Century 'superbugs'.

FOOD FOR THOUGHT

Most of us have heard about the latest media sensation: the "flesh-eating bacteria"...

*This condition is caused by the group A. streptococcus bacteria. The bacteria is actually quite common, and causes a variety of mild infections, such as strep throat. In some cases, however, the organism multiplies and spreads very rapidly to many areas of the body, including the bloodstream. In 5%to 10% of infected people, this can then lead to a condition known as **necrotizing fasciitis**, where-in the infection causes the breakdown of muscle and fat tissue.*

Although the condition is not particularly common, 2-3000 people die from necrotizing fasciitis each year, while 10-15000 people suffer severe infection requiring surgery and sometimes amputation.

The disease occurs mostly in adults, and although the exact reason for its development in particular individuals is not known, there is believed to be an element of host susceptibility involved. The same type of bacteria can cause severe infection in one person while leading to only mild infection in the next. Medical professionals do believe, however, that most cases can be prevented if given timely treatment.

The bacteria seems to prey on wounds in which subdermal tissues are exposed. It is essential that such wounds be carefully cleansed and regularly disinfected (for example, after surgery or injury).

Tea Tree oil has been shown to inhibit many different strains of the Streptococci bacteria, even in very diluted solutions.

> *Definitely merits further study, wouldn't you agree?*

*Since starting this book, I have heard that a few British Health Authorities are doing tests on TEA TREE OIL *MA*, to assist them in combating the recent spread of MRSA 16 (Staph Bacteria), that is plaguing our hospitals.... Is our medical profession coming around to 'natural' alternatives at last???....

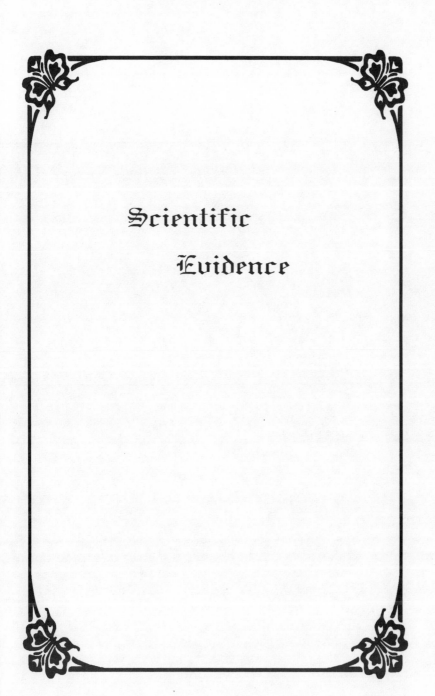

Scientific
Evidence

"The oil of the *Melaleuca Alternifolia* is a pale yellow viscous liquid with a spicy aroma. It is composed of a complex mixture of Monoterpenes, Terpinen-4-ol, Cineole and other hydrocarbons". (Pena 1962).

The first official project by A.R. Penfold (1923-5) stated that " The oil of the Tea Trees *M.A.* contained essential oil which exhibited antiseptic and bactericidal properties 13 times stronger than carbolic acid". (Rideal-walker coefficient).

Doctors in Australia began to use the oil of *Melaleuca* in the 1930's. Abstract on therapeutics printed in the Medical Journal of Australia read ....." it is too early to determine its actual therapeutic place and powers, but sufficient information has become available to justify extensive trials in diverse conditions." (Anon 1930).

"Most synthetics lose some of their effectiveness when applied to blood, pus, serum, (organic matter). Tea Tree oil actually increases its effectiveness in the presence of the same".

Penfold (1920's) suggested that it increased "from 10% to 12 1/2% in the presence of organic matter."

Dr Garrod of London demonstrated that Tea Tree oil was as much as seven times more effective on organic matter (in the growth inhibiting and destruction of micro-organisms) than it was in the sterile conditions of a test tube. *(ANECDOTAL: "One more good reason why we should use natural products rather than try to concoct synthetic alternatives").*

The Australian Journal of Dentistry printed an article which said "An antiseptic which more nearly answers the ideal than any previously tested" (Macdonald 1930).... "and in general surgery it should be of even greater value".

The 'Ideal' was;

      1) Of high antiseptic power
      2) Non-irritant of tissue cells
      3) Non-toxic
      4) Good penetration properties
      5) Active against a wide range of organisms

One of the first scientific papers summarising personal applications was written by E.M. Humphrey (1930) *"The cleansing and dressing of dirty wounds"...."A New Australian Germicide"...."dis-infection properties in Typhoid Bacilli was over 60 times more powerful than soap."....."Dissolved pus - left the infected surfaces of a wound clean"....."No apparent damage to skin tissues"......"An efficient antiseptic mouthwash"..."Benefit to dentistry and infections of the naso pharynx"..."outstanding deodorant properties"... "gargle for sore throats".. "an outstanding treatment for several parasitic skin diseases"... "nail infections".....Paronychia which resisted previous treatments for months cured within four weeks."*

Melasol - a soluble Tea Tree oil marketed by one of the early 1930's commercial outlets- Australian Essential Oils Ltd. - "used to disinfect and dress a large diabetic ulcer, which healed without re-infection" (Halford 1936).

In 1936 the crew HMS SUSSEX were treated, much to their relief, for athletes foot (Tinea pedis) during their stay at Alexandria in Egypt.

Mr H. James, Managing Director of Australian Essential Oils Ltd., pioneered valuable research into his products; 'Melasol', used as a disinfectant and inhalant was reviewed in 'Preparations and Applications'. In the British Medical Journal (Anon 1933) and the Lipophilic properties exploited in a germicidal soap.

By 1937 abstracts of successful treatment of a wide range of throat and mouth infections (nasopharygitis - catarrh - tonsillitis - mouth ulcers -thrush - phtous - stomatitis - sore throats - dental nerve capping and haemorrhaging - pyorrhoea - gingivitis - paronychia - empyema - various gynaecological conditions - Epidermophyton - infections of the skin (psoriasis) - impetigo - contagiosum - pediculosis - ringworm - tinea - candida - skin injuries. (Penfold and Humphrey.)

A magazine "Poultry" Nov. 1936 advocated the use of Ti-Trol oil (commercially available with Melasol) to prevent cannibalism in poultry, with the rapid healing of wounds and deodorising properties.

In 1939 a chemist R Goldsborough reported a 3% Tea Tree oil shampoo was used extensively as a treatment for dandruff.

As previously stated in Chapter 1, Tea Tree oil was used extensively during The Second World War - during the 40's and 50's demand had apparently all but ceased, so not a lot of research work has been documented; until 1960.

In January 1960, Henry Feinblatt M.D. F.A.C.P. an American doctor from New York did a controlled scientific study of Tea Tree oil M.A. His work titled "Cajuput-type Oil" and "Treatment of Furunculosis" was published by the Journal of the National Medical Association... "Application of neat oil on boils - 2-3 times per day seemed to hasten recovery and reduce the need for surgery".

In 1962 Dr Eduardo Pena from Florida published his work in Obstetrics and Gynaecology, Vol 19 for Melaleuca Alternifolia oil; "Its use for Trichonomal Vaginitis and other Vaginal Infections".
The conclusion was - "highly effective in the treatments of Trichonomal Vaginitis, Moniliasis Cervicitis and Chronic Endocervicitis--- The oil is highly fungistatic---- A 40% solution of 'MA' oil produced no side effects. Melaleuca Alternifolia is non-poisonous and non-irritant... A 20% solution is effective for Cervicitis although effective against bacteria it has no detrimental effect on healthy tissue"....."A 4% of the M.A. oil has proven safe as a daily vaginal douche in approximately 1 litre of water and an effective treatment for conditions considered......Tea Tree oil of the Melaleuca Alternifolia is a penetrating germicide and fungistatic--- dissolving pus and debris".

In the 1960's Feinblatt concluded....."Tea Tree oil mixes with sebaceous secretions....to gain entrance in the top layers of skin....affecting subcutaneous layers, carrying disinfecting action deeper than emollient creams...non-toxic, non-irritant, the oil can be used in stronger solutions than other preparations... it provides powerful germicidal activity without irritation...the oil encourages more rapid healing without scarring than other conservative treatments.

In 1970 G.H. Fawcett and D. M. Spencer suggested that essential oils may provide fungicides that are biodegradable, non carcinogenic and less phytotoxic than the normal preservative agents used in modern cosmetic and toiletry products.

*A lot more research is needed in this area, but it is an exciting concept...
Have we found a way of eliminating carcinogenic and teratogenic synthetics from our skin products in the 21st century?.*

BITES AND STINGS

The evidence here is mostly anecdotal, but reports do suggest that Tea Tree oil can reduce the irritation of many bites and stings, including mosquitoes, wasps, bees, horsefly, ants, fleas, lice, and gnats. There have even been anecdotal reports for some snake and spider bites - again much research is needed in this area, but it is likely that its painkilling and penetration properties can help to dissipate the venom, this would then alleviate trauma to the system.

("I have used it on wasp stings and parasitic bites and found it very effective in reducing pain and itching").

BURNS

Tea Tree oil is included in burn creams. The evidence suggests that its solvent and penetrating properties can remove agents that cause pain and irritation, its anti-microbial action will help to prevent the likelihood of infection to damaged tissue.

In April 1972 M. Walker, did a *'Clinical Investigation of Australian Melaleuca Alternifolia for a variety of common foot problems'* published current podiatry, an award winning report......Pathogens eliminated with 100% pure Tea Tree oil, Males a solution 40% oil and 13% Isopropyl alcohol (then it can dilute in water) and an emollient ointment 8% potency..... included Candida Albicans, Epidermophyton Floccosum and Trichophyton Mentagrophytes (with T. Rubrum infections being the most difficult to eliminate).

FOOT INFECTIONS AND FUNGAL CONDITIONS

A 40% solution of oil eliminated T. Rubrum, Tinea pedis (Athletes Foot)......Bromidrotic conditions (smelly feet) responds quickly and permanently to Tea Tree oil.... corns, bunions, hammer toes, calluses and cracks, fissures around heels reported a significant improvement....over 96% of Walkers patients over a 6 year period improved by using the oil of the *Melaleuca Alternifolia.*

In 1985 Dr P Belaiche of the University of Paris Nord carried out a study of Candida Albicans...the oil of the *Melaleuca Alternifolia* had *"remarkable anti-fungal action"....." It could be used for 8 weeks without irritating the mucus membrane.....It is one of a team of major essential oils...It is an antiseptic and anti-fungal weapon of the first order in Phyto-aromatherapy.* Dr Belaiche's findings are embraced by many professionals and woman's organisations around the globe.

Dr Belaiche successfully treated 8 out of 11 patients with infections of the nail by applying twice a day for several weeks. "It is effective in treatment of chronic Coli Bacilli Cystitis... low level of irritation... no toxicity... high germicidal power".

AS A BACTERICIDE

In 1987 Dr L.J. Walsh, from the Department of Dentistry University of Queensland and a microbiologist Dr Longstaff, used Tea Tree oil against oral and non-oral pathogens. In broth and Agar dilution methods. Tea Tree oil demonstrated high anti-microbial properties, especially against anaerobic and microaerophillic organisms, also with inhibition of all the other organisms that may cause adult periodontitis.

In September 1989 R.L. Barnes of Macquarie University found that the oil of the *Melaleuca Alternifolia* was the most effective if it had a low 1,8 Cineole content of below 4%-5%. It was also the least irritant.

P.M. Altman in 1989 claims in the Australian *Journal of Biotechnology* that the oil of the *Melaleuca Alternifolia* has a minimum inhibiting concentration (mic) of 1% v/v for the lowest level which caused inhibition of microbial growth. (No details of exact composition were available). In the most commonly occurring pathogenic bacteria and fungi including E.coli, Staphylococcus Aureus, Pseudomonas Aeruginosa, Aspergillus Niger, Candida Albicans, Trichophyton Menagrophytes, Streptococcus Faecalis, Streptococcus Pyrogenes and Propion, Bacterium Acnes.

EUCALYPTUS v TEA TREE OIL

Dr Lyall R Williams, Vicki N Home and Saras Asre, from Macquarie University, NSW, tested the activity of 'Blue Mallee' Eucalyptus oil under the same conditions that Tea Tree oil *(Melaleuca Alternifolia)* was evaluated for anti-microbial activity. Their conclusion was *"for the overwhelming and superior antimicrobial activity of the oil of Melaleuca as compared to Eucalyptus oil."*

ACNE TREATMENT

October 1990 a comparative study was completed in the Department of Dermatology, Royal Prince Albert Hospital NSW for the treatment of Acne. 5% Tea Tree oil *M.A.* v 5% Benzoylperoxide.

Both products were effective. Tea Tree oil *M.A.* was slower to start acting, but it produced far fewer side effects. The test concluded that further research was needed to see if a higher percentage of Tea Tree oil would work quicker. (I.B. Bassett, D.L. Pannowitz, R.S. Barnetson).

ATHLETES FOOT

1992 research into Tea Tree oil in the treatment of Tinea Pedis. Department of Dermatology Royal Prince Albert Hospital NSW. 104 patients did a random double blind trial with significant results- Tea Tree oil cream (10% w/w) appears to reduce the symptomatology of Tinea Pedis as effectively as Tolnaftate 1% but seems to be no more effective than placebo in achieving a mycological cure....This may be a basis for popularise of Tea Tree oil in the treatment of Tinea Pedis. (M.M. Tong, P.M. Altman, R.S. Barnetson)

Perhaps a higher percentage over a little longer period would have better results.... ("Anecdotally, I seemed to effect a cure in 6 weeks using a 50% Tea Tree oil & 25% Manuka oil in 25% Olive oil 3 times a day").

Do ONLY use a high quality oil.

April 16th, 1994. 5 scientists from the 'Acaemisch Ziekenhuis afd' (Dermatology Department) concluded that 4 patients with allergic contact Eczema contracted it through the use of Tea Tree oil available in the Netherlands. It is distilled from the *Melaleuca Alternifolia* and mainly containing Eucalyptol, this being the most important allergen.
(*"This does not seem to be a very high quality oil, The pure Tea Tree oil MA, does not contain Eucalyptol (Cineole) in such high quantities"*).

CONDITIONS OF THE NAIL

In June 1994 D.S. Buck, D.M. Nidorf, J.G. Addino from the University of Rochester, School of Medicine and Dentistry, successfully treated Onychomycosis, the most frequent cause of nail disease. Their conclusion, after 6 months, was...."*That Tea Tree oil as a natural topical therapy provides improvement in nail appearance and symptomatology.*"

Do not ingest Tea Tree oil and keep out of reach of children. If swallowed, seek medical attention.

1994. A case of Melaleuca oil poisoning was reported from the Hennepin regional Poison Centre in Minneapolis. A 23 month old boy showed signs of severe toxicity 30 minutes after ingesting less than 10ml of 100% *Melaleuca* oil - he was hospitalised and was asymptomatic within 5 hours of ingestion. He was allowed home the next day. A report suggests that a modest amount of the concentrated form of *Melaleuca* oil can prove toxic.

A high Terpinol-4-ol content is better.

March 1995, C.F. Carson and T.V. Riley of the Department of Microbiology, University of Western Australia, Nedlands. published an article in The Australian Journal concerning, Tea Tree oil *M.A* .- as a popular anti-microbial agent. 8 constituents of Tea Tree oil were evaluated using disc diffusion and broth methods. It was found that Terpinen-4-ol was active against all test organisms.

Rito-cymen had no anti-microbial activity.
Linacool and Alpha-terpineol. were active against all with the exception of pseudomonas Aeruginosa.

All 8 constituents showed minimal inhibitory and cidal concentrations effective against Candida Albicans, Escherichia Coli and Staphylococcus Aureaus.

Significant implications for the development of Tea Tree oil as an antimicrobial agent.

March 1995. C.F. Carson, B.D. Cookson, H.D. Farrelly, T.V. Riley Microbiology Department, University of Western Australia Nedlands.....tested the Meticillin resistant Staphylococcus Aureus to the Melaleuca Alternifolia oil ....all 66 staph isolates tested were susceptible to the Tea Tree oil....of the 66 isolates tested 64 were Methicillin resistant S Aureus (MRSA) and 33 were Mupirocin resistant. The MIC and MBC for 60 Australian isolates were 25% and 50% respectively.....suggests Tea Tree oil may be useful in the treatment of MRSA carriage. Similar results in Britain have been achieved.

Miscellaneous reports.

Dr E.H. Holland of the Australian University found that when a dilution of 1:200 (.5%) of Tea Tree oil *M.A.* was applied to raw faeces it had a significant sterilising action on the test sample. It killed 50% of the micro-organisms and stronger solutions rendered the sample almost sterile. Because Faeces is composed of 90% living bacteria this was impressive.

More and more tests are being carried out. The anti-viral properties of Tea Tree Oil have long been advocated by practitioners in aromatherapy, but there does not seem to have been a lot of scientific research in this area. Recent scientific research is being evaluated at the moment, and all indications seem very encouraging.......

Based on a table of Australian Essential oils, published in "Perfumer and Flavorist" Vol. 4 April/May 1979.

Microbes: -	1	2	3	4	5
Oils:					
Melaleuca	.5%	.25%		.04%	.0156%
Alternifolia	.25%	.125%	4 %	.02%	.0078%
Melaleuca	.5%	4 %	4 %	4 %	1 %
Quinquenervia	.25%				.5%
Melaleuca	.5%	> 4 %	4 %	4 %	.125%
Viridiflora	.25%				.0625%
Eucalyptus	.25%	.5%	4 %	.0625%	.0625%
Citriodora	.125%	.25%		.0312%	.0312%
Eucalyptus	.5%	.25%	4 %	.08%	.0625%
Dives	.25%	.125%		.04%	.0312%
Eucalyptus	1 %	.5%	4 %	.125%	1 %
Fruticetorum					
Eucalyptus	1 %	.5%	1 %	.0625%	.5%
Radiata	.5%	.25%	.5%	.0312%	.25%
Leptospermum	.04%	2.5%	2.5%	.625%	>1.25%
Scoparium	.02%				
Leptospermum	1.25%	5 %	2.5%	2.5%	>1.25%
Ericoides	.625%				

The results are given by the % range of minimum inhibitory concentration-(MIC).   NB: 1000 parts per million = 0.1%
                                  100 parts per million = 0.01%

Microbe Table: 1= Staphylococcus Aureus ATCC 6538
                  2= Escherichia Coli ATCC 10536
                  3= Pseudomonas Aeruginosa NCTC 1999
                  4= Candida Albicans
                  5= Aspergillus Niger

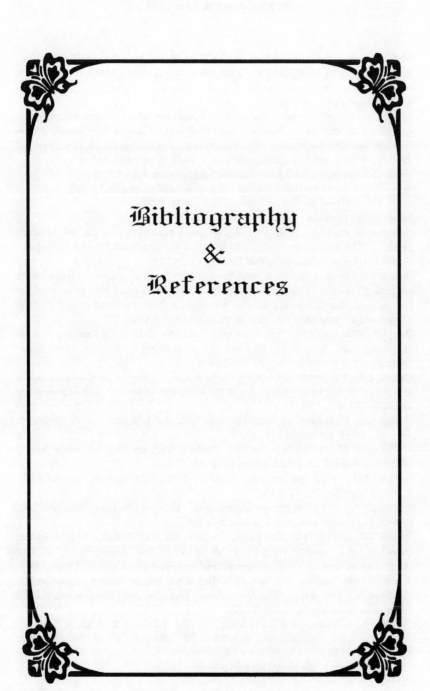

Bibliography
&
References

Ab-Chem, The American Database of; CD-ROM, World-wide from 1977-96.

Altman. P.M. 1988 Australian tea tree oil. *Australian Journal of Pharmacy* 69. 276-278

Altman. P. M. 1989 Australian tea tree oil-a natural antiseptic. *Australian Journal of Biotechnology*3. 247-248

Altman P. M. 1990 (extracts studied from:) Summary of safety studies concerning Australian tea tree oil. In *Modern Phytotherapy-The Clinical 0ignificance of Tea Tree Oil and Other Essential Oils.* Proceedings of a conference on December 1-2 1990, in Sydney and a Symposium on Dec. 8 1990, in Surfers Paradise. CD

Anon. 1930. A retrospect. *Medical Journal of Australia* 1, 85-89.

Anon. 1933a An Australian antiseptic oil. *British Medical Journal* 1, 966.

Anon. 1933b. Titrol oil. *British Medical Journal* 11, 927

Anon. 1990 Tea tree oil and acne. *Lancet* 11 1438.

Atkinson, N and Brice, H. E. 1955 Antibacterial substances produced by flowering plants. 2. The anti-bacterial action of essential oils from some Australian plants. *Australian Journal of Experimental Biology* 33, 547-554.

Barnes B. 1989a (Extracts studied from:) The 'Vaginal' range of formulations containing tea tree oil. In *Modern Phytotherapy-The Clinical Significance of Tea Tree oil and Other Essential Oils.* Proceedings of a Conference on Dec. 1-2 1990. in Sydney and a Symposium on Dec. 8 1990 in Surfers Paradise. CD

Barr. A., Chapman, J., Smith, N., and Beveridge, M, 1988 *Traditional Bush Medicines; An Aboriginal Pharmacopoeia* Richmond Victoria; Greenhouse Publications. (Extracts courtesy of The British Library).

Bassett, L B., Pannowitz, D.L., and Barnetson, R.ST.C. 1990 A comparative study of tea tree oil versus benzoylperoxide, in the treatment of acne. *Medical Journal of Australia* 153, 455-458.

P. Belaiche, 'Treatment of Skin Infection with the Essential Oil of Melaleuca *Alternifolia',* Phytotherapy15 (1985)

- Treatment of Vaginal Infections of Candida Albicans with the Essential Oil *Melaleuca Alternifolia' Phytotherapy 15 (1985)*

Beylier, M.F. 1979 Bacteriostatic activity of Some Australian essential oils. *Perfumer and Flavourist* 4, 23-25

Blackwell, A.L. 1991 Tea tree oil and anaerobic (bacterial) vaginosis. *Lancet* 1, 300.

British Pharmaceutical codex, 1949 (pp 597-598)

Brophy, J.J., Davies, N.W., Southwell, I.A. Stiff, I.A. and Williams, I., R. 1989 Gas chromatographic quality control for oil of *Melaleuca Alternifiloa -4-ol* type (Australian tea tree). *Journal of Agricultural and Food Chemistry* 37, 1330-1335.

Cabot, S. 1989 The use of tea tree oil in clinical practice. In *Modern Phytotherapy - The Clinical Significance of Tea Tree oil and Other Essential Oils.* Proceedings of a Symposium on September 17 1990. CD.

Capt. Cook, A Voyage towards the South Pole. Vol. 1 Strahan & Cadell (1777)

Carson & Riley 'Antimicrobial activity of the essential oil of the Melaleuca Alternifolia. 93 CD

The Dispensatory of the USA 25th ed. (p 1610).

CD ROM Medline, Knight-Ridder, info. 1976-96.

Davies, Dr S. & Dr A. Stewart, Nutritional Medicine.

Drury S., Tea Tree Oil, A medicine Kit In A Bottle 1989&1994.

Fienblatt, H.M., 1960 Cajuput-type oil for the treatment of furunculosis. *Journal of the National Medical Association* 52, 32-34.

Guenther, E. 1968 Report of a field survey. *Perfume and Essential oil records* 59 642-644.

Halford, A.C.F. 1936 Diabetic gangrene. *Medical Journal of Australia* 11 121-122.

Humphrey, E.M. 1930 A new Australian germicide. *Medical Journal of Australia* 1. 417-418.

Extracts relevant: Journal of Allergy and Clinical Immunology 92-93.

Kelsey, J.C. and Sykes, G. A. 1969. A new test for the assessment of disinfectants with particular reference to their use in hospitals. *Pharmaceutical Journal* 202, 607-609.

Lassak, E.V. and McCarthy, T.M. 1983 *Australian Medicinal Plants*. Sydney New South Wales; Metheun Australian Pty. Ltd.

Lawless J., 'Tea Tree oil', The new guide to one of natures most remarkable gifts. 94.

Low, T. 1990 *Bush Medicine. A Pharmacopoeia of Natural Remedies.* New South Wales: Collins/Angus and Robertson Publishers Pty Ltd.

Low, D., Rawal, B.D., and Callaa, W.J. 1974 Anti-bacterial action of the essential oils of some Australian Myrtaceae with special references to the activity of chromatographic fractions of oil of *Eucalyptus citrodora*. *Plants Medica*. 25 184-189.

Macdonald, V. 1930 The rationale of treatment. *Australian Journal of Dentistry* 34 281-285.

Manners and Customs of the New Zealanders, 2 vols, Madden & Co. London 1840.

Martindale, The Extra Pharmacopoeia, 28th ed., 1982 (p678)

Maori Medicinal Plants, Auckland Botanical Society Bulletin 1945. O. Adams.

Medicine of the Maori, W. Collins Ltd. Auckland, 1974-75. C. Macdonald.

Medline CD ROM: Knight-Ridder Extracts. Tea Tree Oil Melaleuca Alternifolia 1925-95.

Merry K.A., Williams, I,R., and Home, V.N. 1990 Composition of oils from *Melaleuca Alternifolia, M linaritfolia* and *m. disitiflora..* Implications for the Australian standard, oil of *Melaleuca Alternifolia-4-ol* type. In *Modern Phytotherapy-The Clinical Significance of Tea Tree oil and Other Essential Oils.* Proceedings of a Conference on December 1-2 1990, in Sydney and a Symposium on December 8 1990, in Surfers Paradise.11.

New Zealand Family Herb Doctor, Miller, Dick & Co, Dunedin, 1884. J Neill.

New Zealand Medicinal Plants, Heineman, Auckland, 3rd Ed. 1987. (Booker, Cambie and Cooper).

Pena, E.F. 1962 *Melaleuca Alternifolia* oil. Its uses for trichomonal vaginitis and other vaginal infections. *Obstetrics and Gynaecology* 19 723-795.

Penfold, A.R. and Grant, R. 1925 The germicidal values of some Australian essential oils and their pure constituents. Together with those for some essential oils isolates, and synthetics. Part111. *Journal Proceedings of the Royal Society of New South Wales.*59

Penfold, A.R and Morrison, F.R. 1937 Some notes on the essential oil of *Melaleuca Alternifolia. Australian Journal of Pharmacy.* 18 274-275.

BIBLIOGRAPHY & REFERENCES

The Perfumer & Flavorist, Vol. 4, Apr/May 1979. Table of anti-microbial activity in Australian Essential Oils.

J. Price, Extracts studied, were taken from: 'The Use Of Tea Tree Oil in Burn Treatment Products', Modern Phytotherapy-The clinical significance of Tea Tree Oil and other essential oils, Proceedings of a two day conference at Maquarie University, Sydney (1990).

Ryan, R.F. 1990 Oil of *Melaleuca Alternifolia* dissolved in liquid carbon dioxide propellant (Bactigas TM) used for the control of bacteria and fungi in air conditioning systems. In *Modern Phytotherapy-The Clinical Significance of Tea Tree oil and Other Essential Oils*. Proceedings of a Conference on December 1-2 1990 in Sydney and a Symposium on December 8 1990 in Surfers Paradise.

Ryman Daniele, Aromatherapy - The Encyclopedia of plants and oils and how they can help you, 1991.

Prof. Sachs *Melaleuca Alternifolia*: (extracts studied came from:) An estimate of its potential as a crop for California. Proceedings of a 2 day Conference at Maquarie University Sydney 1990.

Shemesh & Mayo 'Tea Tree Oil' - Natural Antiseptic & Fungicide', International Journal of A. & Complimentary Medicine (90-91)

Swords, G and Hunter, G.L.K. 1978 Composition of Australian tea tree oil *(Melaleuca Alternifolia). Journal of Agricultural and Food Chemistry*. 26, 734-737.

R. Tisserand, International Journal of Aromatherapy (1989) - Tinea Pedis etc

R. Trattler, Better Health Through Natural Healing.

Turpin, Nina 95. Chapter 4 adapted from, and extract from 'Perfect Health' by D. Chopra taken from 'The Healing Wonder From Down Under'.

Valnet, Practice of Aromatherapy.

Walker, M. 1972 Clinical Investigation of Australian *Melaleuca Alternifolia* oil for a variety of common foot problems. Current Podiatry April 7-15.

Walsh, L.J. and Longstaff, J. 1987 The antimicrobial effects of an essential oil on selected oral pathogens *Periodontology* 8, 11-15.

J. White, Journal of a Voyage to New South Wales. extr. Aberystwyth Library.

Williams, L.R. and Home, V.N. 1988 Extracts from: Plantation production of oil of *Melaleuca Alternifolia (Tea Tree oil)* a revitalised Australian essential oil industry.

Williams, L.R. and Home V.N. 1989 Plantations of *Melaleuca Alternifolia*-a revitalised Australian tea tree oil industry. In *Proceedings of the 11th International Congress of Essential oils, Fragrances & Flavours*.

Williams, L.R., Home V.N. Zhang, X. and Stevenson, I. 1988 The composition and bacterial activity of oil of *Melaleuca Alternifolia* (tea tree oil). *International Journal of Aromatherapy 1* 15-17

Williams. L.R., Home V.N. and Asre, S. 1990s (extracts studied from:) Anti-microbial activity of oil of *Melaleuca (tea tree oil)*. Its potential use *in* cosmetics and toiletries. *Cosmetics, Aerosols and Toiletries in Australia* 4,12-23.

Williams, L.R. Home, V.N. and Asre, S. 1990b Oils of *Melaleuca Alternifolia*. Their anti-fungal activity against Candida Albicans in perspective. *International Journal of Aromatherapy. 12-13.*

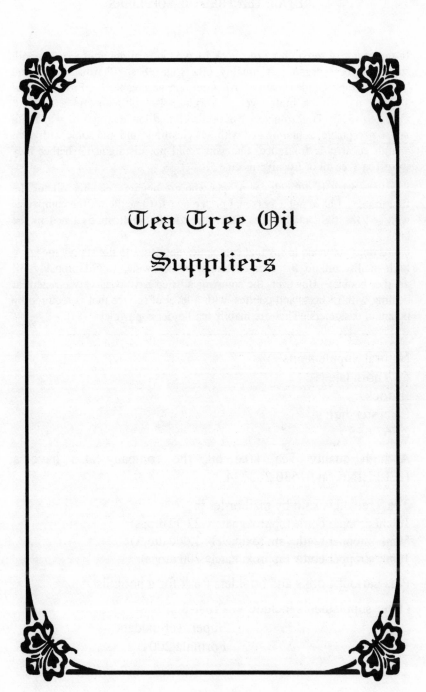

Tea Tree Oil
Suppliers

In the course of researching this book I have found all types of Tea Tree oil, some have been organic, A1 quality, others have been 'Pharmaceutical' and 'Aromatherapy Grade' quality. All three are acceptable for First Aid and Toiletry use with a high level of Terpinen-4-ol (40>%) and a low 1,8 Cineole (<5%). Unfortunately I have also found low quality oils which are not so acceptable, contaminated with 3% cleaning fluid and some with such a high eucalyptus fragrance, that you could not distinguish whether they were Tea Tree oil or Eucalyptus oil.

I realise that it is difficult for people who are buying Tea Tree oil for the first time, so I have put a 'personal preference' list together of the companies who sell the right quality Tea Tree oil, for the applications listed in the book.
(This does not mean to say that companies not listed do not supply the same high quality oil, to list every company nation-wide, would probably fill another book!). However, the companies listed have been very efficient at dealing with requests and queries, with a level of service that is required by potential customers. They are mainly mail order companies:

Natural Supplements
53 Thorndale
Ibstock
Leicestershire
LE67 6PS

A high quality Tea Tree oil, the company also have a HELPLINE on 01530 263734.

Tea Tree oil is sold by mail order in:
100ml dropper bottle (approximately 2,000 drops)
50ml dropper bottle (approximately 1,000 drops)
10ml dropper bottle (approximately 200 drops)

Plus various books and booklets (ask for a book list)

Other supplements include: Prost-8
                              Super Antioxidant
                              Formula 2001

For details and/or retail catalogue please write to:

Essentially Oils Limited
8 Mount Farm
Junction Road
Churchill
Chipping Norton
Oxfordshire
OX7 6NP

Tea Tree products incl. veterinary supplies.

Primavera Aromatherapy Ltd
Mells
Frome
Somerset
BA11 3QZ

plus Tea Tree toiletries.

Videx Animal Health Ltd
5-11 Station Terrace Ind Est
Ely Bridge
Cardiff
CF5 4AR

Telephone: 01222 578578

Natural Tea Tree Oil Pet Care Products.

One of the best Mail Order ranges in the UK

The Australian Body Care Company

Available:
Boots the Chemist
Superdrug

I have also found a few wholesale outlets, who supply good quality Tea Tree oil in large batches, to the trade, these companies were equally efficient and I found them to be very helpful: That does not mean to say that the companies not listed do not supply a good quality oil with efficiency, they would be too numerous to list.

Essentially Oils Ltd
8 Mount Farm
Chipping Norton
OX7 6NP
UK   Telephone: 01608 695544

Australian Essential Oil Company Ltd
Little Barn
Mells
Somerset
BA11 3QZ
UK   Telephone: 01373 812640

A & E Connock (Perfumery & Cosmetics) Ltd
Alderholt Mill House
Fordingbridge
Hampshire
SP6 1PU
UK   Telephone: 01425 656041

M. Wim Tanghe
'Fytosan'
Z. A. Cocause - B. P.
10 - 26150
Die   Telephone: 00 33 75 22 19 13
FRANCE

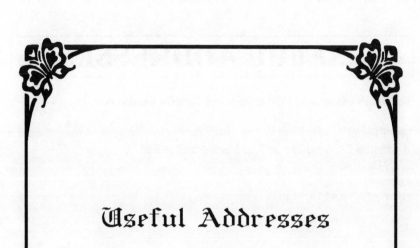

Useful Addresses

USEFUL ADDRESSES

For details of the June 1996 British Tea Tree Oil Conference:

'AusTTeam'
Australian Tea Tree Export And Marketing Limited
P. O. Box 195
Lismore
NSW AUSTRALIA 2480

TEL/FAX: 00 61 66 222 282

'AusTrade'
Australian Trade Commission
Australia House
Strand
LONDON
WC2B 4LA UK

TEL: 0171 887 5326

A database of over 1200 food items based on the nutrient bank from The Royal Society of Chemistry, calculating a balanced diet for you personally. You can select, reduce and increase the foods you enjoy to give you the perfect balanced diet. Going on a diet has never been so healthy or so easy. Available on disc for IBM PC or Compatibles .

Computrition
14 Lower Station Road
Crayford
Kent
DA1 3PY U.K.
TEL: 01322 553041

E. Mail: http://www.dungeon.com/home/computrition/bdt.html

For a Progesterone Fact Sheet to enable your doctor to prescribe an alternative, natural plant extract HRT, send a **large SAE** to:

Natural Progesterone (YAM) Fact Sheet
The Nutrition Line
Burwash Common
East Sussex
TN19 7LX

A relaxing holiday in the Derbyshire Peak District, during your stay enjoy a therapeutic massage and learn from the experts the art of aromatherapy. For a very warm welcome write, ring or fax for details:

The Relaxation Studio
Staden Grange Country House Hotel
Buxton
Derbyshire
SK17 9RZ
TEL: 01298 72808   FAX: 01298 72067

Hair Mineral Analysis, Vega Testing, Customised Prescriptions:
Contact Adrian Blake: Mail Order service available.

12 Cosway Street
LONDON
NW1 5NR   UK
TEL: 0171 224 8944

What's The Alternative? for your health, See Hazel Courteney's column, every Tuesday, in the Daily Mail or read Hazel's informative new book. Send s.a.e. for details or a cheque for £6.95 to:

Hazel Courteney - What's The Alternative?
Infinity Press
P O Box 4629 Edgbaston
Birmingham   B15 3TW

Aromatherapy, Dietry Advice, Exercise Programmes, Toning Tables, Sun Beds etc. **If your figure is not becoming to you, you should be coming to us!.**

> Figure Shapers
> 7 Belmont Terrace
> Buxton
> Derbys
> SK17 6DZ

> Telephone: 01298 22323 (callers welcome)

Tea Tree Petcare products send an S.A.E. for catalogue:

> Videx Animal Health Ltd
> 5-11 Station Terrace Industrial Estate
> Ely Bridge
> Cardiff
> CF5 4AR
> Telephone: 01222 578578

For a list of Aromatherapists, write with an S.A.E.to:

> The Register of Aromatherapists
> 52 Barrack Lane
> Aldwick
> Bognor Regis
> West Sussex
> PO21 4DD

And:

> The Association of Tisserand Aromatherapists
> P O Box 746
> Hove
> East Sussex
> BN3 3XA

> The Tea Tree Oil Information Service
> P O Box 2
> Ibstock
> Leicestershire
> LE67 6ZU

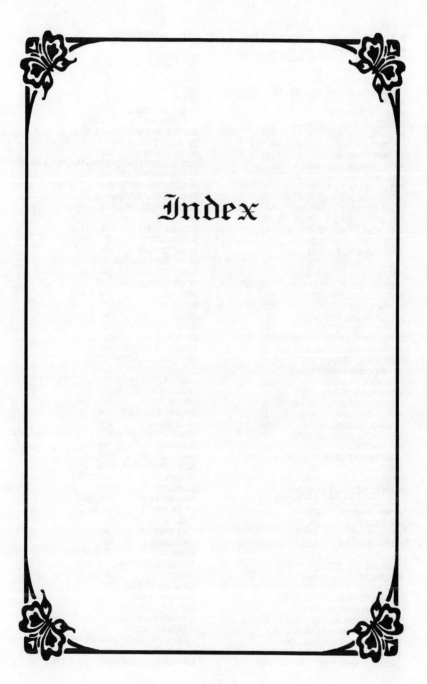

Index